So there's this fat man, a huge black afro wig and a dildo, and they're bouncing up and down on this big bed . . . together . . .

Welcome to Bollywood.

This is studio city, a fantasy fodder factory, the Bombay-based film capital of the Indian subcontinent. Here every year the Hindi film industry pumps out twice as many pictures as Hollywood to satisfy the romantic cravings of its billion-strong audience, from the mobile-wielding middle classes who sit in the air-conditioned comfort of big-city cinemas, to the villagers transfixed by dancing images flickering on a dusty courtyard wall.

Enter Hrithik Roshan, new idol of the silver screen, seducing both the industry and the women of India in a flurry of triceps and biceps, tight T-shirts and slick dance moves.

Bollywood Boy follows Hrithik's meteoric rise through the celluloid firmament. It could be straight from one of the film industry's own big-budget schlockbusters, with its heroes, heroines, villains, exotic locations, a cast of thousands, myriad costume changes and highly charged bop-de-bop dance routines. And like any good cinerama drama, there is the big chase scene as Justine tries to track down the man behind the hype, the hysteria and the silver disco suits.

But there is a dark side to all this, the moment when the lights go out and the hero stumbles – the moment in Bollywood when people die because they have not played by the underworld code. For beneath the glittering surface of India's tinsel town lurk shady racketeers who use the film industry to make serious black money. In Bombay the underworld is king. Welcome to Bollywood.

Justine Hardy has been based in and out of India for twelve years as a journalist, writer and documentary maker. Her first book, *The Ochre Border: A Journey through the Tibetan Frontierlands*, was published in 1995. *Scoop-wallah: Life on a Delhi Daily*, published in 1999, was short-listed for the Thomas Cook Travel Award. *Goat: A Story of Kashmir and Notting Hill* came out in 2000.

Bollywood Boy

JUSTINE HARDY

JOHN MURRAY
Albemarle Street, London

For my brother,
a different kind of star

First published in 2002
by John Murray (Publishers) Ltd,
50 Albemarle Street, London W1S 4BD

Paperback edition 2003

A catalogue record for this book is available from the British Library

ISBN 0-7195-6485 9

Typeset in Goudy 11.5/14 pt
by Servis Filmsetting Ltd, Manchester

Printed and bound in Great Britain by
Clays Ltd, St Ives plc

Up Front

When people in India got a whiff of what comes after this they said, 'Why do it here? Surely it's the godless West that's obsessed with stardom?' When I replied that in India they deify their movie stars, that they build temples to them and pray for them when they have the flu, I was told that things were different there.

Are they? The desire of people to aspire to something just on the edge of what they can imagine is the same the world over. It's just that in India movies bind a country that violence and extremism threaten to fragment, breaking down the barriers built by politics and sectarianism.

With movies, unavoidably, comes stardom. Stardom is craved and worshipped, and it has an insatiable appetite, like ancient gods and the tax-man. It also has its own galaxy, and the galaxy hasn't liked the words, and especially the subtext.

To become a movie star is the destination of choice in India whether you're talking to children in raw slum schools or at fancy foreign film colleges where the bills are paid by Mummy/Daddy. It's an obsession that deserves its own biography. This is not fiction, this is an anatomy of stardom.

Turn down the lights, switch off your mobile, sit back and relax. Welcome to Bollywood.

Contents

Infatuation

SHE HAS A woman's body in recline, her hips, buttocks and breasts rising above a belly of water. Those breasts are surmounted by nipples of wealth, the higher reaches where smooth rich folk live behind tall walls. And on the curves that swoop down to her belly the shore meets land that has been pulled back from the sea, reclaimed to erect a business skyline out of murky wetness where once only the fishermen plied their trade. This is the body of Bombay, and Bombay is a city of bodies.

There is flesh everywhere, skin pressing on skin, offering itself up from Malabar Hill to Back Bay, from Kemp's Corner to the salt-singed arch of the Gateway of India through which a limping empire retreated over half a century ago, back into the sea from whence it had come. Sweat runs off the juice-*wallah*'s arms, dotting the pavement on the corner of Breach Candy as he beheads carrots beside the Arabian Sea. It splashes on to a shopper's powdered neck and Morning Glory sari outside the Heera Panna Shopping Bazaar, and it flies from the straining fore-head of a boy carrying a pile of boxes almost as high as himself. It pricks the backs of businessmen's necks in the air-conditioned cars that idle at traffic lights, agitating them on their way to high-rise meetings in big bank buildings. It slides down the wiry torsos of coolies carrying baskets of cabbages in and out of the crush of limbs in Crawford Market, across town from where the juice-*wallah* drips beside the sea.

Crawford Market has every kind of flesh, alive or dead. Dark blood drips from drawn and quartered cadavers. Rats roam the margins, feeding on whatever they can find, dodging in and out of the cages crammed with poultry and livestock. Green parrots from the Cardamom Hills tug out their flight feathers in paranoid boredom. Once-crested canaries rub their heads raw on their prison bars. Turtle doves in battered braces neither coo nor bill but pine and starve. Roaming pi-dogs piss against the cages of rumpled puppies, litters that will be sold by the dozen and that will end up back on the streets when they get too big to be toys. And a group of excited boys poke at the bloated belly of a rat with sharpened sticks. The rat is too sated to do anything more than bare its yellowed teeth.

Sweat and blood run together down the arms of the butchers who cut and fold, strip and rip. Necks of chickens, throats of goats, mutton anuses, eyeballs and ears, nothing can be spared, every inch can be eaten, every sinew chopped and bargained for, sliced and packaged.

In Crawford Market the air smells of the shit of dead and dying things, but there is sweeter stuff to breathe up on Pali Hill, high above the stink of downtown sweat. Mercedes and BMWs glide around the streets where bougainvillaea grows in pretty bright pinkness over the tall walls of big houses. Every bonnet is buffed to a *crorepati*'s shine, a millionaire's gloss, each almost as shiny and polished as the expensive hair on the sleek heads of the women who recline behind darkened back-seat windows on their way in and out of large driveways. Shopping is the local sport in the hills of Bombay, but it is not the sort of shopping that takes place in Crawford Market's bloody brawl.

From high up in the sweet hills Bombay falls back down to the water, to the old arch beside the sea. Here hundreds of honeymoon couples gather as the sun sets out on the water, a crowd of brand-new saris in fruit-pastille colours, armfuls of wedding bangles, nervous bowed heads beside proud boys in tight jeans and cheap jackets. The scent of jasmine garlands, wound into oiled plaits and knots, floats out with the dreams of young brides over the spangled water, while beside them their new husbands wait to pull the delicate flowers from fine threads, to unwind saris from nervous bodies, to touch fresh, warm skin, voluptuous as fig flesh. Just like in the movies.

Welcome to the capital of Hindi film, the studio city and fantasy fodder factory of the Subcontinent, an industry that pumps out twice as many pictures as Hollywood to satisfy the romantic cravings of its billion-strong audience. Welcome to Bollywood, the celluloid city that hides its alchemy among the alleys that smell of rotting flesh and star jasmine.

Down these alleys, past where Mrs Nirmal throws stones at the pi-dogs to keep them away from her husband's *bhelpuri* cart while her snack man sleeps under a rain tree, beyond the relentlessly tatty tourist shops on The Causeway, is Colaba, named after the original inhabitants, the Koli fishermen, who were plying the waters before records began. A few of them still remain, clinging with the determination of ancient limpets to their pockets of inner city land, to their boats, their nets and their gutting knives. But all around them rise up the symbols of the modern city, skyscrapers etching their jagged silhouette over the harbour, throwing their mirrored images into the water where the Kolis cast their nets in the reflections of modern might and asset management-on-sea.

Right in the thick of this newly risen cool quarter is heat street, Battery Road, the one downtown spot where the stars from the high hills sometimes come out to play. The cars that line up along its length give it away, low-slung, sleek, squatting on fat tyres, shiny boot to glossy bonnet. A tourist carriage rolls past on clattering wheels, its flea-bitten grey horse and driver nodding in time with each slow step. The happy loving honeymoon couple behind the driver stare up at the steps beyond the line of cars and into Bar Indigo – white-hot Mumbai-Bombay, the thrust and grind of the cutting edge, a sea of gym-honed, belly-ringed midriffs that sway

Asset management-on-sea

as the boys go by. As the carriage clatters on past, the happy loving couple take in each detail and store it away for the moment when, back home over family *chai*, they can wow Mummy/Daddy with their brush with Bollywood.

Inside Bar Indigo the hot stagnant street air is chilled and repackaged. Here the air is designer-scented, courtesy of the Paris perfume houses, courtesy of a hundred Non-Resident-Indian stop-overs at Dubai Duty Free, and here it mingles with Marlboro Light smoke over a sea of gleaming heads, cut in London, set in LA and now swinging on Friday night in Colaba. The bar itself is long and low, longer and lower than most bars I know. In London I am average to short. In India I am tall, and bars seem perfectly con-structed so that I can prop myself at just that beautiful-people angle. Even so I'm still about as wrong as you can get for Bar Indigo. I am over thirty, the wrong colour, the wrong type and definitely in the wrong clothes.

On that particular night I was doing the floaty wafty look in white. Dusky and tight was the Spring 2000 season's black in Colaba. Dusky and tight I was not. But the perfect face next to me was. She was about as dusky, tiny and tight as you can get, in black sprayed-on Capri pants, a silk shirt knotted under her canti-levered Wonder-Bra cleavage, and heels that teetered sufficiently to pump her up to the correct angle-at-bar height.

'Hey, Raju, heard your new track at the studio. Shit, man, really cool.' Perfect Face swung her hair and purred as she propped, her comment directed at a gang of gawky young men sporting large amounts of hair gel and almost identical square-toed shoes.

The boy gang ignored her and continued to smoke and talk loudly over their big-price beers. Perfect Face looked around to see if there was anyone else worth talking to. She had been trying to ignore me.

'Hello,' I offered limply.

Perfect Face looked at me, momentarily frozen in social horror. Then she seemed to change her mind, as though she had decided to be a hip-chick angel of mercy who would initiate a desperate outsider into the cult inner circle of Bollywood nights.

'It's too cool here,' she said compassionately. 'See the girl over there?' She pointed to a Lolita with green eyes and a face and body as perfectly and surreally proportioned as those of a doll. 'That's Simmy, she's a friend of Shah Rukh's.' Perfect Face smiled at me munificently as if she had just given me the key to the gates of heaven.

Shah Rukh Khan is one of a testosterone triumvirate, the Khans, three good Muslim boys who hold the Hindi film industry in thrall. Shah Rukh generally plays the moody lover type and, though not conventionally good-looking, he is a killer at the box office. Salman Khan has a six-pack of stomach muscles with enough ripples to front a steroid campaign, and he likes them to be seen, a lot. Aamir Khan is the actor of the trio and is likely to outlast the others.

Perfect Face was examining her pearly fingernails.

'Chitty-chat is that Simmy is going to one of the big award ceremonies with SRK.' She ran her tongue under one of her talons.

The barman looked on in awe.

'Is she his girlfriend?' I asked.

Perfect Face furrowed her perfect brow.

'What is this girlfriend-*shurlfriend*? He is married, very very married. Everyone knows that.' She pouted her perfectly matching pearly lips.

Of course I knew. But since when had Bollywood stars been exclusive to their wives?

'Hey, Simmy,' Perfect Face called out to the doll with green eyes. 'All the chitty-chat is that you're going to the awards with SRK's gang.'

Simmy swung round from her gaggle of friends to see where the barb had come from.

'Nothing doing,' she hissed, her pouting dolly mouth the same pearly shade as that of Perfect Face.

'Oh, oh, this is not what I'm hearing,' shot back Perfect Face.

Simmy narrowed her green eyes but smiled a smile rehearsed a thousand times in front of as many mirrors. She put her tiny hand on her tiny hip and cocked it at Perfect Face in a posture of cosmetically constructed defiance.

'Nothing doing,' she repeated, pointedly turning back to her gang of networkers and naked midriffs.

Perfect Face sulked at her reflection in the shiny bar.

'This is so much of bullshit, she thinks she's so great, *yaar*. If he came in here right now he wouldn't even stop to say "Hi" to her.' Perfect Face was scanning the crowd. She had given me enough of her time.

'Who wouldn't say "Hi"?' I was lost.

'Shah Rukh, of course.' She started to roll her eyes, but they froze halfway and a shudder ran through her perfect little body.

I tried to follow her transfixed expression but the crowd was too dense. Perfect Face was clutching at her chest and panting.

'Bullshit, man, it's Hrithik!' she said as she finally managed to form real words.

I hopped up on to the bar to get a better view.

A young man was swinging up the steps away from the back of a very long, very low, very black car. He stopped outside the bar and turned back for a moment, waiting. He was wearing a light blue leather T-shirt sprayed on to a landscape of muscle, curved and polished like the bonnets of the cars in the street below. His long legs were wrapped in black jeans. Everything clung. He stood on the step, animal shy, animal sprung, his gym-honed body poised for flight.

'Is that . . .?' I put my hand on Perfect Face's arm to try and get her attention.

She cut me off with a wild-eyed expression. 'It's Hrithik!'

'Is he really that hot?'

'You're kidding me,' she gasped. 'Hrithik's It!' And the silence of the church fell on the hottest bar in Colaba as Hrithik Roshan,

Bollywood's newest and brightest, a one-film wonder, the first real box-office challenge to the heart-throb hero stranglehold of the Khan boys, waited outside, not quite sure how to make his entrance.

'Ohmygod, ohmygod, ohmygod, it's Salman,' Perfect Face screeched.

Her hands were in front of her face, her pearly talons fluttering near her mouth as if she was trying to dry her nail polish at high speed.

Another body emerged from behind Hrithik.

'I'm fainting,' Perfect Face announced, though she remained resolutely upright.

Salman Khan, Khan Number Two, The Khan, was right there, right outside Bar Indigo. Salman, famous for his six-pack and his sex life but now proving that he had a nose for a winner. He had picked Hrithik Roshan as his friend when Hrithik was just a tall, skinny boy with a moderately successful director for a father, and enough ambition to aim as high as the Himalayas. Salman had introduced his new friend to the six-pack diet of protein shakes and a pumping-iron regime that would create shapes that bulge nicely in leather, rubber, neoprene or anything else that clings. He told the green-eyed boy that he would be a sensation and watched him grow out of his college jeans and T-shirts and into his spray-on wardrobe.

In contrast to Hrithik's slicked-on look, Salman Khan was wearing a pair of baggy linen trousers and a loose, pale linen shirt, very demure, very Giorgio Armani, very unusual for the king of tight and taut. He bounded up the steps to where Hrithik was waiting, and as he bounded his shirt flew open for all to see. Hrithik looked at the ground in front of him. Salman kept full eye contact with everyone in the bar. His chest rippled, his torso gleamed and a smile spread across his face. He was flirting all the way.

'I'm dying. This is too much. What to do?' Perfect Face, still

I am looking into film-star eyes

standing, still living, clutched my arm in a moment of sisterly bonding.

Salman put his hand on Hrithik's shoulder. He had to reach up a little. Hrithik is tall.

Then the green-eyed boy lifted his head, turned and looked straight at me.

Welcome to Bollywood, city of dreams and dance routines. I am looking into film-star eyes. I am in the movies.

CHAPTER 1

Flirtation

Meet our hero

THOSE EYES, THAT face, that body, they were all part of a film phenomenon heading for the stratosphere.

Hrithik Roshan had just starred in his first film, *Kaho Naa . . . Pyaar Hai* (*Tell Me . . . You Love Me*), directed by his father Rakesh Roshan. When it was released on 14 January 2000 Hrithik walked into the cinema as just another young hopeful. When he left the première he was mobbed. From that moment he shot straight into the number-one fantasy slot of female India. He was the newest, biggest and brightest star in the Bollywood firmament.

India's multi-language film industry produces an average of about 800 films a year. Over half those films come from the Hindi film world of Bollywood, centred in Bombay, and almost every single one of Bollywood's films pops off the production line with a standardized story that goes something like this.

Boy meets Girl. Girl plays hard to get. Boy falls in love with Girl. A big flirty dance number follows. Cue the bad guys, who have an infinite number of ways in which to scupper Boy's love chances. They fail. Boy gets Girl. Another big sexy dance number. Girl then gets tricky and remembers another boy back home in medium-sized town whom her parents have lined up for an arranged marriage. (These home boys always have nice sensible jobs but they are not very hot on the dance numbers. This means the audience knows for sure that they are very boring and will not give our heroine the romantic life she yearns for.) Alternatively, Girl remembers her dying mother, who needs her beloved daughter's constant nursing, or her unmarried older sister, who makes it very clear that she will be disowned by the family if she tries to get married before sister number one.

Not entirely surprisingly Boy gets angry and frustrated, aided and abetted by the bad guys in their standard uniform of dark glasses, black jeans and Eurotrash arm-candy girlfriends. Cue a big aggressive dance number. Girl gets huffy and says that Boy has changed. Boy swears undying love and gives 100% guarantee that he will change his ways, promising never to see the bad guys again. This all takes place during a big dance number with Girl shunning Boy and Boy making big hip-swinging promises. Exit bad guys. Boy gets Girl back. They kiss chastely, a swift and sweet embrace, with absolutely no tongues involved. Then there is a huge finale with a lot of dancing, a lot of glitter and a lot of costume changes. The End.

That is the story line.

There is one thing even more important than the plot, though. At the slightest opportunity the playback singers are cranked up and the costume cupboard is raided. Hindi films are all about the dancing. Let's take a dance number early in the story line. Boy has met Girl and is trying to get in there. They have arranged a date, cue panning shot of the Gateway of India at sunset. Boy, sporting blue jeans, sunglasses and Nike trainers, is staring moodily into the waters of the Arabian Sea. Girl appears skipping down the promenade next to the Gateway in hot pants, pigtails tied with pink ribbons and a matching tight pink T-shirt. Boy is suddenly all smiles, and the soundtrack swells as our hero and heroine start lip-synching furiously in time to the song as they shimmy their way to romantic nirvana. Now she is in his arms, now she rushes away, oh, and now she's back again. Meanwhile the Gateway of

Hindi films are all about the dancing

India floods with pink light, artfully tinted to match her T-shirt and ribbons.

And then suddenly we are in Switzerland. The Gateway of India has been replaced by cows wearing bells and grazing on lush alpine grass. Behind the bell-ringing backing group there is a neat hamlet of cuckoo-clock chalets. Our hero and heroine are frolicking in the grass without having apparently noticed either the change in scenery or the change in their own costumes. Boy is now wearing classic *kurta pyjama* with some natty embroidery work, and Girl is in a full gold and cream sari, its chiffon floating in the alpine air as she spins around her warbling hero. He is so full of love his heart is going to explode. She is just totally in eyelash-batting heaven.

Big change. Now the munching cows are replaced by the glistening naked torsos of a snake-boat rowing crew. We are beneath the coconut palms of Kerala's backwaters in southern India. Our hero is now stripped down to just his *pyjama* trousers and a deep red sash tied jauntily at the hip. His well-oiled six-pack ripples nicely as our heroine arches out over the water in a profoundly provocative manner, her floating sari now replaced by a diaphanous skirt, a big display of midriff and a revealing *choli*, the tight-fitting cropped top usually worn under a sari. Our hero is building to a climax: '*Pyaar hi tha*, love is here, *pyaar hi tha, tha, tha* . . .' He shakes his booty as our heroine drapes herself across one muscled rower after another. Strangely this does not seem to bother our hero. Everyone is in this together. '*Pyaar hi tha*,' chime the glistening rowers in happy chorus.

And here we are back on the Bombay seafront again, back in jeans and hot pants and pigtails. We have come full circle, and as the pink fades from the Gateway of India our hero and heroine switch straight into an earnest discussion about when he should meet her parents. Naturally there is no mention of their transcontinental routine, and not so much as a passing reference to cows or cuckoo-clocks.

There it is, perfect and complete, a Hindi dance number with bells on. It works over and over again as does the story-line formula. In fact Bollywood has been in overdrive on this particular story-line since the Seventies, producing approximately 12,000 floaty, flirty films of which about 30 per cent have been big box-office successes. That makes for around 4,000 hit films with the same story, the same characters, the same dance routines and the same astonishing array of spangled costumes. The new wonder boy, Hrithik Roshan, had just stepped into this industry, into a film genre that has evolved and changed as rapidly and as frequently as one of its current female stars hits the costume cupboard in one film, an industry with plotlines that have mirrored or reflected the country's history and politics for over a century. And now in the new century it was hitting an all-time high with a brand-new star to pull in the crowds. To dance up there is to be lord of all you survey.

I learned not to laugh at the celluloid icons at a *chai* stall in Delhi. During the late Nineties when I worked for an Indian paper

I made some journalist friends. We hung out and drank *chai*. I thought I was pretty savvy. I thought I knew a bit about Hindi films. I had been watching them for ten years and I could sing along to some of the songs and wiggle my hips and bits in time to the trilling tunes.

One afternoon I was taking tea with Niti, a fellow journalist and a friend. Niti is a sensible, unexcitable Sikh with a reputation for good investigative journalism. He and I used to argue with our editor about the same things and we shared a passion for film. As I stood drinking tea, the other *chai*-stall drinkers sat in the backs of their rickshaws, swatting at fat flies with thin arms as they made an inch-by-inch survey of my clothes, and of what lay underneath. It didn't matter. I was lolling against a tree, sipping *chai* with a friend, and I felt safe. We were talking about film. We were talking about Amitabh Bachchan, The Big B, the king of kings, the man who bestrides the Hindi film world. Amitabh Bachchan has even made it to Madame Tussaud's, in wax and in person.

'You see,' said Niti, 'the Big B has the ability to be the common man at the same time as leading him. Do you get me?' He held his *chai* aloft, raised to his hero.

The other drinkers flapped at flies in unspoken agreement.

'Have you really studied his work, have you seen all his stuff? You know, the power of his fight scenes was one of the things that really pulled the Indian male psyche through the political and social lows of the Seventies. He was all the strength that we seemed to have lost. He was our new role model.'

'I've seen some of his films, not all of them,' I mumbled.

'So you know what I am saying then?' Niti's face was alive.

'Well, to be honest it just looks as if he is throwing a lot of chairs around and grunting.' I looked down into my *chai*.

Niti was silent.

'I finally saw *Bade Miyan, Chote Miyan* last night,' I said.

Older Brother, Younger Brother had been a recent hit for the Big

14

Amitabh Bachchan, The Big B

B and had been billed as a rollicking comedy. I had not laughed much.

Niti continued to watch me in silence. The other *chai*-drinkers began to unwind themselves from the backs of their rickshaws and move in on our conversation, a little at a time.

'I wasn't really that convinced, I thought he was quite mannered, quite, oh I don't know, a bit hammy I suppose . . .' I trailed off. 'Maybe just not quite his usual old magic,' I whispered into my *chai*.

There was a moment of suspended silence.

'Are you mad?' Niti sprayed *chai* in all directions.

'What do you mean?' I stopped mumbling.

'Amitabh is the greatest actor in the world. No one else comes close. He is the best thing we have. To tell you frankly, you really don't know what you are talking about. Hammy, what's this? You are very, very wrong.' Niti was shouting, his *chai* splashing out of the glass as he waved it at me menacingly.

My unexcitable friend was enraged. I was now backed right up against the tree, my glass of hot tea held out in front of me as a last line of defence. The other drinkers crowded round Niti, a tight-knit band of fans, and leant towards me as one.

'Do you understand what I am saying?' Niti shouted, his face thrust forward into mine.

I nodded. The small crowd stepped back. Niti wiggled his head in approval. I was released from the tree. We changed the subject. I had been warned.

Can playback dance numbers under starry, starry skies really have this much power? They can and they do. The modern Indian audience is bemused by the Western obsession with *cinéma-vérité* and our fascination with what they see as the squalor of daily life. India's population is now over a billion and nearly everyone is fighting for space, or even just a place to breathe. The oppressive and omnipresent poverty of southern Asia gives every Indian more than his or her daily bellyful of the harshness of reality. They have little desire or need to see it on the big silver screen when they have to live so literally in it all the time.

From the early days of Hindi cinema the current finely tuned Bollywood formula has evolved to give the audience maximum escapism and minimum reality. When the lights go down at the beginning of a Hindi film every member of the audience knows what they are going to get. It is what they want and what they have paid to see: big love stories, big dance numbers, shower-humming songs and fabulous costumes, all played out in a perfectly constructed tinsel boy/girl fairyland.

Out of this comes the biggest draw card of all – romance. The power of hearts and flowers will never diminish as long as the aunties of Asia continue to chitty-chat over endless cups of *chai* about how best to pair up lovely Aisha with clever Anwar. Of course there is love and romance in some arranged marriages, but it is not high on the list of negotiating points on the coffee table as the aunties sip and plan. India's culture of arranged marriage makes the combination of attraction, infatuation, obsession and love a potent and seductive recipe for drawing cinema-going audiences. And those millions of daily film viewers are argument enough for film-backers and producers to stick to the formula.

The Indian cinema audience is huge and excitable, and sexual innuendo is its high-octane flash-point. As the moral guardians of these movie millions, India's film censors take their job very seriously. Entire films, big chunks or even just a slightly raunchy song have been cut by the men who walk the dusty corridors of the Ministry of Information and Broadcasting: a kiss lasting more than two seconds, snip; a show of tongue between meeting lips, snip; a hand on a breast, let alone a nipple, snip, snip, snip.

These busy men were thrown into overdrive in 1993 when a film soundtrack entitled '*Choli Ke Peeche Kya Ha?*' became a big hit. The extreme beauty of the actress Madhuri Dixit, who lip-synched the words as she shimmied and undulated her way into the dreams of tens of millions of teenage boys, had a lot to do with the song's popularity. But what really upset the censors was the title, often repeated by the lovely Miss Dixit, as she pouted and caressed her curves. '*Choli Ke Peeche Kya Ha?*' roughly translates as 'What Do You House Beneath Your Blouse?' Young men started to take to the streets singing the title lyrics and using them as a licence to explore what passing girls did indeed house beneath

The lovely Madhuri Dixit, her choli firmly buttoned up

their blouses. The men at the ministry opened a big manila file, filled it with suits pending and had the song banned. Naturally, with so much publicity, the song became even more popular, and the luscious Miss D became Bollywood's number one sex siren without so much as touching a button on her *choli*.

In the world of Bollywood, India finds a panacea for all her ills. The poverty of life on the streets and in the rural villages is countered by the lushness of movieland sets and locations. The daily grey of arranged married life is made Technicolor by wild love stories in which young men and women defy families, time, space and everything else in their quest for love. Bollywood films take character templates from Indian history and scriptures and tangle them together in eternal love. There are no Romeo and Juliet twists of terminal love. You can't kill off heroes and heroines based on gods and goddesses. In Hindi film the boy and girl are not supposed to die. That would be a disaster, not only for the celluloid boy and girl but also for the box-office takings.

Dil Se (From the Heart) came out in 1999. It was the first Hindi film from a Tamil film director called Mani Ratman. He and his co-producer, Shekhar Kapur, a home-grown Bollywood director who subsequently crossed into Hollywood with his Oscar-nominated direction of *Elizabeth*, put together a seemingly unbeatable package. They brought in the platinum boy of soundtrack CD sales, A.R. Rahman. Then they pinned down Shah Rukh Khan and a very popular and beautiful actress called Manisha Koirala to play the leading roles.

Bollywood began to buzz with gossip even before the crew went on location. By première time the hype had worked itself up to fever-pitch. The critics were poised to welcome a new hit, a new kind of film that would set the trend for Bollywood 2000.

Dil Se looked like a standard story. 'Let us take you on a journey through the seven shades of love,' said the posters several storeys high that towered over major traffic routes in the big cities, tempting the metro audiences with a seductive shot of Shah Rukh and

Manisha arching over each other provocatively, while the world behind them exploded in James Bond pyrotechnics. The publicity was slick and city-centred. The posters were modern and many graphic miles from the familiar hand-painted, chiffon-draped, busty-beauty versions that were, and still are, the usual fare of Hindi cinema. The *Dil Se* campaign had the kind of romantic line and pumped-up visuals that would pull in a big 'initial', the money made on pre-booked tickets, for the opening run. Huge sales of the soundtrack and the promise of lavish dance routines, with locations that spun from the high-altitude deserts of Ladakh in the northern Himalayas to those trusty wafting coconut palms in Kerala, had the audience-to-be panting in the ticket queues.

They seemed such a good idea in the poster promise, those seven shades of love:

Hub = attraction. Boy meets Girl on a misty station platform in the wilds of the north-east.

Uns = infatuation. Boy gets hooked on Girl, pursuing her to her mountain village with some very slick shimmying amidst picture-perfect landscapes.

Ishq = love. Boy gets Girl after big dance number across the deserts and mountains of Ladakh.

Aquidat = reverence. Boy worships Girl, with one small glitch. While pursuing Girl, Boy forgets to mention that there is a very pretty, pre-arranged girl waiting for him back home. This makes for some great finger-wagging dance numbers from Girl on the spot in Ladakh, and from the girl back home when Boy returns to Delhi for some pre-arranged engagement tea parties.

Ibaadat = worship. Boy going way beyond the call of duty in pursuit of Girl.

Janoon = obsession. And this is where the trouble started.

Our boy was a journalist and our girl was a freedom-fighter. Her mission was to make her way down to Delhi from the misty station platform where their eyes had first locked and the *Uns* had kicked in. Once in the capital city she had to take out the President of

India during the Republic Day celebrations. Our boy tried to stop her, to save her from herself and to keep them together.

By now the audience was confused. Our boy had warmed to his pre-arranged girl back home, and so had the audience. The girl back home was a storming dancer and she was also as pretty as a picture. But the real problem came at the end, with the seventh shade of love. There was no big closing dance number, no flocks of pigeons bursting from the Mogul monuments of Delhi, symbolizing perfect love and the flowing and gushing of things to come. Our girl was on a suicide bomb mission and the seventh shade was *Maut*, death. Our boy caught her on her way to work, so to speak, padded up nicely with explosives. He embraced her, and the screen exploded. It was not quite your usual Bollywood ending.

The audience was furious.

The night I went, the auditorium had started out in silence, gripped by the pre-release hype and that eye-locking moment on the misty station platform. Then, as the terrorist plot began to develop, the chatter started, with dialogue in the aisles about after-film restaurant options. While our boy was tracking terrorist units in pursuit of his love, Dilip in row D was trying to decide between Chinese at the Hyatt and Italian at the Intercontinental. By the time our boy, Shah Rukh Khan, went for the terminal embrace there was so much chitty-chat that the audience almost missed the big moment, though not quite. There was stunned silence after the big bang, a pause and then a universal shuffle as a thousand hands reached for mobile phones and dialled friends and family.

'Rubbish, man, I'm telling you this, absolute rubbish. Don't waste your money,' they shouted to their friends as the credits rolled.

No amount of slick playback dance routines and buffed-up gloss could save *Dil Se*. It died within weeks. A little bit of realism and an exploding heart-throb were too much to bear. In contrast, once *Dil Se* went on to the international circuit, it became one of the most successful Hindi films to date. The Non-Resident-Indian jazz bar crowd could not get enough of it, and the soundtrack played in every Asian-Abroad corner of the world, from the back of taxis in Southall, West London, to the hottest funk fusion clubs in Queens, NYC. Commentators could not understand why the film had been such a flop in India and yet such a big hit on international release. They had perhaps forgotten who makes up the core of India's film-goers.

India is one of the few countries in the world still to have a predominantly rural population. Of the suggested figure of 23 million people who see a film each day in India, a large percentage do not fill the aisles in city cinemas: they crouch down in the dust looking up at a rough canvas screen. Often there is a stain on the screen that keeps blurring the heroine's face, the result of travelling film-*wallahs* rolling up their canvases too quickly during monsoon downpours and pushing them into tin trunks that rust. So Madhuri Dixit competes with a stain in a village schoolyard in Madhya Pradesh while her audience of the night sits under an open sky, real live stars acting as the auditorium for the celluloid versions up on the stained canvas. The people in the dust tilt their heads to catch Shah Rukh Khan's every pelvic thrust and strain their necks to get a better view of Madhuri's cheeky *choli*.

These are village people whose lives are an endless round of failing crops, unpaid debts and malnutrition, who live with the constant fear of being cut down by malaria, typhoid or dengue fever, who have watched the promise of Independence come to nothing, who are still trapped in the same grinding cycle of poverty. These people do not want realism. They do not want to see their own story up on the screen. They want to be transported.

Once a fortnight the travelling film-*wallah* arrives to show the latest Bollywood offering, dismantling his roughly erected screen in a hurry at the end of the show before the tax collector catches up with him. Sometimes he plays the film on the wall of a house, half of the audience peering in through holes gouged out by the monsoon. In July and August the soundtrack is often drowned by the rattle of rain on a corrugated iron roof. During the north-west monsoon Shah Rukh Khan and Madhuri Dixit stretch and bulge across soggy screens in badly made tents. A single speaker and the smell of burning dung cakes replace the surround-sound and pop-corn aroma of the urban multiplexes. Yet these people in the dust or the deluge make up the core of Bollywood's audience. They are the real fans who want fantasy not reality, escapism not informa-tion. And when a new face hits the screen they will adore it and cheer for it as long as their dream-catcher sings, smooches, flutters, titters, rages and loves 100% up on the silver screen.

So when Hrithik Roshan walked into Bar Indigo on a March night in 2000 he was a man with a newly formed daily fan club of approximately 23 million.

Or 23 million plus one. I too had been swimming in those eyes in a state of transported breathlessness, just like any good fan should.

'He cuts across gender,' wrote one columnist, soon after *Kaho Naa . . . Pyaar Hai* appeared. She was not famous for her generos-ity in print. 'Men admire him and women adore him. Both sexes are rooting for him,' she informed her surprised readership.

The girls, women and matrons of India were unanimous.

'I went to see *Kaho Naa . . . Pyaar Hai* with my teenage daugh-ter because she was insisting. I was hysterical from the first,' confided a thirty-eight-year-old Delhi exporter.

We were whiling away the time in neighbouring queues at the bank, and she was very keen to give me her views on Hrithik. Perhaps some of the stardust of Bar Indigo had rubbed off on me. I had only just got back to Delhi after gazing into those wondrous eyes in Bombay.

'My daughter had to hold me down because I was getting so

excited,' she explained as she adeptly yanked the staples out of the piles of 500-rupee notes that she had just been handed.

The Non-Resident-Indian accounts manager introduced herself and joined our discussion. She was, she said, forty-five years old, married with two sons and a daughter, and a successful working woman. She tapped a long burgundy fingernail on the job-title badge pinned to her heavy silk sari as if to confirm her status.

'Hrithik Roshan is a very beautiful man. I have seen the film ten times because I like to watch him. He looks to me like Jesus Christ. I am reacting to him very strongly.'

I was surprised by her comparison.

'I am convented. Every day of my schooling I was looking at Jesus Christ. He was the first star for all of us convent girls.'

She ignored the customer waiting in front of the Non-Resident-Indian accounts desk as she elaborated on aspects of Hrithik's Christ-like qualities. I was not sure what the Bishop of Delhi would make of her belief that Jesus Christ would also have looked fetching in a neoprene T-shirt, let alone the nuns who had convented her at Jesus and Mary College, Chanakyapuri, New Delhi, and when she finally managed to drag herself away from the subject, I grabbed my money from the tired man at foreign accounts and ran to the safety of the café next door.

At the table beside me, wriggling on a red plastic chair in tight Capri pants, Anu was ordering a cold coffee with extra whipped cream at the same time as running over Hrithik's finer points with her friend Rani. From their teenage giggles and gasps of wonder it was obvious that they too had seen *Kaho Naa . . . Pyaar Hai*, and they were just as starry-eyed as the Non-Resident-Indian accounts manager.

'I like his biceps, I like the way his lower body moves. I like his hands, his long fingers. I'm sure they feel good.' Anu looked dreamily into her cold coffee, winding her fingers through her thick ponytail. 'Maybe he looks a little effeminate. But I don't think that is a bad thing. Overall, he's hot.' Anu's straw went deep into the cream on her coffee.

Rani did not need to pause for thought.

'He's shy and inhibited – a great change from the shorty Khans. God, you know, I really could eat him. But there's also something vulnerable about him that makes you feel all over-protective. I could take him home for some *filmi fundas*,' she said as she sucked long and hard on her straw.

Filmi fundas, the fundamentals of film: *filmi*, a word that has slid into the language as a catch-all for every glossy dream and disco sari queen – *filmi, fill'mee, adj.*, of film, of Hindi film, the essence of Bollywood (*coll.* Hinglish).

'Imagine, *yaar*, imagine being all on your own with him for an evening. Too good. What do you think his favourite kind of pizza is?' Rani went on.

'How do you know he likes pizza?' Anu seemed a bit non-plussed.

'There is a list of his favourite things on his website. He really likes Ferrero Rocher chocolates, black is his favourite colour, Jan 14 is his favourite date because that's when *Kaho Naa . . . Pyaar Hai* opened . . .'

'Sure, I know, I just forgot about the pizza and stuff.' Anu stabbed her straw up and down in her cold coffee.

I took note of the Ferrero Rocher chocolates.

By now Hrithik's pulling power had already gone far beyond high-street teenage thrills. Within two months of the release of *Kaho Naa . . . Pyaar Hai* he was on the cover of India's leading English-language weekly news magazine. *India Today* is not prone to hyperbole but its Bollywood cover boy gazed from the news-stands in black leather, flanked by stories on the stock exchange in Pakistan and the launch of internet broking in India. 'Heartthr♥b Hrithik',

He gazed from the news-stands in black leather

pulsated the headline. It was as if the latest boy band had appeared on the cover of *The Economist* with bambis hopping around the title words.

From the front cover of a serious magazine Hrithik-talk moved into higher circles. I was at a party at a Delhi embassy famous for hosting the flashiest dos in town. Not that I was there to participate in the fashion stakes. My look for the night was more browns and bags than cocktail chic. An out-of-town Bombay socialite was standing next to me in diamonds and a lime-green silk sheath, waggling a long green nail in the face of a young American who had been unwise enough to ask what she thought of the new wonder boy.

'Of course it is exciting to have someone new on the scene. He is so fresh. Naturally the Khans have proved themselves but perhaps this new boy on the horizon is a sign that they are reaching the end of their shelf-life. You know, all those in the upper crust in London are beginning to really talk about him.'

She turned towards me for confirmation, then took in my clothes and rapidly turned back to the young American.

'This is it, you see. He really is the talk there,' she said, edging away.

It was hard to imagine the clubs of St James's buzzing with chit-chat about Hrithik's biceps, but then the cocktail queen surely knew what she was talking about. And while she planted Hrithik in the social orbit of London, W1, *Kaho Naa . . . Pyaar Hai* continued to break Hindi film records with every passing week of release.

Of course the Bollywood press wanted to know what the 'shorty' Khans thought of the new six-foot wonder boy. All three smiled, gave their best profile to camera, said they thought he was very talented, and wished him luck. In an age of instant gratification when icons are created one night and dismantled the next, it was too soon to see whether Hrithik would last, but the Khans were playing it safe.

Hrithik faced the press with a smile as wide as Chowpatty Beach and humility by the bucketful.

'One fine day you get up and stop traffic. It's hard to digest,' he told a hard-nosed but weak-kneed news journalist from *India Today*. 'My ears go red when I hear girls saying I'm sexy. Look at what I was like before all this, my legs were too thin, my torso too short. I have big ears which keep popping out, hair which never settles, a thin neck and a long nose.'

The female journalist from *India Today* begged to differ, but he batted away her protests.

'I thought I might get pass mark,' he said. 'But now it is out of control. Where did my life go?'

During that spring of 2000 I was moving between Bombay and Delhi on a regular basis, writing and researching, flipping between the high gloss of the financial capital and the dust and harshness of the real capital. Indian film was part of my research. My appetite had been whetted. I wanted to meet big ears, perhaps with a box of Ferrero Rocher tucked under my arm, perhaps dressed in black, perhaps to suggest pizza.

CHAPTER 2

Turmoil

Bring on the baddies

THE JUICE-*WALLAH* on the road beside Breach Candy Swimming Club in uptown Bombay said he could get me a hit-man for 5,000 rupees. It was just your average kind of conversation-over-juice. He smiled at me and his face turned inside out. Under a long Marathi forehead his small dark eyes receded into falling pouches of flesh and his whole face became a ripple of skin, moustache and teeth. The muscles on the juice-*wallah*'s grinding arm are more pronounced than those on his left, the palms of his hands are betel-nut red, stained by decades of juice, and his skin always seems to glisten in the thick humidity.

The juice-*wallah* is part of my life in Bombay. His stall stands outside the formidable gates of the Breach Candy Swimming Club, a central fixture in the city's social round, just five minutes' walk from where I stay on Carmichael Road. When I am in Bombay I swim at the club a couple of times a week, and then I take juice with the juice-*wallah*. He does front-of-house at the stall and his juice-extractor lurks in the shadows behind him, a wrought-iron beast that proudly proclaims itself to be a product of Sunbrite Grinders Ltd of Calcutta. Man and beast are conjoined by the wooden grinding handle. He has a silver whizzer too, a modern electric insult to the fortitude of Sunbrite and elbow grease. It makes the same level of noise as a light aircraft taking off. The juice-*wallah* remains faithful to his old companion. The whizzer is used by those who mind the stall when the boss is not around, by other less muscular members of the juice-*wallah*'s family who have no objection to just flicking a switch and taking off, rather than pumping sweat and wrestling with the great wrought-iron beast.

The whole of the front of the stand is a theatre set of triangular piles, predominantly of oranges, the small sweet indigenous variety, part orange, part mandarin, stacked up in yellow and green. Sometimes there are marigold garlands draped over these piles, as if they have just won first prize in a horticultural show. While the oranges hold the foreground the rest of the ingredients form the wings and the backdrop: neatly topped carrots with Cyclops ends peering from their mounds, the darker, redder, sweeter variety that suit the Indian palate; apples from Kashmir and Kulu, polished to a shine; beetroots, bloody and dark, small and squat; wild, green-haired pineapples; flushed pomegranates, blushing and beautiful beside pale melons that smell of yeast as they overripen in the heat. In the right season there are great bunches of lychees, huge pink bouquets, or mangoes that leave their trails of golden stickiness all over the stand. There are flowers too that sit in vases on either side of the silver whizzer, but there are no flowers around the grinder.

It was April. The flowers beside the silver whizzer were roses, white and red, their petals softening in the sun. The juice-*wallah* was telling me about hit-men because I had been quietly complaining about a man with dyed red hair and a lop-sided smile who was hanging around the house where I stay. I thought the juice-*wallah* might have the rundown on any local loiterers, that perhaps he might be able to have a discreet word with the man. I was tired of the peeping tom's punctual face at my bedroom window, always just as I started to dress or undress. I was just after a subtle word of warning. The hit-man rates came out of left field as the juice-*wallah* slashed into some beetroots and carrots. Dark red juice leaked from the blades of the grinder as my hit-man guide elaborated. He wiped his hands on the front of his *kurta*, adding arterial-red trails to the butchered vegetable stains that were already there.

'Shootings are best. No touchings, no seeing, only killing, so much more value than knifey-job.' He poured the juice into a clean glass and passed it to me. 'Knife killing means seeing all of face, much bigger price.'

'Stabbing.' I took the glass of dark juice.

'You want man for stabbing pervy chap?' He paused for a moment, counting his knuckles first and then the dips in between. 'This will be 7,000 rupees. You want?'

'No, no, I meant that the word is stabbing. I just want the man to go away and stop staring at me. I was hoping that a quiet word with him might be enough.'

'Here men are all the time staring.' He wiped the blades of his grinder and waved away a crowd of listless flies. 'Best time for killing is *andheri rat*. You know meaning of this?'

Andheri rat, the blackest night when there is no moon.

'How did we get on to this? I just wanted someone to talk to this man. You've all been watching too many films, people being shot, actors and directors, underworld hits. You've all got it on the brain. What's wrong with just talking to my pervy chap?'

I looked down at the dark juice in my hand. It had lost its appeal.

The juice man rested his arm on his grinder.

'Much more effective killing.'

🌿

The night of 21 January 2000 had been a perfect *andheri rat* in Bombay. In the Santa Cruz district, in the northern reaches of the city, it had been even blacker because the power had failed. On Tilak Road generators chugged, creating small holes of light in the dense humidity that overlay the city. At this time of day Tilak Road is usually full of cars parked bonnet to boot as their drivers wait for the *filmi* bosses at the doors and gates of the offices that line the street. But on that evening the street seemed almost empty. A doorway opened, throwing a rectangle of generated light out on to the black tarmac. Two figures stepped into the bright square and a car door was opened, the pale interior bulb lighting up the face of the first man, unrolling his shadow into the street behind him.

Two more figures appeared out of the blackness, shouting and running. There was a loud report. The shadow of the man getting into the car lurched and his body smacked back against the open car door with the impact of a bullet. Then he flopped forward, half-way into the car. Two more shots split the darkness and then the driver of the wounded man began to scream.

The two hit-men ran across the street, picked out by the light that spilled from the open doorway. They were not running away but repositioning themselves. The driver screamed again, throwing open the other rear door of the car to drag his boss across the back seat just as a second volley of shots began to slam into the lining of the open door. The wounded man slid on his own blood out of the line of fire. His driver jumped from the back seat into the front and turned the car towards the hit-men. They were still firing as they scattered either side of the car, the driver leaning on his horn and screaming into the darkness as a bullet shattered the windscreen. As the car lights passed, the hit-men melted into the blackness of *andheri rat*. They were on the way back to the man who had hired them, to collect their pay before it became clear that they had not quite completed the job. As the car lurched away the wounded man managed to make a call to his son.

When the driver reached Santa Cruz police station a few minutes later policemen swarmed all over the car. Within another few minutes it was empty and the wounded man and his driver were being taken to Nanavati Hospital. By the time they reached the hospital twenty minutes later, a news crew was waiting for them. People had seen the shooting from behind their windows on Tilak Road and the car was a familiar one in the neighbourhood. The news crew wanted to know if the attempt had been fatal. Santa Cruz is synonymous with Bollywood stars. A shooting up there was headline news.

Back at the police station the victim's car was under close scrutiny, this time by the press looking for clues as to who had been shot. One young television journalist wiped her hand across the bloodied back seat. She was dragged off into the police station and charged with tampering with evidence.

Three hours later a senior doctor appeared on the steps of Nanavati Hospital to address the still swelling crowd of television crews, journalists and photographers. He paused for a moment, slightly taken aback by the volley of camera flashes.

'After an hour's operation my team has made a successful extraction from near the patient's heart wall. The bullet passed through the patient's bicep as he raised his arm to protect himself from the attack. It then passed into his chest cavity.' The doctor paused again. 'Mr Roshan is now in the recovery room.'

Hrithik had been working out at the gym when his father had called. Rakesh Roshan told him not to move from where he was. Hrithik asked why. His father told him that he had been shot. Hrithik grew up very quickly during that short conversation. At the time he was in the middle of making his second film in which he was playing a terrorist, fighting and dancing his way further into the public eye. Now the guns had become real. Bollywood was no longer a playground for the young star.

Beneath the brittle celluloid glitter of Bollywood, out among the fetid alleys of Bombay, the underworld dons rule. India has dual economies, one white and legal, one black and illegal. Bombay is

Now the guns had become real

the epicentre of this financial fissure, and the dons have made the black economy their own. Since the Sixties they have grown fat on protection money extracted from the prostitutes of the city. When the local government tried to make Maharashtra a dry state the dons diversified into bootlegging. When the city began to grow they moved in on the rich pickings of the construction industry. India's export restrictions on the bullion market gave them fresh fishing-grounds to trawl. And when those restrictions were lifted, and their smuggling network ceased to be profitable, the dons went shopping again. Bollywood and politics were the peaches they picked.

Then history gave them a blank cheque.

On 6 December 1992, rioting Hindus destroyed an important Muslim mosque, Babri Masjid, at Ayodhya in Uttar Pradesh, claiming that the area was a sacred Hindu site. The backlash in Bombay was immediate. As television images of the destruction of Babri Masjid were transmitted across the country, bringing with them memories of the bloodbath of Partition, Muslims started to riot in the Mohammed Ali Road area, the heart of Bombay's Muslim community. In response the predominantly Hindu city police fired indiscriminately into the crowds of rioters. Incensed Muslims then attacked police stations and Hindu temples. Hindu extremists retaliated, rampaging through the city and burning Muslim homes and businesses. The riots were finally brought to a halt when the leader of Shiv Sena, the city's powerful militant Hindu-centric political grouping, called off his bullies. Over a thousand people had been killed, 70 per cent of them Muslims in a city which is predominantly Hindu, and an estimated 150,000 people had fled from Bombay.

The dons took advantage of this state of civil unrest and used it to hoist themselves further up the ladder of illicit power. Two months after the riots, in March 1993, thirteen bombs went off in one day across the city, aimed at the institutions that symbolized the Hindu business community. The Stock Exchange was gutted as were the Air India building, the Sheraton Sea Rock Hotel and the Centaur Hotel. Bombay's biggest don, Dawood Ibrahim, was said to have masterminded the attacks in retaliation for the deaths of his fellow Muslims during the riots. Dawood was living in Dubai at the time and he then moved to Karachi, but his change of domicile did not mark an end to his grip on Bombay's black economy. From the safety of exile in Pakistan he continued to rule his army of extortionists in Bombay, each one of them controlling a separate area of operations. Dawood picked his army carefully and appointed one of his darkest operators, Abu Salem, to trawl Bollywood. Dawood's *filmi* flunkey was known as Bollywood's *Bhai*, tinsel town's Big Brother. He watched the Hindi film industry from his own offshore lair in Bahrain. Producers and directors were followed and threatened until they handed over a share of their latest film deal. Most of them had dealt with the world of organized crime at some point in their careers – a little help here and there in the early days to get a project off the ground, a bit of dirty work that they had farmed out, a few wild parties with free-flowing alcohol stocked by the dons: nearly everyone had dues to pay. As far as *Bhai* was concerned no one was untouchable.

Producers, directors, distributors, dance choreographers, composers, even the stars were given a choice. Pay or die.

In 1996 an attempt was made on the life of a director, forcing him to move abroad to protect his family. In 1997 a powerful music distributor who had not made enough fuss of a particular music producer with underworld connections was killed. In October 1999 a film distributor was beaten up outside one of the main cinema complexes in Bandra, the heart of residential Bollywood. A month later, there was a further assassination attempt, this time on one of the big film laboratory owners who had been holding out against *Bhai*'s demands. The *filmi* crowd began to get jumpy. The list of celebrities with police protection doubled and the city security forces complained that they were running out of personnel.

In 1998, when Rakesh Roshan first announced his plans for *Kaho Naa . . . Pyaar Hai*, a call from *Bhai* came through. He was demanding 5 crore rupees, that is 50 million rupees, about £750,000. Roshan refused to pay. The demands continued. The secretaries at Roshan's Film Kraft offices in Santa Cruz West were ordered to check the identity of every caller before putting them through to the producer. But still the calls managed to get to him. By the time the film was about to open in January 2000 the demand had become more flexible. Roshan could either pay the original demand or sign away the overseas distribution rights. Still he refused.

Just before the opening of *Kaho Naa . . . Pyaar Hai* Papa Roshan decided to have a party to celebrate the launch of Hrithik, his golden boy, on to the big screen. He picked a club, Fire and Ice, a new *filmi* favourite. Situated in a sedate district of central Bombay, Fire and Ice is about as discreet as it gets in Bollywood. Here the stars can flex their egos in comparative privacy.

The pre-release hype for the film was in full swing. Rakesh Roshan was about to launch his son on the unsuspecting women of India, his six-pack shining, his biceps pumped, his green eyes ready to laser into millions of teenage hearts. Dad the director was feeling good. He had not had a big hit for a while.

A stranger came into the club and made his way to where Rakesh was sitting. The stranger leant over and said that he had a message from *Bhai*. The emissary evaporated into the crowd. Rakesh said nothing and continued with the party. His wife asked for the air-conditioning to be turned up. She was worried that her husband was sweating.

At the end of the party Rakesh drove home with his son. He told Hrithik not to go out without a driver, as a security measure. Hrithik laughed.

Three weeks later Rakesh Roshan was shot.

A few days after the shooting, Hrithik was on set doing a big dance scene for his new film. One moment he was thrusting and grinding for the camera, the next his world collapsed as he caught sight of himself in a mirror.

'I realized that this was crazy. My father was lying in hospital and I was dancing around like some kind of idiot.'

Hrithik announced that he would be leaving the industry.

Hundreds of journalists went gasping into editorial meetings. No one did this kind of thing. No one left Bollywood just as they hit stardom.

Bollywood rides on a river of gossip kept at full spate by countless film magazines that dominate the news-stands in glossy, tacky sheaves. Pumped and preened Bolly boys and babes smile and pout from the covers in outfits that are a tribute to all things that cling. Cover stories tempt the *filmi*-hungry reader with rivalry and love drama. 'Who's The Sexiest Man In The Industry?' shouts a headline between a picture of Hrithik clad in frightening denim dungarees and his rival, Salman Khan, in, well, obviously not much more than his six-pack. 'Akshay Used And Abused Me!'

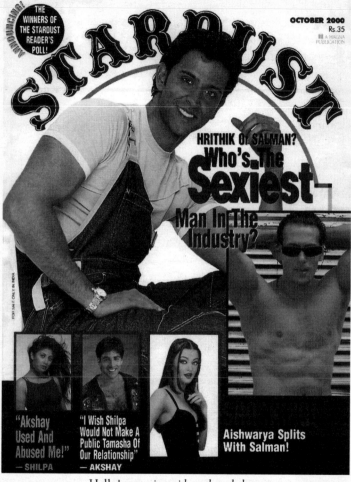

OCTOBER 2000
Rs.35
A MAGNA PUBLICATION

STARDUST

HRITHIK Or SALMAN?
Who's The Sexiest Man In The Industry?

"Akshay Used And Abused Me!"
— SHILPA

"I Wish Shilpa Would Not Make A Public Tamasha Of Our Relationship"
— AKSHAY

Aishwarya Splits With Salman!

FOR SALE ONLY IN INDIA

Hello! *magazine with teeth and claws*

claims *filmi* kitten Shilpa under a pouting picture of her with her hair blowing in the breeze. Next to Shilpa is a snap of the heavily gelled Akshay: 'I Wish Shilpa Would Not Make A Public *Tamasha* [drama] Of Our Relationship.' And inside Shilpa's article continues: 'Unbreak My Heart. I Got to Know after We Broke off that Akshay Was Cheating on Me all Along.' They are *Hello* magazine with teeth and claws. They grasp every hint of a story that flickers through the *filmi* world and make them stretch over about 150 big, bright pages of unimportant vital inside information. At about 50p each they are a great deal more than cheap thrills. They have the highest monthly magazine circulation figures in India and they are the longed-for fare of most middle-class and middle-aged city matriarchs. Few men own up to reading *filmi* mags but millions do, in just the same way that countless men in England skulk in the loo on Sunday mornings with *Hello!* rolled up inside *The Economist* or *Computer Weekly*.

The female *filmi* magazine fans of India treat the contents of these magazines with a reverence they do not deserve. They are passionate about them. I see it around me all the time. When I am in Delhi I go to a beauty salon close to where I live. La Belle is on the fourth floor of a five-star hotel. In the midst of its floral chairs, gold fittings, space-pod hair-dryers and trolleys of alarming hair tints and shimmery nail colours, I slump down ready for a regular pedicure and manicure. India allows me the luxury of being scoured, primped and polished to a shine for just £6, and there I can put my prettified fingers on the pulse of what is happening in female India.

Each time I go, a plump Punjabi matriarch is there too. Mrs Kanwar goes to La Belle every few days to have her hair done and her legs massaged. She always brings me up to date on the family. Her husband, a bank manager with terrible problems of 'liver dysfunctionality'. Her son, a supervisor at a video store, and his 'not so sweet' wife who have three apparently perfect children. The constant dramas with the domestic servants. And then I get the tip of the week, usually along the lines of how to keep today's *chapatis* fresh for tomorrow. She also tries to marry me off to her nephew, a lanky computer software engineer in Florida with a bad hairstyle. She thinks we would make a lovely couple because, she says, I am 'so sweet'. But none of this family frou-frou matters as much as her regular update on exactly what is happening in Bollywood. This is what she really cares about. This is what really matters in her world.

Mrs Kanwar's good friend, Dolly Singh, is usually there too. Mrs Kanwar is round and smooth. Dolly Singh has frazzled edges and hair that looks as if it has high voltage behind it. She does not talk nearly as much as her good friend. She is usually having the hair whipped off her top lip. The flying and plucking action of the beautician's thread over her fairly luxuriant moustache keeps her quiet. She winces a lot but she seems happy to listen as Mrs Kanwar gives her update on the family, *chapati* storage, my nuptial future and what is what in Bollywood.

It is when Mrs Kanwar is not so chatty that I know the new editions of the *filmi* magazines have just come out. She will be ensconced under the dryer, the control at full throttle, drinking in the glossy pages of pouting babes and movie-muscle rivalry. Mrs Kanwar favours the main four, *Stardust*, *CinéBlitz*, *Filmfare* and *Movie*. It takes her a good hour to survey the big four and then she is ready to give a highly detailed account of life, lust and loss in Bollywood. The *filmi* magazines are her inside track.

Mrs Kanwar's inner world is shaped by those magazines. I needed to find someone who shapes the magazines. While I was in Bombay, fresh from my first encounter with Hrithik Roshan, I rang Meena, Magazine Queen and editor-at-large on one of the main *filmi* monthlies.

When I got through to her breathy tones she was off-hand at

first, speaking to me as if I was a minor itch that would not go away. Then I made it clear that I would be writing about her and her views on all things Bollywood in the foreign press.

'You are going to quote me by name?'

I assured her I would.

'Cool. When do you want to meet?'

'Tomorrow?'

'Sure.'

'What about breakfast?'

'At the Taj?'

The Taj Mahal, India's most famous five-star hotel, built in 1903 by one of the greatest Parsi industrialists, J.N. Tata, dominates the seafront beside the Gateway of India. There the beauties and deal-makers of Bombay glide among an excess of glittery chandeliers, springy carpets and lounge muzak, and there they compare mobile phone gimmicks and watch brands over weak coffee and doughy croissants.

'How about Leopold's?' I countered.

Leopold's is an old Parsi café. Variations on the bag-lady theme go down better at Leopold's than at the Taj.

'You like all the tourist-*shurist* thingy?' Meena had the urban middle-class habit of rhyming-*schyming*, Bollywood-*Shollywood*. Very Yiddish-on-Arabian Sea.

'Yes, I do. Can you make nine?'

'So early?' Meena was horrified.

'Ten?' I tried.

We compromised on 11.30. Power breakfast on Indian Standard Time is not an early-*schurly* thing.

Leopold's Café and Bar was once as central to the city's social heart as continental breakfast at the Taj Mahal Hotel is now. Leopold's and its kind sprang up in the mid-nineteenth century as the Parsi community began to make its mark in Bombay, bringing its Persian social clubs to the city. In essence they were safe clean places where the swelling numbers of factory workers from Bombay's cotton mills could get cheap and nourishing cake and tea. Like their Parisian equivalents the cafés were full of space and light, with high ceilings, fans that turned above marble-topped tables, and wide open frontages with views on to the constant cabaret of street life. It was in rooms such as these that Bombay youth once discussed life, love and politics over Persian chicken and thick, sweet coffee.

The glory days of the Parsi cafés have passed. Bombay is now modern Mumbai-on-the-move, and the idea of lingering over life and coffee has been abandoned in the constant rush and scurry for the next big thing. Leopold's has become a hippy haven where the back-packing and pony-tailed congregate over cornflakes and *lassis* before taking the bus to Goa. It is a postcard from the past, picturing the world of old Persia. There is a devotional niche behind the bar that holds a sad-eyed portrait of the last Shah of Iran. His crown seems heavy, pushing his forehead down to his eyebrows, and his great velvet cloak looks too big on his narrow shoulders. His presence is as weak and tired as the hollow-bellied hippies bent over their bowls of comforting cereal. Leopold's brings together those who are a long way from home.

The morning after I had called I sat waiting at Leopold's for Meena. Half an hour after the agreed time a *filmi* magazine-cover figure swayed into the shadows of the café's interior out of the hard sun on the street.

'Oh my God, what is happening in this place, every single piece of road is dug up. My driver parked miles away. I've had to walk for hours to get here. I'm so hot and dusty, I must look awful. So sorry to be late.' Meena extended a perfect hand to me, tipped in very blue nail varnish.

There was not a strand of hair out of place, not a speck of dust on her tight white silky trousers and sparkly designer T-shirt or on the very high, very spiky sandals that made her sway as she walked.

'So clever of you to recognize me.' She was the only highly polished Bombayite in a room full of back-packers and academically rumpled locals.

'So sweet here, isn't it?' she said as she picked her way with me back to the table where I had been waiting.

She perched warily on the edge of one of the chairs at an angle where she could see herself properly in the nearest mirror. Then she scanned the room, tilting her sunglasses down her nose, before sighing and pushing them firmly back into place.

'Good to meet you. I have been telling everyone that I was coming to Leopold's for an international interview. They all thought it was so funny, so cute,' she tinkled, as she lay her mobile phone, her Filofax and her black Prada handbag on the table. 'So adorable this place. I used to come here when I was a kid with my friends, so much fun.' She rested her perfect chin on the tips of her blue fingernails.

Meena could not have been more than twenty-five. The back-packers stared at us, looking at Meena with something between disdain and hatred, and a girl in a floppy dress, with hennaed hair and a face full of frown lines, snorted into her *lassi* as Meena chirruped about the cuteness of youthful days at Leopold's.

'I just love this. I have so many Parsi friends from school. You must be knowing . . .' She rattled off a list of twenty-something scions of the buoyant Parsi houses of Tata, Wadia, Godrej, Readymoney, Todiwallah, Jeejeebhoy and Mistry, each and every one a millionaire from the pram.

I did not know any of them. Meena looked at me more closely.

'So who do you know in Bombay?' she asked, tapping a nail on her mobile.

'I'm more Delhi- than Bombay-based.'

'Oh.' She scanned the menu intently to close the subject. I was *jungli*, a wild out-of-towner from the dusty, unsophisticated north.

She called a waiter over.

'Do you have plain *dosa*?'

'Is it on the menu?' the waiter retaliated.

'No, this is why I am asking.'

'Then we do not have.' He smiled.

43

Having drawn a blank on thin South Indian pancakes Meena tried again.

'Are these freshly made?' She pointed to the menu, one perfectly blue nail resting on the word *idli*, South Indian rice dumplings served with coconut *chutni*.

'How fresh do you want them?' The waiter put one hand on his hip and began to twirl his order pen between his fingers.

Meena rolled her eyes at me.

'Are those good?' She looked at my big plate of *wadas*, South Indian doughnuts, as soft and warm as fairground food.

'Delicious. Would you like to try them?'

'I can't eat that sort of stuff, just too too fattening.' She waved away my offer of a *wada* as if it was toxic.

'Just cold coffee, no ice-cream.' She snapped the menu shut and sent the waiter on his way.

'So which magazine is it you are writing for?' she asked as she began to scroll through some numbers on her mobile.

I listed the newspapers and magazines on whose behalf I was tracking the Hrithik phenomenon and the *filmi* scene. Meena stopped scrolling and gave me a smile that would have melted the heart of any Bollywood producer.

'So what is it you want to know?'

'What was it like when Hrithik said he was going to quit films after the assassination attempt?' I bit into a *wada* and Meena pursed her lips.

'God, you have no idea. It was so awful.' She closed her eyes for a moment.

'The assassination attempt?' I asked.

'No, no. That happens all the time. But imagine Hrithik being the very hottest thing this town has seen for God knows how long and suddenly *bhaff*, he's gone!' She clapped her hands together dramatically and puffed through rhododendron-red lips to make her point. The back-packers at the next table looked up from their *lassis*, startled by the sudden noise. Then the waiter reappeared with Meena's cold coffee and she took a long, elegant suck that left a perfect dark red ring around the straw.

'Do you mean it was a bigger deal that Hrithik was pulling out of films than that the dons had tried to kill his father?'

'God, *yaar*.' She wiped a finger across her lips and then leant towards one of the mirrors to check her lipstick.

'My God, every woman in India was in love with him,' she told her reflection.

'But *Kaho Naa . . . Pyaar Hai* had only been out for a couple of weeks. How could they all have seen him?'

'Hype was such that we had him on the cover of every magazine for months before the film. The whole industry was so desperate for a new star, something fresh, someone to take on the Khans. God, they are all so old now, all of them are mid-thirties.'

'That's not so old.'

'*Yaar*, over thirty and forget it.'

'I'm thirty-three,' I told her.

'So sorry, nothing personal meant.' Meena paused. 'You are looking much younger than this,' she said, without much conviction.

'Thank you.'

'Welcome. Are you done with these?' she asked, pointing to my now abandoned *wadas*.

'Please, help yourself.' I pushed the plate towards her.

'Just to try.' She tore a tiny corner off one of them and dipped it into the coconut *chutni* on the side, swallowing it down with a suck of iced coffee while pushing the plate back towards me.

'It was like the whole thing had been a big tease. One minute we have a new star. The next minute he's saying that he's not going to be making any more films because of what has happened to his dad.'

'You can see his point though.'

'What do you mean?' Meena was puzzled.

'Well, one day he is just another young hopeful and then his first film comes out and he's a huge star when he wakes up the next morning. He gets knocked over by a wave of adulation and then someone tries to kill his father.'

'This stuff is happening all the time,' Meena shrugged as she picked at the *wadas* again.

'What, assassination attempts?'

'*Yaar, yaar*, most of the stars have protection. There is a list of them. Amitabh Bachchan has free protection. The government picks up the bill for him. But he's different. The rest of them have to pay and they don't like it. They think Rs.555 per protection guy per twenty-four hours is too much. God, they are pulling down so many millions per film and they can't even come up with that. It's pathetic. So if they get shot, well . . .' Meena let the sentence die.

'Rs.555, that's very exact.'

'This is the price. I found out for myself. Not so much, *naar*?'

At about £8 a day even I could afford to have a bodyguard on my very un-Bollywood salary.

'You should do it, get a few of them next time you are going to a party here and everyone will think you are some hot-shot.' Meena gave me a sweet smile.

A small gang of pubescent boys had gathered outside the open window where we were sitting. Others were joining the group. Meena was the star of their show and they watched her every move.

'I think you've got a fan club.'

Meena batted away the compliment. 'Nothing doing.'

'You look like Rani Mukherjee.'

Rani Mukherjee was one of the biggest stars of the moment, and Meena really did look quite like her. The gaggle of lads outside definitely thought so.

'What rubbish is this? Rani is gorgeous.' Meena rolled her eyes.

I shrugged and the fan club outside gazed on in adoration. At last Meena smiled with her whole face and then she waved at the waiter. She ordered another cold coffee as she checked herself again in the mirror. She only made eye contact with the waiter via her reflection. He winked at her. She snarled back.

'Hrithik?' I asked again.

'*Yaar, yaar.* So he does this big *tamasha*-drama on all of us who have been building the hype around him. Even before *KNPH* came out we were making all this song and dance about him in the mags. Do you know about the whole Provogue drama-*sharma?*' Meena started in on another *wada*, tearing off tiny pieces very carefully with her fingernails.

'I heard about it.'

Hrithik had been booked by Provogue, a designer house, to appear at a big Delhi fashion show. When he hit the catwalk the usually calm Delhi fashion crowd went mad and the whole event turned into a mass of screaming girls and swaying older women, all begging Hrithik to get back on the ramp every time his fine rear end disappeared off stage.

'It was like there was this huge great train thing that the mags had set in motion even before the film opened. The film opens and the train is going twice as fast, then *bhaff*, he sticks on the brakes and says he's not going to play any more. What is this?'

'Understandable though,' I said.

'Nothing doing. You start a *filmi*-train, you stay on it. He's too much of a Mr Clean Guy. He needs to look around him a bit more and see how much you need to feed the press so we can fuel the hype. Look at Salman Khan. We get such good stuff out of him all the time. He plays by the rules.'

Salman Khan, Hrithik's ripple-chested friend at Bar Indigo, is the wild boy of the old guard who provides the *filmi* press with a steady stream of stories about behaviour that is more in tune with a rebellious teenager than an A-list movie star. Within days of Hrithik hitting the hoardings with *Kaho Naa . . . Pyaar Hai* the *filmi* mags had decided to pitch the two against each other: Salman, the body, the stud who picks up his leading ladies and drops them the second they start to cluck, the streetfighter who tears bars apart, the big star whose every move sells magazines; and Hrithik, the new squeaky-clean boy with muscles to match those of the Khan but

Salman Khan, The Body, The Stud

manners straight out of every Mama's dream son-in-law photofit. The main *filmi* magazines on the news-stands, the big four beloved of Mrs Kanwar at La Belle beauty salon, filled pages of their issues debating the kissability factor of new boy Hrithik as against old Mr Pucker-Up Khan. Would Pritti from Pune and Mira from Mysore rather ride off on the back of Salman's throbbing Harley Davidson for a frenzied night in black lace or cosy up on the sofa at home in their teddy-bear slippers with the green-eyed Hrithik and probably a fluffy kitten? *Stardust* was even making it a monthly event to compare Salman's and Hrithik's biceps and other bulges. *Filmi* India had developed muscle mania and Salman and Hrithik were at the forefront. Each of the magazines had their favourite. Meena's maga-zine was undoubtedly Salman-centric.

'He's such great copy. You know he is just an editor's dream, he makes stories, boom, boom, boom.' Meena clapped her hand on the table. Then she narrowed her eyes and leant towards me.

'Want to know something really hot?' she said in a very Bollywood stage-whisper.

'Of course.'

'It's the latest on Salman and Ash.' She began to smile.

By the general consensus of the *filmi*-mag-reading public, one of Salman Khan's greatest selling-points is his inability to keep his hands off his leading ladies. One of his recent co-stars, Aishwarya Rai, was possibly the most beautiful of them all. A former Miss India and Miss World, she had made the natural sideways glide into Bollywood and had shot straight to the top. It had quickly become urban legend that she was a good girl with a clean track record and that her parents were only too keen to find her a nice boy as far away as possible from the fleshpots of Bollywood. To Salman Khan she was jailbait.

'Catcher in the Rai', Meena's mag had banner-headlined the story. Then the reader was sucked into some scorching prose, laid out over a particularly beautiful black-and-white photograph of Miss Rai:

A man is like a mustang . . . wild and unleashed, galloping recklessly into the sands of time, flying high on the joys of bachelorhood. Until that one moment, when that perfect someone walks into his life, takes the reins in her hands and tames him despite all resistance. Leaving the spirit of the mustang gasping, tucked away in the closet.

The whole of the opposite page was taken up with a bare-chested picture of Salman, flames licking at his triangular torso, a wild horse of the media. Mrs Kanwar had been ecstatic under her dryer.

'The latest?' I asked Meena.

'They're an item, it's official. They've been smoochy-*moochy* all over Goa, all kissy-*wissy* at the Leela Resort, not even bothering to go back to their rooms, like they want everyone to know. How stupid is that? Not so squeaky clean Ash baby any more.' Meena shook her head like a maiden aunt. 'Word is her parents are so mad that they have made her swear that she will not make another film with Salman. What rubbish. Why not use the chemistry?' She waved at the waiter again. 'This is lumpy. *Chalo*, go and get another one.' She pushed her second half-drunk glass at the waiter.

He peered into the condemned glass.

'*Dekho*, look, it's disgusting.' She dipped the straw in and out impatiently.

The waiter took it away, still looking for the lumps. The backpackers had now abandoned any pretence of conversation. They were as gripped as Meena's adolescent fan club outside, as our star was only too aware.

'She is asking for trouble.'

'Who is?' I was beginning to lose the plot.

'Miss Ice Queen Ash. She is all pally when it suits her, then she makes it oh so clear that she thinks she is in another league in the beauty thingy. And all this *tamasha* about keeping Salman a big secret. Big joke, *naar*, who is she kidding? Everyone knows they are having an affair, and she goes around as if she is the first girl he's kissed.' She laughed, her hands either side of her face, then suddenly stopped. 'Oh my God, poor thing! Perhaps she thinks Salman the stud is going to marry her.' She snatched the third cold coffee from the waiter. 'She can't think that, she must be mad. He's bedded everyone. Why would he settle on her after the whole risky-*frisky* thing in Goa?'

'But doesn't every girl hope that the man they're mad about is going to be "the one"?'

'*Yaar*, *yaar*, but not Salman, everyone knows it's like an itch with him. He has to scratch-*snatch* all the time.' Meena was distracted. She was spinning lines for her next edition. She was spin-

ning for Bollywood, lacy, racy, pacy Meena, queen-in-waiting of
the gossip column. Above our heads the fans turned amidst hippy
talk of trance parties on Goan beaches, and the man behind the
pile of fruit on the marble counter stared past us to the action
outside on Colaba Causeway.

'How quickly did Hrithik change his mind about not making
any more films?'

Meena sat back, pursing her lips and crossing her legs elegantly.
She curved her foot up to examine her toes. I had interrupted her
train of thought.

'Oh drama-*sharma*, the whole thing. He was out of circulation
for maybe two, three days.'

'Wouldn't you have gone under cover for a bit in the same situation?' I asked.

Meena looked at me and was about to reply when her mobile began
a digital version of 'Lara's Theme' from *Dr Zhivago*. She answered it
without looking at me. A rapid-fire conversation followed, mainly in
English but with lapses into Hindi. It was about a party. Meena was
keen to go but the caller seemed to be having difficulty getting her an
invitation. She turned away from me and changed her tone to an
exaggerated whisper, now mainly in Hindi, hissing her responses, the
sibilance rising and falling as she made her points, her blue fingernails
tapping on the table. The conversation went on.

I followed the murals around the walls of Leopold's as Meena
hissed and tapped. Above the bar was an interior scene of the café,
the apron-wearing waiters looking more Parisian than Parsi, the
Parsi clientele certainly looking more Hollywood than Bollywood.
All along one wall above the tables was a curious hand-picked set
of scenes: Big Ben next to the Eiffel Tower, the Taj Mahal beside
the Great Wall of China, the Pyramids and the Sphinx at Giza
framed against Red Square. Meena was still talking as I got to Red
Square. I returned to the finer points of the Eiffel Tower.

'So sorry, where was I?' She snapped the telephone down on the
table and turned back to me with a practised smile.

'Hrithik.'

'Okay.' She paused. 'Have you met him?'

'Not yet.'

'Have you got an interview?' She narrowed her eyes.

'I'm planning one.'

'Good luck, he's not at all easy to get hold of.' Meena tipped herself forward in her chair. 'Love to know if you get hold of him.' She smiled again but it was less polished and more competitive. Her blue nails drummed on the table.

I asked the waiter for the bill and paid for Meena's rounds of cold coffee.

'That was fun. We must do it again,' she said, looking over my shoulder to the street outside where her fans were still hovering. 'God, it's too hot out there. How can I get back to my car in this heat?'

'I'm sorry to have taken up so much of your time.'

'No, no, not at all.' The smooth smile was back. 'Remember to have a look at my stuff on Salman and Ash in the next issue, it's going to be hot.' Then she teetered out into the midday heat, her tight white bottom shimmering as she sashayed.

Her promised low-down on Salman and Ash's love life came out a few weeks later:

Love is like a dose of cocaine . . . Before you take it, you're curious as hell. And once you do, you're hooked. Though you might live to regret it! Why? Why do we fall in love? Perhaps love can only be explained by the senses . . .

As I'm floating in my spool of philosophical thoughts on my way back from the office to my cosy nest in New Bombay . . . the shifting image of a couple distracts my attention. A vision of a couple entwined in each other on a motorbike. Alabaster skin, ruby lips, a beauty mark at the corner of her mouth. Actress Aishwarya Rai emerges from the darkness . . .

As a colleague once rightly put it . . . 'When two people kiss, one person always holds out a cheek' . . . In this case,

Ash was on the giving end. The lady was softly nibbling at Salman's ear lobes, whispering soft little nothings. Occasionally, she would also kiss him at the turn of a traffic signal. The couple drove on to catch a highway leading to Panvel and disappeared also into the horizon . . .

It has all the ingredients . . . A fairytale princess as lovely as an angel. A charming prince, lord of the land, handsome and strong. And a love story that's caught the interest of everyone in the world who loves a lover. But like every relationship, where the balance always tilts in the favour of one, this is no exception. Being the most beautiful woman in the world doesn't guard you from the inevitable hurt that love is bound to create. Ask Aishwarya.

*

'What do you think of Aishwarya Rai and Salman Khan?' I asked my hit-man consultant, the juice-*wallah* on the road beside the Breach Candy Swimming Club.

'Ahh . . .' He settled himself on the edge of the pavement, pulling one very thin ankle over his thigh, the pose of the street philosopher. 'Such a beautiful girl.' He refolded the edges of his *kurta* to keep them off the road. 'Such a man is wanting all of womens.'

Two teenage schoolgirls walked along the other side of the road, perfect in white *salwar kameez*, neatly folded blue *chunnis* or scarves fixed across their shoulders, their hair pulled tight into oiled plaits tied with blue bows. The juice-*wallah* and I watched them. The girls walked by, eyes fixed on the road in front of them. My street philosopher smiled.

'I am thinking the blame lies with the parents. They should be making marriage for this lady. Running around all over the place with *filmi filmi* peoples and she is thinking love, love, love, all the time. She needs a good husband. This is what she needs. Salman

Khan, big star but not big husband.' He stopped for a moment and looked at me.

'And where is your husband while you are running all over this place?'

'I don't have a husband.'

'No husband, what is this? What are parents thinking? You must find good husband for childrens and for future.'

Ash was being cast as the fragile infatuated female, and the affair with Salman was beginning to affect her work. Once one of the few stars famous for being punctual and courteous, she had taken to arriving late on set, making crews sweat it out. There were also reports of the odd tantrum. The magazines were in clover, Ash's directors less so. Their box-office kitten was showing all the signs of the Bollywood primadonna syndrome.

Her behaviour did nothing to dent her popularity. Miss Prim was in love and behaving badly, and *filmi* mag-reading Indian women sighed from a thousand Saturday afternoon beauty salons and fantasized about frenzied nights on Salman's Harley. Ash was the leading lady in town and everyone was just waiting for a director to pair her with Hrithik. It was the most obvious casting – wonder boy and golden girl shimmying across the screen to create a beautiful new couple for the *filmi* mags to feed on. It was what always happens in Bollywood. The best boy and the best girl do lots of films together and enough versions of happy-ever-after to satisfy every audience from the village wall to the metro multiplexes. Ash was the newest number one girl and Hrithik was the boy who was turning Bollywood upside-down. 'When,' Meena's magazines asked, 'when are you going to put them together? We are waiting, India is waiting for that *filmi* moment when you let us know that Ash and Hrithik are going to trip the light fantastic and make us all dance and sing their numbers from the shower to the office. What are you waiting for?'

I added the question to my list. If and when I met wonder boy I would ask him.

CHAPTER 3

Adulation

Meet a heroine

WHEN I WAS about eleven I used to dream that I could just ring up
Paul Newman, that I knew his number and could call him whenever the mood took me. We would talk about robbing banks in
Bolivia and spaghetti sauce, just normal day-to-day Hollywood
movie-star stuff. But that was twenty-two years ago. By the age of
thirty-three I should have grown up. Still, in Bollywood you *can*
just call the stars. You may not get through, but you can have a go.

I had five numbers for Hrithik. Two came from friends of friends
who seemed to have his number for no particular reason. The
other three had been given to me by the man who had arranged
the Provogue fashion show in Delhi where Hrithik had turned the
audience into screaming rock chicks.

It took me several days to settle at the desk by the window in
Carmichael Road and just ring up a movie star, and when at last
I did sit down and open the Hrithik page in my contact book I
immediately found other vitally pressing things to do. I spent a lot
of time watching the cars go by and counting how many times the
guard outside the Belgian Consulate next door spat betel-juice in
the space of half an hour. I made a deal with myself: the next time
he spat I would pick up the phone. He spat. I dialled the first
number.

The first three numbers put me through to a recorded message from a sweet voice that sounded as if it was wearing a sari. 'The network is not connecting, please try later.' The fourth number on the list was Hrithik's 'number of residence'. I was fiddling furiously with a pencil in my hair. I did not really want to try it. A man answered in Hindi. In my panic I stabbed the pencil into my head.

'*Halo, halo?*'

'Please may I speak to Hrithik Roshan?'

'Not possible, out of station.'

'When will he be back?'

'Not for some time.'

'Next week, the week after?'

'No.'

'I am calling from England,' I lied, trying to untangle the pencil. 'I would like to try and arrange an interview with Mr Roshan.'

'Then you are calling Monday.'

The telephone went dead.

On Monday I spent a long time rearranging the pens and pencils beside the phone in order of length and then thickness. Then in order of which ones I liked best. The guard outside the Belgian Consulate seemed to be on an extended *chai* break so I did not even have his spitting habits to count on. Instead I counted the book titles on the shelves around the sitting-room wall that began with H for Hrithik. There were thirty-three, my age, a sign. I picked up the receiver.

This time a woman answered.

'Would it be possible to speak to Hrithik Roshan?'

There was a pause at the other end.

'He is out of station,' she replied, but her voice was more welcoming and elegant than that of the man I had spoken to first time around. 'Who wants him?'

Apart from every woman in India, I do.

'I was hoping to be able to fix up an interview for an English magazine.'

'He is away until the end of the week. You could call then.'

I was flying back to London at the end of the week.

'Perhaps you should speak to his secretary, Mr Ashok. One moment, please. I will give you his number.'

I tried Mr Ashok.

'Mr Ashok is out of station.'

'Is he out of station with Mr Roshan?'

'Who is wanting to know?' asked quite a polite girl at Film Kraft, Papa Roshan's family *filmi* firm in Santa Cruz.

I explained who I was and how much I hoped to interview Hrithik.

'You will call tomorrow.'

And so I called.

'Mr Ashok is not here as yet.'

I grabbed a pencil from the array in front of me and stabbed at a lethargic fly. The fly flew off and the pencil lead broke and shot up my nose.

'When do you think he will be in?' I snorted.

'After 2 p.m. You will call then.'

I called at 2 p.m.

'Mr Ashok is not coming today.'

'But you told me to call back at 2 p.m.'

'This is the case but now he is out of station.'

'But that's what you told me yesterday and you told me to call today, and then you told me to call back at 2 p.m.'

'Mr Ashok was out of station yesterday and now he is out of station today. You will call back tomorrow.' She was firmer than she had been the day before. Perhaps she was not the same girl. Perhaps she practised martial arts in her spare time.

I called the next day, and the day after. And so the week passed.

A couple of days before I left Bombay Mr Ashok put in a surprise appearance and I got him on the line.

'Hrithik is out of station until day after. What is it you want?' His voice was not encouraging. His Hindi accent was overlaid with something else. I could hardly understand what he was saying.

57

'I realize how busy he is at the moment but . . .'

'What are you saying?' Mr Ashok interrupted.

'I was hoping to be able to arrange an interview.'

'For what purpose?'

'For a magazine.'

'In India?'

'No, for a magazine in England,' I said.

Mr Ashok paused. 'You will call day after and speak then.'

Outside the window where I was sitting, the Carmichael Road fish man was squatting on the steps with Severin, the diminutive South Indian Christian fireball who watches over the house where I stay. Severin may be small but she does not put up with any lip. She was giving the fish man a lecture about the freshness of his goods. Her voice flew up at me, and the fish man bent over his basket as if to deflect the blast. I should have put Severin on the telephone to Mr Ashok. She would not have had stage fright. She looked up at me.

'What is this so sad face?' she asked.

'I've just been jilted by a movie star.'

Severin's laughter ricocheted back and forth across Carmichael Road, bouncing off the shiny black gates across the road and the gleaming cap badge of the guard outside the Belgian Consulate who had yet to start on his first betel-spitting session of the day.

'You will take *chai*?' she asked through her laughter.

The fish man stayed on the step looking at his toenails while Severin bustled inside to make consolation tea.

'But you see no one is in town right now,' explained a young man lying beside me at the pool. I had abandoned the phone and headed for sea and sky at the Breach Candy Club after Severin's cheer-up *chai*.

The juice-*wallah* had not been at his pitch outside the gates as

I passed through the hallowed portals. Next to the entrance there is a large sign that warns 'Members Only – non-members not allowed without special permission'. But for 200 rupees you can buy special permission Monday to Friday, and another 100 rupees gets you in at the weekend. The Breach Candy Club is beside the sea, a place to swim elegantly without taking to the waves beyond the high wall that separates the club from the beach. The swimming-pool is the shape of India and there the children of international bankers and brokers learn to swim with Bollywood boys and girls in the shallow end, their fluorescent water-wings paddling over the states of Tamil Nadu, Karnataka and Kerala. Semi-naked foreigners, greased up with suntan lotion, tend to set up camp on one side of the pool in the sun. Bombayites in baggy shorts and designer labels linger in the shade on the club-house side. There is no sinister reason for the division. It is just that the foreigners like to fry in hot silence over sun-curled books, and most Bombayites like to chat under umbrellas. Waiters weave among the beached bodies bearing trays of iced coffee and ice-cream. Gardeners water stunted bougainvillaea and tired roses in pots beside teenage Spanish, Italian and French beauties in spaghetti bikinis. The swimming-pool is as blue as the sky above the chosen people at the Breach Candy Club.

The young man beside me wore chic sunglasses and the ear-piece of a mobile telephone.

'Where are all the stars then if they're not here?' I asked.

'They're in London. They are there and you are here.' He laughed and flipped the front of his telephone shut.

'When you say everyone, who are you talking about? How come you're still here?'

'I am right in the middle of making a film.' He adjusted his swimming-trunks unselfconsciously, stretched and yawned, rolled towards me and propped himself up on one elbow so that we were face to face. He smiled.

'So you are a . . .' I waited.

'Director.' He stretched again and yawned a little more. 'I'm Sunil, good to meet you.'

I tugged at my bikini top. I was propped on one arm too. I did not want to look down to check my cleavage but it felt over-exposed.

'Hello, I'm Justine. What's your film called?'

He took the telephone earpiece out and slowly wound up the wire.

'*Snip!*' He smiled.

'Good title. Is it a Hindi film or an English one?'

'Both, about *adha, adha*, half, half,' he laughed. 'You know, very now, very Hinglish *masala* movie-style.'

'And what's it about?'

Sunil moved a little closer.

'It's about a hairdresser. Her parents are Indian but she was born in England. She comes back to Bombay and kind of goes mad. You know, one of those new generation, fusion, dark comedy kind of things.'

'A hairdresser? Why a hairdresser?'

'It's cool. Did you see *The Hairdresser's Husband*, Patrice Leconte's film, so cool. Everyone was in love with the hairdresser and everyone wanted her.' Sunil's accent was Beef Wellington soused in a mild *masala*.

'I went to Harrow and then film school in the States,' he explained.

'Are you shooting at the moment?' I asked.

'*Yaar*, but we had a bad morning. You know what it was like earlier today?'

It had been hot and still since sunrise, and a haze hung over the city. When I had headed out early to run on the racecourse, the haze had been so thick that the horses out on the track had seemed to be floating through the dust they kicked up as they galloped.

'We were shooting this scene where one of the characters, a

Snip!, *a fusion, dark comedy kind of thing*

heavy mafia type, has been shut out on a balcony. He really needs the bathroom and he ends up having to pee over the edge of the balcony. We shot it at my place, right up at the top of Carmichael Road. You know how cool the views are up there?'

I did.

'I wanted to have this great panoramic sweep of the city while the guy pees and what do we get? Thick Bombay soup.' Sunil rolled his eyes.

'So who is out of town?' I asked again.

'All the big stars. They're heading for London for the big Bollywood Award thing.'

'Where's it being held?'

'What's that place called where there's been the big millennium screw-up?'

'The Dome.'

'That's it. They're having the awards there.' Sunil looked up and waved at someone behind me. 'Hey, Sophiya.'

A beautiful Indian girl was walking towards us. She wore a tiny bikini under a chiffon shirt and a very large pair of fluffy slippers shaped like teddy bears. She bent down and kissed Sunil full on the lips.

'Hey, babe.' She had a perfect London estuarine accent.

'This is Sophiya. She's my star, the hairdresser. Soph, this is . . .'

I introduced myself to Sunil's star. Born in Portsmouth, half-Bangladeshi and half-Gujurati, Sophiya had launched herself in Asia via music television in Hong Kong. From there she had moved to Bombay. She had been in the city for six years but had never seemed to find the time to start learning Hindi. She was perfectly formed except for her very large feet in the fluffy teddy bears.

'Can I come and watch you filming over the next couple of days?' I asked Sunil.

'Why not? What have we got coming up?' He directed the question at Sophiya.

'I don't know, sweetheart. You're the director, aren't you?' she shrugged, waving at someone over Sunil's shoulder. 'Hey, babe.' She jumped up and walked over to a tall, lean, polished man in a pair of turquoise trunks.

He smiled slowly as Sophiya and her big fluffy slippers approached, the black noses of the brown bears bobbing up and down among the lolling bodies by the pool.

'Isn't that Sanjay Dutt?' I asked Sunil.

'It is.'

Sanjay Dutt is one of Bollywood's biggest *filmi* heroes, and one of the first to be as famous for his muscles as for his acting.

'Why isn't he in London with everyone else?'

'He's still not allowed to leave the country. He's on licence.'

After the Bombay riots in 1993 the police raided Sanjay Dutt's house, suspecting underworld connections. They found an AK56 and so completed the link between Sanjay, the gun, the dons and the riots. He had ended up in prison and now, though released, he was still on a legal leash.

'Is he up for any awards?' I asked as I watched the star smiling deeply into Sophiya's eyes with his famous hooded, big-screen eyes.

'Maybe he is, perhaps for best actor in a negative role.'

'Negative role?'

'Oh you know, the bad guys. Negative equals bad. What else would you call it?' Sunil raised his eyebrows.

'Best villain?'

'Okay, so best performance in a villainous role – which do you think sounds better?'

'Maybe negative role sounds better. I'm not sure they have that category at the Oscars.'

'They wouldn't. That would be far too political for Hollywood. Imagine them having a category for anti-heroes, it'd be McCarthyism with bells on.' Sunil stretched and reached for his mobile.

'So where do I go tomorrow for the shoot?' I asked.

He gave me the address on Carmichael Road. It was five minutes' walk from where I was staying.

As I made my way back to the changing-rooms, a Sikh walked into the pool. His perfect black turban matched his trunks and he set off across chlorinated Jammu and Kashmir, his head held high, his turban perfectly dry.

It was ten o'clock on Sunday morning on Carmichael Road. The sleek cars that would have been sliding out from behind big black gates on a weekday were parked out of sight. Instead the dog walkers were out, weaving between the piles left by other dogs that had already taken their ease as they strolled. The pooches had a groomed air about them. Their minders were less polished, thinner and dustier. Naturally their charges were more interested in the efforts and strains of their fellows than in taking the air. There was a lot of dragging of small dogs away from large mounds. The result of this doggy cabaret is that the human walkers on Carmichael Road take to the streets rather than risk the pavement.

As I made my way up the road to Sunil's apartment building an elderly gentleman wearing a *kurta* shirt over a pair of green track-suit bottoms puffed past me, followed by his wife in a billowing pink *salwar kameez* and trainers identical to those of her husband. He was as tall and thin as his wife was short and round. Behind them came a second couple, a bit younger and a bit faster, he in full *kurta pyjama*, she in a pale yellow *salwar kameez*. As the road curved around the Belgian Consulate, the younger pair took the elderly couple on the inside bend. The older man moved up another gear and came back at them at the top of the bend, but he was sadly let down by his wife who just could not find that other gear among her billows. Her husband slowed back to her pace and eyed the leading pair with disdain before turning the same expression on his panting wife. The watchman outside the consulate had been keeping a close eye on their progress, so much so that he had neither chewed nor spat his betel for the duration of their neck-and-neck contest on the consulate curve.

Sunil's apartment was set on the top floor of a great semi-circular block built in the Eighties, when Indian apartment architects went in for new wave curves and sweeps, so Eighties, so advertising, so now, so then. Above its black marble entrance rose tiers of balconies overlooking the city. Sunil's mafia character had been given a great view to pee over.

The lift opened right into the apartment and I stepped out into Sunil's film. His mafia character was bouncing up and down on a sofa in a pair of dark glasses and a huge afro wig. After four or five bounces he launched himself over the end of an ornate iron bed, wig and belly flying, and as he hit the mattress the gathered crowd cheered: Sunil, his cameraman, the sound men, the producer and Sophiya, her head now full of curlers and the rest of her tightly wrapped in a baby-pink candlewick dressing-gown. This time she was wearing large white fluffy slippers, more permed polar bear than teddy bear.

'Hi, hi, come, come in. See what Munnu's up to. How fantastic he is, just like a gymnast.' Sunil took me by the hand and pulled me over to the now beached figure of Munnu, the mafia character.

'Bloody bastard Sunil, you were not saying about all of this bloody bullshit jumping thingy and all this English bloody bullshit. Why can't we speak Hindi?'

'This is Justine, she's from England.' Sunil introduced me.

'What? Bloody voice coach, *yaar*?' Munnu set his wig straight and sniffed.

'No, she's just here to watch.'

Munnu pushed his sunglasses up through the wig and sat on the bed with a mournful expression.

So Eighties, so now, so then

Sunil smiled and led me through the glass doors that opened on to the balcony. 'Really he's a fantastic actor, he just doesn't feel that comfortable in English. The next scene we're doing is the dildo scene. This is good. He'll be fantastic because he gets to do this one in Hindi.'

'A Hindi dildo scene?' I was stunned.

'Too good, really funny.' Sunil looked out over the edge.

From where we stood the city rolled out beneath us, her hips and buttocks running down to the Arabian Sea from our high perch on one of her breasts. She shimmered, melting away at the edges.

'This is where we did the peeing scene yesterday. Can you see how good it would have been without the fog?' Sunil leant out further over the edge holding the sides of his head.

'I can, but perhaps the smog made it more interesting,' I offered.

'Oh sure! How interesting is it to have one of the greatest city views in the world covered in pollution haze?'

'Oh I don't know, it's quite brooding, quite . . .' Sunil was no longer with me. He was staring down over the edge with a look of mild panic.

'Oh bullshit, my aunt is coming. She doesn't know we are filming in the apartment. Bloody hell.' Several hundred feet below us a woman was extracting herself, her maid and a small balding dog in a fluffy white coat from the back of a large car parked by the marble steps of the entrance. She looked powerful. Her dog looked like one of Sophiya's slippers.

'Why has she come to see you then?' I asked.

'Not me, my parents.' Sunil looked at me with a hunted expression. 'This is my parents' place. They have gone away for the duration while we are making the film.'

'You live with your parents?' I asked in surprise.

'Of course.' Sunil peered into my face. 'Why do you ask?'

'No reason,' I lied.

'We looked at so many other apartments around and there was

nothing as good as this. It was the most obvious thing to do. My parents were totally cool about it. They really want this film to work for me.'

The Sippys are one of Bollywood's big *filmi* families. Sunil's uncle, Ramesh Sippy, had directed *Sholay*, one of the most successful Hindi films ever made. Sunil has a big shadow to walk out of.

'Okay, let's go, it's dildo time.' He pushed himself away from the balcony. 'Auntie*ji* will just have to look the other way.'

The day's scenes were set in the hairdresser's apartment. As a result of a twist in the plot, involving a snipped ear and a failed actor, Sophiya's character is forced to take Munnu the mafia man in as an unwelcome flatmate. While she is out hairdressing he decides to do a little dressing-up of his own, but as nothing in her flimsy wardrobe comes anywhere close to fitting his generous frame he has to resort to her very impressive wig collection. Sunil was shooting several scenes with Munnu trying on a series of the hairdresser's wigs, dancing around her bedroom with great enthusiasm, and experimenting with her eye shadow, her nail polish and her curling tongs. As Sunil was making a hip and swinging fusion film these scenes were going to be the core of a new kind of song-and-dance number. Forget cowbells and an alpine village setting. Instead the audience for *Snip!* was going to get a strange balding Bombay mafia guy in an afro wig doing somersaults on the absent hairdresser's bed while playing around with her blue disco nail polish.

And the dildo was not just for effect.

'It's an important part of the plot,' Sunil explained. 'You see Munnu is sitting on the sofa with a guy called the Egg Man. He is very important but I won't give you too much detail. They just know each other from the underworld and they are the two who speak in Hindi when they are together. Got it?' Sunil was directing the cameraman as he spoke.

I nodded uncertainly.

'So the Egg Man has found out where Munnu is staying and he

comes to see him. They are sitting on the sofa together and I'm going to have just them in the frame. See here.' He pointed to Munnu's trampoline sofa. 'The Egg Man doesn't know that Munnu is staying with a girl. They are just sitting chatting on the sofa and then the Egg Man feels something under his butt. He pulls out the hairdresser's dildo and asks Munnu what it is.' Sunil was trying not to laugh. 'Do you want me to tell you what Munnu says or do you want to work it out from the dialogue?'

'I think I'll probably miss it. I'm weak on punch lines in Hindi.'

'Okay, so Munnu tells the Egg Man that it's "soup *hai*", for making soup.' Now he was laughing.

I was not laughing. Sunil looked at me.

'Don't you think that's funny?'

'I don't really understand the context. Why does Munnu decide to tell the Egg Man that the dildo is for making soup?'

'Oh, oh, I forgot to tell you that bit. Munnu of course has gone soft on the hairdresser and in one scene he does this big romantic gesture thing of cooking her dinner. He's making soup and he finds the dildo and uses it for whizzing the soup.' Sunil raised his eyebrows at me. 'Got it now?'

'Got it.'

Sangeeta the producer had her hands full. She had been left to explain the situation to Sunil's aunt. Auntie*ji*'s small dog was attacking one of Sophiya's slippers, and Sophiya was dancing around the dog, driving it into paroxysms of hysterical yapping. Sunil went to greet his aunt. Sophiya was ordered to stop torturing the dog and Sangeeta took me back out on to the balcony to get me out of the way of the film scene and the family saga. We watched through the windows as Sunil first calmed his aunt and then progressed to directing Munnu, the Egg Man and the dildo, so leading to the 'soup *hai*' bit.

'Sunil has put so much great stuff in the script, stuff that people just have not done before.' She pushed her hair back with her sunglasses.

'With things like dildos and cross-dressing mafia characters aren't you going to have problems with the censors?'

'God, I expect so but we are not worrying about that at the moment. That is a headache for another time.'

'Who do you think will want to see *Snip!*?' I asked.

'The new generation who have had enough of the old formula. They want to laugh and not be treated like idiots. Brushing your teeth is more of a mental challenge than watching the average Bollywood film.' Sangeeta pointed to a couple of vultures hanging in the thermals above us. 'Such a great view they have, such perspective. Do you think they are watching us?'

'Perhaps.'

'I just hope the press and critics are going to be kind. They can be so vicious with anything new that shows signs of challenging the old Bollywood formula.' Sangeeta was still watching the huge birds circling above. 'I'm not sure we really know what we are letting ourselves in for.' She smiled up at the vultures. 'Come, I think they are having a break.'

Munnu had lost his temper with Sunil and was waving the dildo in his face, shouting in Hindi that he was being interfered with too much.

I slunk away from Sunil's set but Sangeeta caught me at the lift.

'Please call when you are next here. We would so like you to see how it is coming along. Thank you for being with us today. So sorry it was all a bit chaotic.' She shook my hand and smiled.

'I have to find out what happens. I'll call.'

As I reached the bottom of the building Sunil's aunt was repacking herself and her entourage into her large car. After the fight with Sophiya's slipper her dog seemed to be taking out its humiliation on the driver's leg. The aunt ignored the driver, the dog and me.

That afternoon of dildo soup was my last chance to call Mr Ashok again. Hrithik was still away.

70

'Perhaps you call when you are next in town,' Mr Ashok suggested with irritating nonchalance.

I left Carmichael Road and Bombay without having managed to talk to Hrithik, without being able to ask him about his dance moves, his biceps, his preferred spaghetti sauce, just normal day-to-day Bollywood *filmi*-star stuff.

The first International Indian Film Awards to be held outside India took place on a strangely sultry English May summer evening in Greenwich. Doe-eyed Indian-origin teenagers, raised on *filmi* fare in Reading and Rickmansworth, had made the trip so that they could see their heroes and heroines in the flesh, and they started to line up behind the cordon hours before the first stars were due to arrive, happy to wait and wallow in the buzz of the moment.

I had a prime spot behind the cordon, so close to the action that I could look right into the stars' eyes as they got out of their cars and catch trails of jasmine-heavy scent as they wafted in chiffon and silk down the red carpet. But my real stars of the night were standing right next to me: Jyoti and her friend Amrita, both of them Milton Keynes born and bred, both wearing mini-skirts, wisps of T-shirts and impossibly high platforms. They had an encyclopaedic knowledge of all things Bollywise. Amrita had been a bit of a Salman Khan girl. Jyoti had been dancing in front of her Shah Rukh Khan poster since she was five. She showed me how. She dreamed of being a make-up artist to the stars, an ambition that she wore on her lips and eyes and cheeks. Amrita was a little less starstruck. She thought she might go into her father's software company. But their allegiance to their childhood pin-ups was now in doubt. Both of them gave almost identical responses to my main question.

'Have you seen *Kaho Naa . . . Pyaar Hai?*' I asked.

'Are you kidding?' gasped Jyoti. 'I've seen it about six times, and there's one scene I have watched, God I don't know, maybe a hundred times. That scene in New Zealand when Hrithik does the dance in the nightclub – I have to lie down every time I see it.' She clutched Amrita's arm, once again overcome at the very thought of it.

'You know that move he does?' said Amrita.

I did. It's a sort of hip flick thing from the pelvis, with one hand held out in front, the middle finger bent forward, rigid and provocative, half Indian classical style, half Michael Jackson. It has become Hrithik's dance trademark, the one that makes the girls lie down on the floor. I had tried it in a friend of mine's bedroom one afternoon, watching Hrithik doing his thing on the television and enlisting my friend's seven-year-old son as my tutor. Hrithik and the seven-year-old had thrust and ground in perfect unison. I had not been so good, more Agnetha from Abba than Michael Jackson does *bhangra*.

Amrita gave me a demonstration of the Hrithik flick right there behind the cordon, perfectly balanced on her platforms. She was good. Everyone else around us applauded. They knew exactly whose dance she was doing.

'Will you teach me?' I asked.

But we never got any further because the stars started to arrive. The crowd surged and the Dome's security boys faced their first fan riot. Shah Rukh Khan emerged from the back of a huge black Mercedes. The live news crews sent to cover the show were drowned out by the wailing and moaning of thousands of teen-agers suddenly faced with the man whose picture they had worshipped on their walls, the man they had danced with in their dreams for as long as they could remember. Shah Rukh Khan looked at the crowd with a smile as wide as his limo was low.

'How huge is his nose?' Jyoti shrieked at Amrita as he passed close enough for us to see the pores on his famously large and much-loved feature.

Each car wafted in another star. Shah Rukh was followed by Aishwarya Rai, sheathed in pale gold crêpe-de-chine.

72

'Do you think Salman is coming?' Jyoti was jiggling up and down to get a better view.

'God no, far too uncool.' Amrita nudged nearer to the cordon to get a closer look at Aishwarya. 'She has to be the most beautiful thing ever. I have to be like her. Look at her jewellery, my God, look at it!' Amrita was finding it hard to breathe.

Aishwarya disappeared in a cloud of diamonds and adoration.

After Aishwarya came the still delicious Dimple, queen of Bollywood in the late Eighties and early Nineties, now still as beautiful, still as polished, but also the mother of two increasingly popular new stars, her daughters Rinke and Twinkle. As Dimple and her daughters took to the red carpet in folds of shimmering silk, and as Dimple's deep red nails hooked into her great mane of hair for the camera, even the security guards smiled.

'God, she's so much prettier when you see her in the flesh,' Amrita shouted to Jyoti.

'Which one?' I asked.

'Dimple, of course. She's so old and she still looks so good.' Amrita slid her hair back with her index finger just as Dimple, all of forty-four, had done.

'You know she makes candles now?' Jyoti told Amrita. 'Apparently they're really beautiful, you know really original an' all.'

'But I thought she was an actress,' I butted in.

'Sure but she makes candles now too,' Jyoti shrugged.

'How do you know all this stuff?' I asked.

'The *filmi* mags, of course.' Jyoti raised her eyebrows at me. Was I stupid or what?

The arrivals slowed down and the volume of chatter around us increased, the accents a mixture of London and downtown Mumbai. There was a name that bounced in and out of every conversation, a heartbeat in the crowd. Why wasn't Hrithik coming to the awards?

'He should be here.' Jyoti jutted her bottom lip.

'How could he have been nominated?'

Jyoti and Amrita looked at me in surprise.

'He's only made one film so far and it came out this January. These awards are for last year's films. He isn't even eligible for an award yet,' I lectured.

'He still could have come,' Amrita said defiantly, rolling on the edge of one of her platforms.

I muttered something about him filming and being very busy. Jyoti and Amrita spun on their impossible heels and ignored me for a while.

It was one of those rare hot summer nights when London becomes suddenly foreign. I closed my eyes and inhaled. The air smelt of cheap scent, sweat and burning incense. The conversations might have been those of a Saturday night in a crowded Bollywood-Bombay bar. But this was Greenwich, a part of London now temporarily Indian, temporarily exotic, temporarily outstripping the dreams of even the Dome's spin doctors.

Another car arrived and a bearded Indian climbed out, his dark eyes sparkling at the crowd.

'Who's he? I haven't seen him before.' Amrita stared after the man and his wife as they headed down the funnel of red carpet.

'Shekhar Kapur,' I said.

'Who?' Jyoti was jutting her lip again.

'Did you see *Elizabeth*?' I asked.

'Elizabeth what?' Amrita peered at me.

'The film about the queen.'

'About the queen? You mean this current queen?' Jyoti looked slightly disgusted.

'No, it was about Elizabeth I. Joseph Fiennes played her lover,' I started.

'God, yes, he is so sexy, a bit thin but really sexy.' Jyoti rolled her eyes.

'Was that guy in it?' Amrita pointed to the disappearing Shekhar Kapur.

'No, he directed it.'

Disappointed they both turned away as another car arrived. The back door opened but instead of a floating sari we got an expanse of thigh under a short tight black dress and a pair of sunglasses. It was an English actress. She seemed self-conscious among the chiffons and the silks, and she plucked at the hem of her dress as she got out of the car. Jyoti and Amrita thought she looked gorgeous.

The cars had dried up and the news journalists moved inside with their passes and camera crews or else packed up and headed home. We were left to hunt for the monitors that were covering the action from inside. Jyoti and Amrita were going to watch the show and then go clubbing with some friends in Basildon. I was going to go home and get a better view on television.

Naturally the almost-live coverage missed out on the best bits of the evening. By the time I was ensconced there were sixteen leather-clad thighs strutting their stuff on a small revolving stage. The dancers threw their chests out in homage to Salman Khan, and then they clenched their thighs and the little macho muscles in their cheeks as they dived to the ground in a press-up star around the tiny bouncing figure in their midst. Kylie Minogue was shimmying over her floored dance troop in a very short gold dress that perfectly showed off the crease between her thighs and her buttocks. It wasn't quite a Bollywood number, though there were hints of disco *bhangra* in Kylie's come-back song. And Kylie was coming back with her buttocks on parade. It was host entertainment time at the International Indian Film Awards as covered by Channel 4. The beauties that Jyoti, Amrita and I had seen on the red carpet now smiled elegantly from tables around the stage, discreetly suggestive in their softly falling saris. The pop princess bouncing on the stage looked naked in the face of so much skilfully draped subcontinental elegance. We at home got an advertisement break middance. We missed the power cut at the Dome. We missed Kylie tumbling off the edge of her small stage in the dark and almost into the arms of Shah Rukh Khan at the top table. Naturally SRK had performed gallantly, we were told, lifting the pixie popster back on to her stage and thanking her for throwing herself at him. We, at home, were assured that she blushed most fetchingly. We, at home, were sorry to have missed the golden flash of buttocks tumbling towards the top table.

It took several minutes to get the power up and running but most of the guests seemed unconcerned. For the Indians in the audience a power cut was business as usual. The Londoners were acutely embarrassed. The show's hosts suffered still more PR humiliation when the gala dinner was served an hour later than programmed. The Indians did not even notice. Dinner at 10.30 p.m. seemed early to them. Your common or garden banquet in India rarely hits the table before midnight.

Channel 4's camera team seemed a bit unsure what to do with so many Bollywood stars scattered around and so the camera kept homing in on the two faces they knew, Shekhar Kapur and Shah Rukh Khan. SRK wore a smile as wide as the Dome's deficit and Shekhar Kapur had a look of suitable mystery and directorial intrigue. After another commercial break for those of us at home, Shekhar Kapur took to the stage to present the award to 'The most influential star of the past five years'.

'I am so glad and proud to be here tonight, and more than that I am proud to be part of Bollywood. It is the most, and I say again, the most important part of me.'

He was forced to pause as the audience clapped and whistled.

'When my last film *Elizabeth* came out, the one in which I committed the unthinkable crime of deflowering your Virgin Queen on celluloid, one New York critic wrote: "Mr Kapur has simply given us a Hindi film in fancy frocks".' He paused and smiled. 'It was the greatest compliment I could have been given. My roots are in Bollywood and I am prouder of that than anything else.'

The audience roared again as he opened the award envelope.

'And the artist voted "The most influential star of the past five years" is Shah Rukh Khan.'

76

Shah Rukh Khan, the most influential star of the last five years

Another wild burst of applause followed as SRK rose from amongst his retinue – his wife, his assistant, his assistant's wife, his assistant's wife's friend. There was no sign of Simmy, friend of SRK from Bar Indigo. He twinkled at the audience and hugged the award to his chest as Shekhar Kapur handed it to him. When he was told that 61 per cent of the polled public had voted for him he laughed.

'Thank you all and as for the other 39 per cent, what's wrong with you guys?' Then he bowed low, unable to continue as the clapping and cheering drowned him out. He made his way back to his table with a smile and a swagger. We, the viewers, got to see him jiggling his award on his knee in time to the music as the show went on – after a pause. There had been another slight delay due to complications resulting from the power cut. There was another commercial break to tide us over. The Indians at the Dome remained unconcerned. The locals began to fiddle with their jewellery or their cuffs. The wait ended with the return of the sixteen leather-clad thighs, now accompanied by six hot young Hindi actresses. This time around it was pure Bollywood *bhangra*, a compilation of big film show tunes, a different number for each of the six stars as they made their solo appearances among the leather-clad lads. The show's choreographer seemed not to have factored into the Bolly-on-Thames *bhangra* moves the likelihood that some of his solo dancers were going to be in flowing saris. The first girl up was wearing a short clingy number so she did just fine, Hindi-jiving at high speed. The prancing boys flexed their muscles and flicked their hips in almost perfect Bollywood style. Solo girl number two tripped over the hem of her heavy sari as she tried to waft across the stage amid the flashing thighs and the wiggling hips, but she was borne aloft by the muscular boys and hardly anyone noticed, except the British press who lapped it up. We, the viewers, were on our feet hippy-flicking, head-wiggling and hand-flapping to the Hindi hot one hundred themes. Well, I was.

The award for 'The best male lead in a negative role' came next, to be presented by Aishwarya Rai, described by Channel 4's commentator as 'another ex-Miss World to have made the move into Bollywood'. On a huge screen above the stage we were spun through clips of the nominees and so treated to the full range of tortured expressions, from the faintly mad to the certifiable, and then back again via deeply menacing with bristling eyebrows. Sanjay Dutt, the star by the pool at Breach Candy whom Sophiya had snuggled up to in her bikini and her fluffy slippers, was on the list. He won and SRK graciously took to the podium again to accept the award on behalf of the winner.

The locals began to look tired as they entered their fourth hour of the show. It was already one-thirty in the morning and there was still one more entertainment and several awards to go. The Bollywood boys and girls were just getting into their stride and, as it had been outside before the show, the buzz was all about Hrithik Roshan. As the locals in the audience flagged amid the throb of Bolly gossip, I fell asleep with the bedside light on and still wearing my glasses. While the remnants of a bag of honeycrunch popcorn ground their way into the sheets, I dreamt of dancing *bhangra* in a tiny gold dress amid a sea of thighs.

By the time the show at the Dome finally ended at about 2.30 a.m. it was 7 o'clock in the morning in Bombay and the *filmi* journalists were already on the line to Roshan Villas.

'What does Hrithik think of Shah Rukh winning the award for "The most influential star of the past five years"?' they asked the sleep-hazed maid who answered the telephone.

She had no idea. Hrithik *sahib* was away filming. She had not seen him for days.

'Where is he filming?' they asked.

'This information I am not at liberty to pass on,' she informed them.

I started to ring at about midday Bombay time. I was trying to get in touch with the ever-elusive Mr Ashok, Hrithik's assistant. By some quirk I got straight through.

'*Yaar*,' a voice snapped down the line.

'Is that Mr Ashok?' I asked.

'Who is wanting to know?' he snapped again.

I reintroduced myself and told him that I was hoping to find out how Hrithik felt about Shah Rukh picking up the big prize.

'I have no comment to make.'

'Could you just pass a message on to Hrithik to say that I called. Perhaps I could call back at a time that suits him?'

'Not possible, he has a very tight schedule and is filming all day. We are in Udaipur. He is working all the time,' Mr Ashok assured me.

I left my number just in case, not really expecting him to write it down.

The day went on and I was in the middle of a piece on the victims of the Kashmiri conflict, tapping away on my keyboard in West London, every thought a lifetime away from Bollywood. The phone rang. There was an empty echo on the other end, a delay.

'Hello, hello,' called a voice through a wind tunnel.

'Hello,' I shouted back.

'Hello, hello,' called the voice again.

'Hello, can you hear me?' I asked.

'Hello, hello,' called the voice again, the voice from *Kaho Naa . . . Pyaar Hai*.

'Hello, please, can you hear me now?' I cried out. My hands were sweating. I was shouting very loudly.

The line died.

I pressed the recall button maybe twenty times.

'Hello, hello, hello . . .'

I dialled 1471 to try and get the number.

'You were called at 2.43 p.m. We do not have the caller's number to return the call.'

I slumped down beside the phone. So close, it had been so close. But he had tried to call me. Hrithik Roshan had tried to call me.

CHAPTER 4

Rivalry

Bring on the girls

THE CITY WAS febrile, the buildings and pavements sweating in the humidity, when I returned to Bombay in August at the tail end of the monsoon. Every morning Mrs Nirmal, the *bhelpuri* man's wife, hung a wet sheet in the doorway of their one-room house on the corner of First Pasta Lane. It softened the ferocity of the air blowing in through the door and made the room a few degrees cooler for a short happy period. The juice-*wallah* at his stand outside the Breach Candy Club wore a towel wrapped around his head like a turban to stop his sweat running into the juice. Up in the Bollywood hills, in Juhu, Pali and Bandra, they just turned up the air-conditioning and carried on as usual.

In the shadow cast by her elegant breasts, Bombay keeps her secrets. Just below Cumballa and Malabar Hill the children begging at the traffic lights on Grant Road seem almost oblivious to the heat, but then they are tougher than most. They do not tap mournfully on the window, heads rolled to one side in submissive entreaty, like other children at other traffic lights. On Grant Road they reach right into the car and pluck at your clothes, your face and your hair until they get your attention. If you wind up the window you have to push their fingers away as they try and pull the glass back down. Each time they press their faces up against the car I close my eyes, knowing that I will never be able to get used to it.

These are children who have no childhood. As soon as they can walk they join the fight to extract money from those heading for the triangle between Grant Road and Falkland Road. The traffic-light children play to the crowd, preying on their guilt, trying to separate them from the money in their pockets. But many of the men in the crowd are in no mood to give alms. They are headed for Kamathipura, the red-light district.

While most of Bombay rests on Sunday, the traffic-light children and the brothels are busy. The nautch-girls of Grant Road do not have a day off. Nor do their lives in any way resemble the romantic Mogul notion of dancing girls who live in a world of playing fountains, tinkling ankle bells, shy faces behind chiffon veils and the jasmine-scented laughter of the harem. The girls on Grant Road and Falkland Road, like the children at the traffic lights, live on the edge of deprivation and disease.

As I made my way through Kamathipura one Sunday afternoon, a thin man and a thin dog were picking through a pile of *dhaba* café rubbish outside the Original Cinema on Falkland Road, the man's searching fingers next door to the dog's mouth. On the other side of the road a row of carriages, the open victorias that take the tourists around the Gateway of India, were parked among the brothels, their traces hanging loose, a Roman-nosed sheep asleep in the shade of one set of great wheels. There was a horror flick showing at the Original Cinema. The hand-painted sign above the entrance portrayed a curvaceous beauty being strangled by a hideous snake of car-tyre proportions, its fangs dripping with venom. 'The Killer is Back' the sign assured the crowd of skinny men who had gathered beneath it, torn between the over-painted, over-voluptuous girl having the life squeezed out of her and the over-painted, over-tired girls having the youth sucked out of them as they waited in every doorway along Falkland Road. Seventy per cent of the prostitutes in Bombay are HIV positive.

I had to push through the crowd of young men outside the

The open victorias were parked among the brothels

cinema. Every one I bumped against reached out and grabbed at me, pinching my breasts, sticking a hand between my legs, confident in their numbers, over-stimulated by all the flesh on offer on celluloid and on the street. I did not retaliate. In other parts of the city I would have turned around and slapped the Eve-teasers, but in Kamathipura there is little point. These men are here for sex.

I retreated into the Delhi Darbar café. It was clean and the waiters wore uniforms, and though there were no women in the *dhaba* the men inside were older and less excitable than the youths in sexual ferment outside. A waiter brought me 'special *chai*' in a small flowery cup.

The comfort of the *chai* was fleeting. Every sip, every gesture I made was watched by the men in the room. Any conversations they might have been having faded, leaving just the noise that surged in and out of the kitchen as the waiters swung back and forth through the connecting door. I left half the *chai*, paid and went back out on to Falkland Road. I had wanted to ask directions, but I had lost my nerve. Everyone in the café would have heard. I felt the need to protect what little remained of the privacy of the woman I had come to see.

The juice-*wallah* at Breach Candy had told me about Deepa. He had seen her in a few films, never in big parts but always in good dance sequences. He had liked the way she moved and the colour of her eyes.

'Like a cat, all bright and golden like the sun, and her arms, they moved like . . .' he had smiled as he remembered, searching for a simile, 'like sari in the wind.' He had waved his arms about, quite unlike silk on air, and had laughed with sad eyes.

Then, about ten years ago, Deepa had disappeared from the screen. The next time the juice-*wallah* saw her was on Falkland Road.

'Maybe one year past, maybe a little more.'

I had not asked him what he had been doing there and he had not offered an explanation.

'At this time I was stopping watching films. If this is the thing it is doing I am not watching.'

He had seen Deepa near the Delhi Darbar café.

'Do you think I could try and find her?' I had asked.

'Why not? But do not tell me what has happened to her. This I do not wish to know.'

But he had told me how to find the café.

As a foreign woman on your own it is impossible to wander down Falkland Road as if out for a Sunday stroll. Men stare, groups of pimps growl and peer, and the nautch-girls scuttle away as you approach, nervous that you might take their picture. I tried to look nonchalant, smiling at the girls, asking how they were. Most of them ignored me though a few caught the moment, the link with another woman, and smiled back fleetingly.

A few houses down from the Delhi Darbar three women were sitting in a doorway. Two of them, both young girls, sat on the top step like a pair of matching dolls, their childlike faces painted, rouged and powdered, pale masks above their dark naked shoulders and arms. Both had bands of fabric wrapped around their breasts, but all the fragile areas, the base of their throats, their upper arms, the parts of their body covered by most Indian women, were exposed. They were thin under their tight skirts, but their faces seemed bloated. There was a bruised quality about them, the crude China blue of their eye-shadow highlighting the blackness of the circles under their blank eyes. One was deftly picking through the hair of a much older woman who sat on the step below, her head lolling to one side on a frail neck. There was a greyness to her skin, and the sockets of her eyes had sunk back into her head. She lay in the younger girl's lap, limp and exhausted.

I went up to them, smiling and asking how they were. They looked at me blankly. I asked their names. The two young girls turned to each other and then back to me, their faces empty. The older woman had her eyes closed. The girls did not speak Hindi or perhaps they just found my accent incomprehensible. I do not speak Gujurati or Marathi, the main languages of the streets of Bombay. I shrugged and smiled and was about to move on when the older woman opened her eyes. The whites were burnt out, the irises the colour of cats' eyes.

'We are all just fit and fine, as you see,' she said in English.

She started to cackle, her wasted body bending forward as her laughter turned to coughing. The other girls joined in, giggling and bouncing on the step like children.

'How old are you?' I asked the two young girls in Hindi.

'Twenty years,' one of them replied. The older woman's lead seemed to have given them licence to reply.

I raised my eyebrows and smiled.

'Maybe eighteen,' she tried.

I said nothing.

'Maybe sixteen.' She paused and spat. 'What age is it you want?'

'No age in particular.' I introduced myself.

The girls turned back to each other and laughed again. The older woman straightened a little and put a hand to her thin, lice-picked hair.

'This is Maya, and this Miriya.' She waved her hand at the two girls behind her. 'And I am Madam Deepa.' She put her hand to her chest, her fingers stretching against the papery skin that hung off her collar bones.

I had found the juice-*wallah*'s heroine. Madam Deepa could only have been about forty-three according to the juice-*wallah*'s calculations but I had judged her to be about sixty.

She continued to speak in English. I explained that I had come to Falkland Road to find her. She looked up and down the road and waved the girls inside.

'Go, go,' she shouted, hurrying the girls back into the gloom of the room behind them, a dark rectangle of shadows and dankness where damp towels were hung out on the door and the bed.

'What is it you want? Why have you come to find me? Get away, leave,' she hissed at me.

Her shouts had aroused interest on the street. A man got up from a card-playing group on a step a few doors further along. Madam Deepa waved him away as she hissed at me but he came and hovered.

'Can I take you somewhere to have a cup of tea?' I asked.

'Why should I want to do this? I do not know who you are. Who are you?'

I introduced myself again. I told her about her fan, the juice-*wallah* at Breach Candy, and how sad he had been when she had stopped appearing in films. For a moment her face cleared, the gaunt pain lifting into a remembered smile, her cats' eyes opening, making her look younger, just for a moment.

'Why does he know that I am in this place?' she demanded, but her voice was softer.

I lied to her, telling her that one of the juice-*wallah*'s fruit suppliers had seen her and recognized her eyes. It was plausible. There were cheap fruit-sellers further down Falkland Road. She jiggled her head, accepting the explanation.

'There is nowhere we can take tea in this place. It is a man's place. Women are not coming to this place. It is not safe for me to leave my girls. Now it is a busy time.' She tugged at her frayed sari, trying to cover her sagging skin.

She looked up and down the street again. The crowd outside the Original Cinema were filing in for the afternoon showing of the big snake movie. The man who had left his game and hovered had returned to his cards. Madam Deepa turned back to me.

'We will go to Delhi Darbar's family room.' Her thin body doubled over again as she coughed. She told me to wait and disappeared into the room behind her.

I never asked her why she changed her mind and decided to talk to me. Perhaps I brought a momentary reverberation from her former life.

Ten minutes later she reappeared. She had changed into a clean, bougainvillaea-pink sari, and her thin hair was freshly oiled and twisted into a coil at the base of her neck. The tight pull of the knot had lifted the skin of her face, and the oil had darkened her hair. She looked a different woman to the broken vessel that I had first seen on the step.

'Come.' She led me out on to the street, twenty yards down the road, back into the Delhi Darbar.

We marched right on through, past the knowing smiles of the waiters, past the lascivious looks of the *chai* drinkers, up the stairs and into the family room, a small musty place furnished with only a table and four chairs. A narrow window looked out on to a back courtyard and on to the heads of men from the *dhaba* urinating into the open gully that separated the café from its neighbour.

'It's more peaceful up here,' I said.

As I sat down with my back to the window, Madam Deepa laughed.

'Family-*wamily*,' she snorted. 'In this street "family room" is where *grahak*, tricks, bring my girls if they do not find our premises to their taste. No kiddies and mummy/daddy here.' She pressed a bell beside the door and settled herself opposite me.

I was still studying her transformation and its echoes of Deepa the dancer whom the juice-*wallah* had described with the soft focus of besotted memory.

'Now, tell me what it is you want,' she said.

'You talked about your girls.'

'Every girl in this street is my *beti*, my daughter. What else do they have? Who else will fight for them?'

'And you, Madam Deepa, what are . . .'

One of the waiters came into the room. Madam Deepa shouted at him to knock first next time. He smiled or smirked – it was too quick to see. She ordered a pot of special tea and a plate of vegetable *pakoras* and then paused. I asked for a couple of other things. I wanted her to eat. The waiter sidled out, staring at me over his shoulder.

'I think he believes I am interviewing you for a job.' Madam

Deepa giggled, a rippling, girlish sound at odds with her tired body.

I blushed.

'I am a prostitute.' She returned to my question, resting her chin on her hand as she looked past me through the window. 'But now I am watching for the girls more. My body is old and tired and sick.' She prodded one of her fallen breasts under her bright *choli*.

'And before?'

'Before this was a different life. I do not speak of this now.' She closed her eyes.

We sat in silence. The waiter came back, banging metal plates on to the table. He had not brought delicate flowered cups this time but plain metal beakers. No one spoke. The waiter slammed the door behind him. I poured the tea and passed a beaker to Madam Deepa. It sat in front of her among the plates of *pakoras*, fruitcake and vegetable *samosas*. She did not move. I waited and drank my tea. She continued to stare past me. I moved my chair so that I could look at her face and smiled into her eyes, picking up the *pakoras* and offering them to her. She turned her face to look at me.

'I was a dancer,' she began as she took one *pakora* and put it on to the plate beside her. She took a small sip of her *chai*.

'My friend told me that you were very good.'

'This may be so.'

'Did you enjoy it?'

'I was so happy.' She picked up the *pakora* and then her hand stopped in mid-air. 'So happy.'

Silence fell down around us again. Two flies copulated lazily beside the *samosas*. Madam Deepa slammed her hand down on the table. We both flinched.

'Bloody bastards.' She took a pink napkin from a sheaf in a glass and wiped away the corpses. 'It was not a time then for people who were not from *filmi* families. What choice was there? I left home, I left everything to come here to be a big star. I said bye-bye to all my family. I said to myself that I would only go back to Alleppey in a big fancy car. But I had no big starry mummy/daddy.' She put her face in her hands, her fingers working at her forehead and pulling strands free from her oiled hair. 'I had all the right things, a pretty figure, good dancing, emoting eyes, good English.'

'Your English is lovely to listen to, it's so fluent.'

'We have very good schools in Kerala. I speak better English than most of these *filmi* kids with their fancy educations, but no famous mummy/daddy, and I was not going to bed with the director bastards.' She started to laugh, a slow sad sound. 'And no going to bed meant no more films, and no more films meant I ended up as this. Funny, *naar*?'

Neither of us laughed.

Deepa had failed to get further in films because she was not from a *filmi* family and she would not sleep with the directors.

'Why didn't you go back to Kerala?'

She had finally put a corner of the *pakora* in her mouth and she chewed it slowly and thoroughly.

'I told them I would go back as a big star.' She put her hand up in front of her face. 'Enough, this is enough.' Her mouth and her eyes were full.

I left her to go and pay the bill. I wanted to leave her alone with the food.

I could not ask her any more questions. I had pushed her far enough. How had she, a *filmi* dancer with a high moral code, become a prostitute on Falkland Road? I imagined her trying to find a job and being turned away as unsuitable because of her colourful movie past. How close to starvation had she come before she abandoned her principles in order to survive and eat? Did she still believe in anything? Perhaps she did. She cared for her girls, she had become their guardian and their mother in the dark amoral world in which they lived.

Downstairs in the café the cashier did not smile politely as he had when I had paid first time round. He looked me up and down,

A never-ending frieze of film posters

taking his time and examining me minutely. I paid and then sat for a while, fiddling with things in my bag to pass the time. I was away for at least ten minutes. When I returned to the family room Madam Deepa was sitting exactly as I had left her. None of the food had been touched.

'Could I have this packed for Maya and Miriya?' I asked.

'As you wish.'

A waiter packed the cake, the *samosas* and the *pakoras* without grace, jamming them together into a flimsy box so that the cake crumbled into the *pakoras* even before he had closed the lid, and as we walked back through the café, cold laughter followed us out on to the street.

When Madam Deepa reached the steps where I had first seen her she did not turn to say goodbye. She walked away from me erect and broken.

Walking back along Falkland Road and then Grant Road, I followed a never-ending frieze of film posters. They were slapped on

91

to every surface: on a wall beside an advertisement for a venereal disease clinic, on a door next to a notice offering 500-rupee abortions, under a flapping sign that extolled the virtues of Dr Nirav's powder cures for 'itching of parts'. Each film poster was offering up a few hours of escape from the poverty and humiliation of Bombay's back streets. In the musty gloom of the Original Cinema, the people of Kamathipura could be among heroes who walk on air and heroines who dance while rose petals are scattered at their feet. Deepa's sad journey from the posters to the streets had been short and cruel.

The second time I'd met Sophiya, Sunil's hairdresser star, on the dildo-soup set in her pink candlewick dressing-gown and signature slippers, she had told me to call when I was next in town. I walked away from Madam Deepa in Kamathipura in the late-afternoon sunshine and called Sophiya as soon as I got back to Carmichael Road. She was going to be at the Oberoi later on and we agreed to meet there among the rich folk of easy virtue and principles.

Waiters moved through a fine fog of cigar and imported cigarette smoke in the bar at the Oberoi. The volume of the early evening crowd dipped and rose in waves. There was one table in a corner near the door with a slight cross-breeze. I could not see Sophiya anywhere in the haze, and a corner table meant that I would get a view of everyone coming and going. I asked one of the waiters to help and he waved me graciously into a stubby little leather chair, hovering beside me while I decided what to have. He did not hurry me and he did not look me up and down. I found myself staring at the cocktail menu and feeling pathetically grateful for his courtesy. He even managed to maintain his poise when I asked for just a glass of water. A group of men huddled together over the next table looked up one by one to check me out. Their expressions were not so far from those of the men on Falkland Road, they were just dressed in flashier clothes and fiddling with expensive phones rather than snookering their hands in their pockets like the crowd outside the Original Cinema.

I drank the glass of water and watched the entrance to the bar for a while. I called Sophiya's number as the stares of the men next door became more confident and more uncomfortable.

'Sorry hon, I'm in the café. I was so bloody hungry I just had to get something to eat. Come on over, it's just across from the bar,' she said.

I paid the waiter, gave him a big smile of thanks and shrugged at the pack of leering men at the next-door table as I got up and set off across the great marble expanse between the bar and the café. Just as the woman at the front of the café was about to ask where I wanted to sit there was a yelp from a waving figure at a distant table. It was not a big wave. The whole of Sophiya's right arm was strapped against her body in a complicated splint and sling.

As I walked across to her she curved over the table and kissed me on both cheeks with a puff of puckering lips.

'What happened to your arm?'

'Great, isn't it?' She stroked the complicated structure. 'I was compèring one of these fashion shows that I do yesterday evening. Big dance number at the end, I'm doing the whole thing, right in there, no problem, legs, arms, the whole thing, da da da.' Sophiya waved her good arm wildly. 'Next thing I know my shoulder's gone and I'm in hospital screaming my tits off, begging for drugs, as this doctor tries to pop it back in. Sit down, sit down.' She wiggled the fingers of her strapped hand at the chair in front of me.

'It sounds disgusting.'

'Oh boy, so right, on a scale of vile it was disgusting central.'

Almost half of Sophiya's face was covered by a huge pair of sunglasses and her hair fell right down her back in a mass of extensions and plaits. Its length and volume dwarfed her fragile body.

Her smile was a little crooked, almost hiding slightly lop-sided teeth with the full curve of her mouth. Under the sunglasses, the big hair and the kooky smile layers of sheer silk hung off her thin frame, half-hitched on her right side by the strapping and sling on her arm. Sophiya was a mixture of big and small, tiny face, bones and body, saucer eyes, big nose, mouth, hair, sling and feet, an explosion out of a dressing-up box. I had forgotten the hair, its hugeness and whole separate personality.

'Hope you don't mind that I'm stuffing my face, I just had to have something, I felt so sick yesterday with this thing.' She wriggled her strapped arm.

There was a large plate of antipasti in front of her. Sophiya carefully rolled a slice of red pepper in some pastrami and popped it in her mouth, letting the juice from the pepper run down her chin. She giggled and rubbed it away with the back of her hand, sloshed some wine into her glass and into the glass next to me and then pulled a cigarette from a packet lying close to her good arm.

'Light me, babe.' Sophiya smiled and leant towards me.

There were no matches on the table. I reached over to the lighter that was lying next to the packet and lit her cigarette. She inhaled deeply and sighed out the smoke.

'You've finished on *Snip!* now, haven't you?' I asked.

'Yeah, I did a TV interview this morning about it and it's on the entertainment news at nine. I was so out of it this morning I really think I talked a load of crap but it might be a laugh to watch it. The cute guys at the business centre will let us see it on their TV.'

She shifted her chair slightly to clear her view, her good hand running through her hair as she scanned the room. Then she checked her watch, turned her attention back to her food and began to pick, her cigarette waving over the plate. She inhaled and slid a slice of salami into her mouth at the same time.

'Was *Snip!* your first feature?' I asked.

'Sure, my first starring feature, but I did a dance number in one of Sanjay Dutt's recent films. He was great, totally fit and so sexy.

He's really back on track after all that prison rubbish.' She rolled her tongue around another piece of pastrami, licking it into her mouth, and checked her watch again. She seemed to swallow her mouthful without chewing.

'It was in *Khubsoorat*, wasn't it? I've seen it. I only really went because I thought *Beautiful* was such an un-Hindi title. You were great. I've just clicked that it was you. You made Sanjay Dutt look as if he could actually dance.' I realized I was gushing and stopped.

'Thanks, he wasn't bad, was he?' Sophiya smiled. 'What time do you make it now?'

There was still a quarter of an hour until the entertainment section of the news.

'Come on, babe, let's go down there now.'

Sophiya uncurled herself from her chair and gathered up the wine and what remained of her food. She tucked the bottle under her sling and carried her plate out in front of her, balancing it on the palm of her hand and smiling full and wide at the whole café, ignoring the embarrassment of the waiters hovering around her. Everyone watched her leave.

I followed her with the glasses of wine across the marble to the stairs that led down to the business centre. The one bit of Sophiya that I had not seen in the café was her feet. Now they were padding in front of me in the same fluffy teddy-bear slippers that she had been wearing at the Breach Candy Club. She looked like Minnie Mouse off to a party with a wine bottle tucked under her arm.

'Good evening, Miss Haque.' A thin man behind the desk in the business centre bowed. 'Such a pleasure to have you here with us.' His two juniors, one at a computer and the other on the phone, also bowed to Sophiya.

She smiled and shook the manager's hand but did not take off her sunglasses.

'Could we use the TV in the conference room for a while?' she asked. 'I'm on the news.'

'Of course, why not? It is our pleasure.' He popped out from behind his desk and ushered us into the conference room with another sweeping bow.

The room was beige and the air was stale and heavy with old cigarette smoke. Sophiya said nothing but she seemed satisfied by the large television set on a dark cabinet arrangement at the end of a long table.

'Can I bring you something, water, snacks? Anything you need please just to let me know.' He hurried around the conference room, setting the chairs straight round the table and gathering up some used teacups and full ashtrays.

Sophiya waved the wine bottle from under her sling at him.

'It would be so great if you could get us some more of this and just put it on my bill at the café.'

'Of course. Is there anything else I can get?' the manager asked, smoothing the front of his pinstriped trousers, checking his tie knot and trying to read the label on the bottle being waved at him.

'No, no, that's great.' Sophiya was holding the door, waiting for him to leave.

'May I say again what a pleasure it is to have you here?' He bowed in the doorway.

'Thank you, yes, thanks a lot.' Sophiya nudged the door a little and the manager backed out of the room.

She rolled her eyes and dropped into one of the chairs, swinging her teddy-bear feet up on to the table and taking off her sunglasses.

'Bless 'im, but bloody hell they do go on.' She gave a movie-star smile. 'Can you sort out the telly?'

'Why did you choose Bombay?' I asked as I fiddled with the remote control.

'I was doing all the stuff out of Hong Kong and it just seemed that the audience that liked me was here.' She filled the two glasses that I had put down on the table.

'Had you been to India before?'

'Nah, Portsmouth-born, then London girl through and through.' She laughed and her whole face came alive behind the huge sunglasses.

'Wouldn't you have more access to the viewing public if you spoke Hindi or Marathi?'

'Didn't seem much point. Everyone in music TV speaks English and I don't want to crap around in local telly. I've got a big following. The young urban gang here really like my accent and the whole Indian-London thing. It's getting me a load of work.' She lit another cigarette. 'It's made it really pretty easy to get into film.' Two trails of smoke swirled out of her nostrils.

The news started on the large television screen.

For the next hour we sat through the latest low-down on Bollywood. We watched clips from Shah Rukh Khan's new film. We followed the coverage of a première party, packed to bursting with big stars in jewelled saris and wannabes in overly tight Western dress. We listened while we were told all about the problems one female director was having with violent demonstrations on set while she was trying to make a film about Hindu widows. We sat through a round-up of what was hot and what was not: Capri pants, cropped T-shirts, cork platforms and strange fluorescent beany hats were the things to have; tailored suits (for women), formal shirts (for men), and anything too ethnic were right out. Sophiya stared at the screen, smoking through each new topic with studied concentration.

The news ended.

'So what the hell was all that about then?' She filled up her glass and smacked the bottle back down on the table. 'What a bloody waste of time. We've been sitting here for hours. I must have been so crap they cut my interview. Poor Sunil, he'll be really pissed about that. We need all the coverage we can get. What the hell do you think happened?'

'Perhaps they're holding it over for tomorrow.'

'Oh, don't try and make me feel sodding better.'

She fished into her cigarettes and then tipped the packet upside down. A small shower of tobacco floated down on to the table. 'All gone, time to go home. No more smokes, time for bed. This is hurting.' She dunked her head towards her strapped shoulder. 'Either I didn't drink enough wine or the painkillers are wearing off.' She slumped over the table, resting her head next to one of the full ashtrays.

'Can I drop you off?' I asked.

'No, I'm just around the corner. Sorry about this evening. Will you come out again? Jules and I are going up to Olive, that great new place up in Pali Hill, soon. You know, over the other side of town.'

'Who's Jules?'

'My boyfriend, my manager, just about everything really. You'll like Olive, it's funky, kind of London-meets-Bombay with a bit of Italy on the side.'

We made our way to the front of the hotel. I waited for my car on the steps and watched Sophiya walking out into the night towards the Gateway of India, her huge slippers as incongruous in the buttery humidity as her sunglasses were in the darkness. It was the second time that day that I had watched an almost-star walk away from me – first Madam Deepa, erect and broken, a flimsy box of snacks in hand, as she disappeared into the gloom of her brothel on Falkland Road, and now Sophiya, all big hair and fluffy slippers, fading into the darkness.

While Sophiya was trying to get airtime for *Snip!*, Hrithik was in trouble.

Roughly half of India's female population was dreaming of him as boyfriend, fiancé or husband material while leafing over his pumped-up body in *CinéBlitz*, *Filmfare* and *Stardust*. But Hrithik was in love. He had been in love before he hit the silver screen and, unlike most of the Bollywood pack, he had made no secret of the fact that he was not up for grabs.

Many of the *filmi* fraternity are convinced that the box-office value of all new stars depends on their remaining single. They are inclined to forget that some of the industry's biggest stars, Amitabh Bachchan, Shah Rukh Khan and Aamir Khan among them, were well and truly married even before they hit the head-lines. Still, the *filmi* family shake their heads and insist that single status is essential for stardom. They cite Salman Khan's super-studdom as an example, and they point to Dimple, the *filmi* dream I had seen at the Dome with her daughters. She had withdrawn from the industry when she got married and she only returned to the big screen when her marriage broke down.

Hrithik ignored the *filmi* magazines' catty comments about his stellar position depending on his staying single. He stuck with his girlfriend Sussanne, and the magazines had no choice but to print pictures of the happy young couple together.

'Love like this only happens once in a lifetime. Why would I let it go because a few people think it might affect my career?' Hrithik said in reply to the constant questions from *filmi* reporters about his love life.

'So how did you lovebirds meet?' Meena the mag queen had asked in the early days of Hrithik hysteria.

'It started at a traffic signal. I was driving and when I stopped at a signal another car stopped beside me. There was a girl in the car who looked very pretty and very sad at the same time. When I saw her I thought I knew her. As a kid I had met her and then she had gone off overseas to study. That same evening I spoke about her to a friend of mine. My friend turned back to me and said: "My God, I saw her this morning and she was speaking to me about you because she had seen you too!" It was like, what a coincidence! So that common friend helped us to get together and that's how it started.'

It all seemed too perfect, too scripted. In Hrithik's launch film,

Kaho Naa . . . Pyaar Hai, his character meets the girl of his dreams at some traffic lights. The only difference is that in the film he is a struggling musician on a bicycle, while his dream girl, in her fancy car, is naturally the daughter of a phenomenally rich drug baron. The magazines fell on this coincidence, snapping like hyenas. Hrithik responded calmly and politely:

'You know when Dad thought of this scene for *KNPH* he told me about it and I thought "Oh no!" But at that time he did not know how Sussanne and I had met. For me it was like a sign that maybe we were meant for each other. I think it just meant that I could do the scene better on film because I knew exactly what it felt like. That was perhaps the strangest and best thing about *KNPH*.'

And all the matriarchs in the beauty salons read the interview and sighed: 'Such a lovely boy.' And all the young girls who were in love with Hrithik drew moustaches and spots on pictures of Sussanne in the *filmi* magazines and picked holes in her dress sense with their fellow Hrithik-loving girlfriends.

I had been in Delhi the week that Hrithik decided to reiterate to his fans that Sussanne was the girl of his dreams, his forever woman. Mrs Kanwar's husband had just had a particularly liverish attack and Dolly Singh was ill too, suffering not from liverishness, but from a nasty dose of fever. Mrs Kanwar had not been nearly as interested in the health of her husband or her friend as she was in Hrithik's championing of monogamy.

'All very nice now, you know,' she said wagging her finger at Hrithik's cover shot on *Stardust*, his lightly haired chest gleaming from the top of a shiny T-shirt, its sleeves rolled right up to give maximum exposure to his biceps and triceps. 'Nothing so nice for a lovely girl like her as to have such a pretty young man all sweetheart on her.' Mrs Kanwar banged the masseur on the head. '*Aram se halka*, not so hard.' She spun the magazine around to give me a full view. 'Lovely, *naar*?'

'Yes, he is very pretty.'

'But what if he roams around a little?' She tapped one of her nails on the picture again.

'What do you mean?'

'He is a man, *yaar*.'

'Yes, I know. So what?'

'So men are doing men's thingies.' Mrs Kanwar tapped even more adamantly on Hrithik's picture.

'Thingies?'

The salon was silent, waiting for Mrs Kanwar to reply.

'Kissing-*wissing* rubbish and all, don't make me say these things. It is most embarrassing for me.' She flapped her hands in front of her face. 'Too much, too much. To tell you very frankly, what I am saying is it's nice and fine for him to play Mr Clean and all, but what if he does men's thingies with others and gets caught? Not so sweet Hrithik baby then, *naar?*'

Uma the manicurist, bent over her bottles of Beachy Peachy and Sexy Shimmer high gloss polish, was shuddering with suppressed giggles. As Mrs Kanwar reached her climax Uma snorted.

'What's so funny? I don't think you would be finding it so funny if it was your husband-*wusband*,' Mrs Kanwar huffed, and she crossed her arms beneath her ample bust as if to underline her point.

'Do you think your husband is getting better?' I asked as Uma bent down over her polishes again.

'*Yaar, yaar*, I suppose. He will be fit and fine soon enough.' Mrs Kanwar was not to be drawn from her sulk and I left her to her tales of Hrithik and his lady love in her *filmi* fantasy world.

'Do you think his girlfriend Sussanne is pretty?' I asked a friend of mine's fifteen-year-old daughter. Mira had sworn lifelong devotion to Hrithik the day *Kaho Naa . . . Pyaar Hai* came out, along with half the girls in her class at school.

'Pretty stupid.' She scowled at me. How could I be so insensitive? How could I understand what it was like to be fifteen and in love with Hrithik Roshan almost to the point of hysteria every time his biceps put in an appearance?

Budding teenage Mira needed to know everything about her hero. She would scowl at the newspaper man in her local market if the *filmi* magazines came in even half a day late. Though normally shy, she would quiz almost total strangers for news of Hrithik. And although she had regarded me with relatively polite indifference for years, I suddenly became her number one new best friend when she found out that I was on the Bollywood trail.

'Have you heard the story about how Hrithik and Sussanne met?' I asked Mira.

'Obviously.'

'Don't you think it's romantic?'

'Is it?'

'Well, quite romantic, and don't you think it was a bit weird that it was repeated in the traffic-light scene in *Kaho Naa . . . Pyaar Hai?*'

'I suppose.' Mira was not going to give ground.

'Apparently when Hrithik first read the scene in his father's script he wanted him to take it out because he thought it was too personal.'

'How do you know?' Suddenly Mira was interested.

'Oh, someone told me when I was last in Bombay.'

'You know someone who knows Duggu?' she shot back, using Hrithik's nickname.

'I do.'

'Have you met him?' She was shouting now.

'Not yet.'

'So you mean you are going to?' Now she was clinging to my arm, her fingers digging in deep.

'It may take a while but I plan to.'

'When? When are you going to meet him?' Now Mira was dragging me upstairs to her bedroom.

'I'm just not quite sure yet. I'm working on it, though.'

'When you see him can you get him to sign a T-shirt for me? You have to, you really have to do this for me.' She was pulling things out of her bedroom cupboard, and cropped T-shirts, pedal-pushers and teen bras flew through the air and landed in a wanton pile beneath a full-face poster of Hrithik gazing out over her teenage turmoil with eyes of unutterable beauty. Mira presented me with a white T-shirt on which a small pink kitten holding a love heart was embroidered roughly in the left breast area.

'You really really have to do this thing, you know?' she pleaded.

Mira was asking for the thing I hate almost more than anything else – having to beg for an autograph. But every fibre of her being was imploring me.

'I'll try,' I muttered gracelessly.

From then on I could do no wrong in her eyes. In her teenage world there was only one degree of separation between me and her hero.

Sussanne Khan may not exactly have been the most popular girl in India, and Hrithik may have tested the devotion of Mira and her fellow millions, but they were still waiting for the release of his next film in a state of constant breathlessness.

Fiza promised to turn the standard Bollywood formula inside out. Hindu star Hrithik was cast as a young Muslim caught up in the Bombay riots of 1992 and 1993. Furthermore the film was being directed by a poacher turned gamekeeper, a *filmi* magazine editor who was brave enough to chance his luck and be judged by his own tribe. Khalid Mohammed had been the editor of *Filmfare* for fifteen years when he decided to take his turn in the director's chair. Before his editorship *Filmfare* had contained little more than a routine monthly rundown on what was in production, what was about to come out and how current films were doing at the box office. Packed full of statistics and monochromatic location reports, it had about as much appeal for the general film-going public as *Computer Weekly* would have had for Mrs Kanwar and the ladies at La Belle. Mohammed had been a *filmi*-mag revolutionary. The hitherto staid auntie of the Bollywood press now contained at least as much kitty-katty chitty-chat as any of its *filmi*-family competitors. Mohammed made full use of *Filmfare*'s new persona to hype his film. What his readers wanted to know was whether he would be as radical with the Hindi movie formula as he had been with the original format of *Filmfare*.

The hoardings for *Fiza* were going up all over the city by the end of August, but at the bottom of Carmichael Road there was a different drama being played out.

The road falls steeply, down from the heady heights where Sunil's mafia man had taken his ease over the city's panorama, to Peddar Road, the main road that runs from Cumballa and Malabar Hills to downtown Colaba and the Bombay Harbour seafront. Where the steep drop hits the main road there is a wall of advertising hoardings as high as apartment buildings. When I run down the hill to the racecourse in the morning haze I see Bollywood stars magnified a hundred times, telling me I need to buy a mobile phone, a watch or a car. On Carmichael Road the art deco apartments of old Bombay are framed by the million-rupee smiles of modern Mumbai.

Now these hoardings had become a war zone. On one side of the site Shah Rukh Khan, eighty foot high and with a thirty foot-wide smile, was inviting me to buy Pepsi. Hrithik was to the right, blown up to the same dimensions, the same idea, different drink. He was the new face for Coca-Cola. I ignored them both and ran on down to the juice-*wallah* outside the Breach Candy Club.

The stall was empty. I ran on towards the racecourse and came back half an hour later, limp and exhausted. The heat was already sucking away any hint of cool in the early morning air. The juice-*wallah* had arrived. I sat under the tree beside his stand while he methodically cleaned his machines, reassembled them and set out the first pile of vegetables ready for slaughter. The back of the hoardings at the top of the road rose above us. It was the first time that I had seen the juice-*wallah* since I had been to Falkland Road.

'What do you think of all the Bollywood stars advertising Pepsi and Coke?' I asked him.

'All those big smiles, it should not be right for them to show all those teeth. All this soft drink *bagwas* is making teeth drop out, plonk, plonk.' He dropped two carrots into the grinder. 'They are not telling you any of this up on the big fancy poster, are they?' He squashed the carrots down into the turning blades. 'Carrot juice, *acchha*, now this is good for teeth.' We both watched as the dark orange juice began to drip through into a small glass. 'And for eyes and hair and nails and stomach,' he continued.

'Do you think it's okay for them to be plastered all over the city advertising these things?'

'*Yaar*, why not?' He paused for a moment. 'Danger being in that young not so smart people are thinking that perhaps Hrithik Roshan is getting so much of muscles from drinking Pepsi.'

'Coke. He advertises Coca-Cola.'

'Whatever. Coca-Cola has so much of money and he wants so much of money. If this is how he is wanting to earn his money let it be. The big company wants the famous face, the famous face wants the big company's money. It is suiting all parties.' He shrugged and took my five rupees for the carrot juice.

I was walking away when he called out to me.

'Did you find her?'

I turned back to him.

'Yes, I did.'

'Just tell me if she is fit and fine. This is all I want to know.'

'Yes, those were the words she used.'

'*Thik hai*, okay, this is enough.' He put his hand up to stop me from saying any more.

CHAPTER 5

Jealousy

Boy loses girl

THE FIZZY POP wars made it to the front pages. In the gossip columns of the *filmi* magazines it was rumoured that Hrithik was going to be paid the rupee equivalent of almost half a million pounds for signing up as the new face of Coca-Cola. The first advertisement was going to be made with Bollywood bells on. It was to be directed by Rakesh Roshan, and Aishwarya Rai was going to be Hrithik's leading lady. Wonder Boy and Wonder Girl were finally going to get it together.

It was going to be set on a desert island, a perfect place for a Cola war to begin, and it had a perfect story-line.

Boy meets Girl beneath swooshing palms and blue, blue skies. Girl has a thirsty look in her eyes. Boy reads it as thirsty for . . . well, she's got that haughty come-hither look. She must want him to dance. Cue interesting costume on a Charlie-Chaplin-meets-Marcel-Marceau theme and a tap routine with Boy sporting a cross between a squishy, very 'in' beanie hat and a bowler. Boy dances along the boardwalk, tap, tappety, tap, hippy, hippy flick. This is all very nice but Girl still has that thirsty look in her eyes. Boy dances a bottle of Coke right off the boardwalk and into his hand. Then green eyes and smouldering looks are replaced by a curvaceous, salacious Coca-Cola bottle which appears to be just as good at dancing as Boy and does not apparently need a bowler hat. Coke bottle gets Girl's lips wrapped around it. Boy just gets to look on with a cute smile on his face. The End.

It was such a lovely little story and it was going to be Rakesh Roshan's first outing as a director since the runaway success of *Kaho Naar . . . Pyaar Hai*.

'We are very excited about this project,' Papa Roshan told the *filmi* press.

'We are very excited about this project,' said Hrithik. 'And I am going to be getting a whole new look for it that is going to surprise people.'

'We have not confirmed dates yet,' said Aishwarya Rai's assistant.

'We have a very exciting and exotic location for the shoot,' said Papa Roshan.

'We are going to have a very exotic background to the ad,' said Hrithik.

'No comment,' said Aishwarya Rai's assistant.

'Is Aishwarya definite for the ad?' asked the *filmi* reporters.

'No comment,' said Papa Roshan.

'Are you looking forward to working with Ash?' the same *filmi* reporters asked Hrithik.

'No comment,' he replied.

'What do you think of Ash doing the new Coke ad with Hrithik?' they then asked Aishwarya's boyfriend, Salman Khan.

'Is she doing it? I don't know. You better ask her.'

Father, son and film crew packed their bags and headed for exotic Mauritius. Aishwarya was still to be found in Bombay.

'I think she is not fresh enough looking to be in the ad with Hrithik,' Papa Roshan was reported to have said from his exotic location.

'Miss Rai will not be going to Mauritius,' confirmed her assistant. 'It was not possible to match the dates.'

'No, I don't think she is filming right now,' Salman Khan replied to the questions. 'Why not ask her yourself?'

'Miss Rai is not available for comment at the moment,' said her assistant.

Another girl was flown out to Mauritius.

'The shoot is going fine, thank you,' said Papa Roshan when the journalists called again. 'If you will forgive me I am working and we have a very tight schedule.'

So the journalists camped at the airport and lay in wait.

The cast and crew flew home.

'It was a really exciting shoot,' said Papa Roshan. 'We hope you will like the story.'

The resulting newspaper and magazine articles kept referring back to the amount that Hrithik had been paid for the advertisement. Hrithik started to concentrate his energies in other areas, dropping into children's hospitals and donating money to the disenfranchised of India.

'I think I've lost my house keys,' I told Severin. I was standing in the kitchen doorway, trying to finish a cup of her *chai*, find my keys and get dressed all at the same time.

'What is this? You have lost them day before as well.' Severin took the cup away as I tried to do up my shirt. 'So much of this starry starry thing. I think your head is having so much of tension all the time. What is this thing that is so important that it is giving you so much of tension?'

'It's just my keys.'

'Today keys, tomorrow blouse, next day what then?' she asked, handing me back the cup now that I had finished buttoning up my shirt.

'What do you think of Hrithik Roshan?' I asked.

'Is this it? Is this what is making all of this tension?' She rolled her eyes to heaven. 'You must go to church and make prayers to keep you out of all these troubles. These are not good people. You

must pray to God. I am praying to God at all times to help me.'
She paused for a moment. 'And also to St Anthony so that he can
be helping you with the finding of the keys.'

'I don't think Hrithik Roshan is exactly the work of the devil.'

'You must not say these things. This is harassy.'

'Heresy.'

'This thing also.' Severin was in full spate. 'All things for
money. All the things they are doing for money. Parading all over
the place and doing all sorts in front of how many millions of
people. And what about the girls? What kind of mummy is letting
her daughter run around in so many wet saris showing all her
pieces to anyone who cares to look? I cannot even think on this.'
She shook her head between her hands, her eyebrows screwed up
in pain.

'You don't really think that someone like Hrithik Roshan is
bad, do you? He's so clean-cut.'

'But still he is making so much of money to be giving him
tension.'

'I don't know that it gives him tension.' I gave my cup back.

Severin paused for a moment, staring at the cup.

'But they were shooting his daddy, *naar*?' There was a note of
triumph in her voice.

'That was the underworld and that was because his father had
made a mistake in the eyes of the *gundas*, the underworld heavies.'

Severin tossed her head dismissively.

'You still haven't told me what you think of Hrithik.'

'Stop troubling me with all this.' She flapped her hand at me.

'I still don't have my keys.'

'Take these.' She took her own set out of the corner knot in her
chunni.

'Do you think he is good-looking?'

'Baby boy face.' Severin flapped even more furiously. 'This is
not important thing. Stop this troubling.'

'Do you like Pepsi or Coca-Cola?'

There were bottles of both in the kitchen fridge. They were recent additions to the household in the same way that Shah Rukh Khan and Hrithik were recent additions to the local hoarding landscape.

Severin's hands steadied to a flutter and she peered into my face.

'What is this? Are you mad?'

'No, just asking.'

'*Chalo*, go now.'

I turned to leave.

'If you are losing my keys I cannot be taking this,' she called after me. 'Coca-Cola, Pepsi, too much of tension, too much.'

Her refrain faded behind me as I left the house.

A press release was issued from Roshan Villas.

We are aware of the speculation surrounding the recent Coca-Cola shoot in Mauritius. There has been extensive misreporting in this matter as to the participation of Miss Aishwarya Rai in the advertisement. Miss Rai was not available for the shoot during the dates that had been fixed. There was no other reason for her absence in Mauritius. We look forward to your reaction to the forthcoming ad and hope that it will give you as much satisfaction as it has given us to make it.

The release was made on behalf of Rakesh and Hrithik Roshan.

The magazines rolled their editorial eyes and went in for the kill. The covers of the next editions shouted it out loud: 'Ash snubs Hrithik', 'Roshan vs Rai, Ageist vs Beauty', '"Ash too old for Hrithik," says Rakesh Roshan', 'Ash skips Mauritius for Salman'.

Hrithik deflected the questions diplomatically and focused on the pre-release publicity for *Fiza*.

'Why do they always misquote everything?' he asked one of the few journalists he trusted, someone he had been at school with. 'My father was just saying that he thought it would be good to have a new face in the ad, someone who has not been seen before. So they decide he is saying that Ash is too old for me. Come on, she's the same age as me. How can she be too old?'

'But that wouldn't make headlines, would it?' his friend replied.

Further trouble was brewing. In *Fiza* one of Hrithik's leading ladies was Jaya Bachchan, the wife of Bollywood's long-term superstar Amitabh. Jaya had been a bigger star than her husband in the early days of their marriage, but she had given up her career when they started to have children. Once the children hit their twenties she had made a tentative and carefully picked return to acting, appearing in a few plays and one slightly art-house film. With *Fiza* she was coming back into the mainstream. The press began to focus on the fact that she had chosen to star with Hrithik while her own son Abishek was struggling to launch his career in the shadow of the Hrithik phenom-enon. Moreover, in *Fiza* she was playing Hrithik's mother, a Muslim woman whose life falls apart when her son disappears during the Bombay riots. The *filmi* magazines sharpened their claws.

'Oh perfect, *yaar*, a mother playing a mother, but not to her own son.'

Sophiya's boyfriend Jules called me a few days after my evening in front of the television in the business centre at the Oberoi.

'Do you feel like meeting up tonight? We're going to go to Olive.'

'How's Sophiya's shoulder?'

'She's still all strapped up. She did a show yesterday like that and she looked so cute, strutting her stuff all trussed up like a turkey.'

'Did she dance?' I asked.

'Did she ever.'

'Good on her.'

'So are you going to come out tonight?'

'Yes, I'd love to.'

'Olive is on Pali Hill. Most taxi drivers know it, but if there is a problem just tell them it's at the top of Union Walk. I guess we'll be there from about eight-thirty and there are some other people coming as well. It's going to be a great night.'

But before a night out on Pali Hill I had a date in a graveyard. I was looking for someone buried far out in the nether regions of the Bombay Christian Burial Ground at Sewri. A friend had told me that A.M. Jacob, the man on whom Kipling based the character of Lurghan Sahib in *Kim*, had been buried there on 9 January 1921. He hoped that I might be able to trace the grave. But my date was not with a tombstone. It was with Mr M.G. Tivarekar, the clerk-in-charge. He was going to lead me through the burial records of 1921 so that I could find a plot reference from amongst the thousands of names, each one whispering from the fading pages of Bombay's colonial chapter.

Mr Tivarekar was eighty-five years old but his memory was as sharp as the pencils lined up on his desk. According to the thermometer on the wall the temperature in his office was 35°C and the ceiling fans were at full tilt. Even so Mr T was firmly encased in a tight and very home-knitted jumper in a curious shade of *eau de Nil*. He had been the clerk-in-charge for thirty-five years, ever since he had taken early retirement at fifty from his position at the Post Office, and he saw no reason why he should ever retire from his retirement job.

'They can retire me into one of these plots I have been keeping my eye on for all these years when the time is right. Until that time I will just keep on doing what I have come to know,' he said as he clambered up a rickety set of library steps to hunt out the record book for 1921.

112

His assistant and I stood at the bottom, sweating in anticipation. Mr T wobbled calmly on to the top step, fingering his way past the thick volumes of the First World War, past the slimmer volumes of 1919 and 1920, before coming to rest on another fat volume, 1921.

'A terrible year for cholera during the monsoon,' he mused.

Mr T would have been six.

'Our *mali* and his whole family died in just three days. My *chachaji*, my paternal uncle, he departed also.' He paused for a moment, the heavy book rocking gently in his hand.

We stood below him, our hands reaching up to steady him.

'No, I think this is not right. I think it was *mamaji*, my maternal uncle.' He opened the book. 'What of it, I will find it here. He is in D section of Church of North India plot, D14 if I am right on this.'

He was right on this and it was his *chachaji*. He did not come down from the steps until he had found the entry in D14. His assistant and I were becoming increasingly nervous. Each time Mr T turned a page he swayed a little more. At last he sighed his way back down the steps and snapped the book shut on his *chachaji* as he hit solid ground.

'Enough of this now. It is our duty to help with your enquiry.'

Back behind his desk he adopted a more official air, licking his finger with precision as he made his way backwards from where the book reopened naturally at the page of his *chachaji*'s demise in November 1921. When he reached January he began to work his way down each name, line by line, death by death.

'Are there any film stars buried here?' I asked.

Mr Tivarekar looked up at me, his fading liquid eyes focusing with intent.

'Are you looking for the grave you are telling me to find or are you searching for film stars?'

'Both, I suppose, though so far I have only really been studying the live film stars.'

Mr T laughed.

'I am very happy to pass time with a madam such as you. You

are very witty. This is good for passing time but perhaps not so good for marriage. Do you have a marriage here?'

The eternal question of India. I gave him the usual line on happy single life.

'This is a very fine thing. Some ladies would be saying this thing because they could not be finding a husband but I think you are being truly sincere on this. I think perhaps many men would like to have you but you are running too fast for them.' Mr T broke out into laughter that crackled around the room.

'Any film stars?' I asked again.

Mr Tivarekar carefully put a ruler under the name that he had reached. He sat back and crossed his hands in his lap.

'You will take tea?'

'That would be lovely.'

The flirtation with information had begun.

'We have those of many churches in this place, Church of North India, Church of East India, Church of England, Christians of all walks. All types are here.' He turned stiffly in his chair and lifted a picture of Jesus off the shelf behind his desk. Jesus had floppy blond hair and blue eyes, a cross between a modern football hero and a Seventies hippy. 'To Him all these types are equal.' Mr T tapped his finger on the glowing Christ. 'There are no stars here, all are equal before such as He.'

He smiled at me with the same beatific expression as the blond in the picture.

I smiled back.

'See? He is making you smile in such a way.' He replaced the picture on the shelf, adjusting and readjusting it to get it just as it had been. 'If you are smiling like this, all in your life will be simple.'

'But before they all became equal underground were any of them in films?'

Mr T reapplied himself to the page of January 1921 in the grave record. He was not going to answer my question. The tea came and was poured in silence. In silence we drank. Mr T continued his slow progress down the page.

He found the grave I wanted and wrote its number on a piece of paper. Then he sent me out with the head *mali* of the Church of North India plot. I had been a day out, much to Mr Tivarekar's delight. A.M. Jacob had died on 9 January and had been buried on the 10th.

I was led through ranks of cherubim and seraphim weeping over the grand slabs of civil servants and their loyal wives. Angels spread their wings over Mrs Lillian Augusta Lowe and her daughter Joan Enid, 'taken from us by fever aged 5 years 1 month & 4 days'. Beneath Joan was 'Dorothy Mildred aged 4 months & 13 days'. The angels overhead raised their eyes to heaven through a banyan tree. Piles of leaves were being burnt among the plots, casting a pall of smoke around the gravestones and their heavenly attendants. We passed a long section devoted to the Church of South India where the gravestones carried photographs of the dearly beloved. Alphonzo John and Lily De Souza stared out from their headstone in their Sunday best while an over-suckled bitch slept on the grave under their ever-fixèd gaze. As we walked on, the plots became increasingly neglected, the stones awry and the statues broken. Right out in the furthest corner of the cemetery we found the plot from the grave register. At D12 we unearthed the corner of a great white marble slab. It was too deeply buried for me to be able to read the inscription. We returned to Mr Tivarekar through the heat and the smoke to ask for a digging party at a later date. He was examining the ceiling thoughtfully when I sat down in front of his desk again. My request was granted. We made a date for the unearthing of A.M. Jacob's slab.

'You will take more tea?'

I nodded.

We waited in silence and drank in silence once more. Mr Tivarekar sucked the last drop from his cup, put it down carefully and waved his assistant and the cup away.

Angels spread their wings over Mrs Lillian Augusta Lowe

'We have some of these stars as you call them,' he proffered.

'Wonderful.'

'But this is not information that has been put about for perusal of the general public.' He lowered his chin to his chest and closed his eyes.

'I don't understand.'

'Some of our great stars of yesteryear were coming from backgrounds that they rubbed out and wrote fresh.' Mr T had started to whisper, a fine spray of saliva descending through the thick afternoon sun on to his desk.

'I don't really understand what you mean by "wrote fresh".' I leant towards him.

'I was thinking that you were more clever than this,' he tutted. 'What is the thing we are always wanting most in our *filmi* stars?'

'Oh, where do I start? Good at dancing, good at raising their eyebrows?'

Mr T shook his head.

'Good at jumping around trees, good at wearing lots of costumes, brilliant at running across hillsides, arms outstretched . . .?'

Mr T continued to shake his head.

'I don't know. How many more guesses do I have?'

'None of these, none of these, you are missing the most important thing.' He sat back in his chair. 'What is it all ladies are trying to find out of pots of cream? What is it they are always looking for in the matrimonials for their most precious sons?'

I shook my head.

Mr T jutted his chin.

'You have it, He has it.' He turned to point to the picture on the shelf behind him. 'Skin, skin, skin, all are wanting fair complexion.'

'Pale skin?'

He nodded.

'And?'

'So some of our as you say "stars" were Anglo.'

He was talking about the children of mixed race, those born to English and Indian parents.

'So they were Christians?'

Mr T nodded.

'But Christian is not the problem.' He stopped and applied himself to the ceiling again. 'Maybe a small problem,' he admitted. 'Many of these Hindi films are having trainfuls of Hindu deities and monkeys but no Lord Jesus. However, main problem is Anglo.' He stopped for a moment, peering beyond me in search of a word. 'Not so *pukkah*, shall we say.' Mr T steepled his fingers and narrowed his eyes, one eyebrow raised in full Bollywood style.

'So they covered up the fact that they were Anglo-Indians and pretended to be fair, full-blooded Indians?'

'This is what I am saying.'

We both paused, staring into the pool of sunshine on Mr T's desk.

'And when they died they were buried here anonymously or under different names?' I continued.

'Some were buried under different names but some used their real names because they had changed their names in the first instance for their life in cinema. It is not so hard to pick out an Anglo from the name.'

'But there must have been rumours.' I stopped for a moment. 'Like in Hollywood. I think everyone knew that Merle Oberon was half-Indian.'

'Is that so?' Mr Tivarekar looked up in surprise. 'Merle Oberon, *achcha*.' He rolled her name around his memory. 'Such a pretty lady.'

'The story went that she tried to cover her tracks by keeping her mother as her *ayah* and never letting her out of the house.'

Mr T shook his head. 'Why is it that you have so much interest in these people who are breaking every day the commandments: "Keep honour for your mother and father."' He paused. '"Thou must not lie, cheat or steal." Every day they are doing these things, every day.'

'But in a way that is part of their work.'

'What is this? What kind of work is it that makes it necessary to break these commandments?' He banged his hand on the desk.

'Their job is to pretend that they are other people, so it's hard for them to know who they really are.'

'Perhaps pretending is not breaking commandments.' He put one hand to his mouth and looked up at the ceiling again, his other hand stretched out towards me to stop me interrupting the thought he was chasing across the peeling plaster. 'But to tell you very frankly I think they are most of the time forgetting who they are in this chasing of roles to perform.'

'Does it really matter that they hide the fact that they are from a community that is looked down on by most people?'

'It is not a Christian thing that the Anglos have been so poorly treated in this country.' Mr T tapped his fingers together. 'I am not saying that any of all this is correct procedure.'

'I don't really see why it is so bad to pretend if it means that you are going to be able to get round the bigotry of society.'

'Bigotry, this is a fine word. I have not heard this word for so long.' He rolled the word over and over on his tongue, sucking the sound of it. 'What other way is there for defining this word bigotry?'

'Oh, prejudice, racism, intolerance, anything like that.'

'Yes, yes, a very good word, and very correct application in this case,' he concluded.

'Do you really think it is wrong that they effectively reinvented themselves to help their careers in the face of all that?' I asked again.

Mr T adopted selective hearing.

I tried another tack. 'Would I be able to see any of their graves?'

He took his glasses off and pinched the bridge of his nose.

'Is this the reason you have come here?'

'No, I came for the A.M. Jacob grave but now I'm just chancing my luck.'

Mr T smiled.

'So you have taken chance and I cannot respond. Sorry for this.'

'Mr Tivarekar, you are protecting them. That's very good of you, but it's annoying for me.'

'No, no, I am just doing my duty.' He put his glasses back on. 'They come here for peace, and peace they must have. This is my duty.' He opened one of his desk drawers. 'Now you will write in my book. I will take all your details and I would like to have a photograph of you. Do you carry one?'

'I'm not a movie star, Mr Tivarekar.'

'But surely you are carrying a picture?'

I was, a nasty set of passport photographs for visa applications. I passed the sad collection to him. He went through them until he found a couple of me smiling. I did not look very beatific but Mr T seemed satisfied.

'Good, this is nice one, smiling.' He took a stapler from another drawer and pinned me down next to my address in his book. 'Now I will be able to see this smiling face when I am sending you a Christmas card. You will come back and see me again, even after the digging of A.M. Jacob is done?'

'It will be a pleasure.'

He examined the weakening light falling on his desk.

'This is the time for you to go. There is not so much of light and you should not be here as it gets dark. People are often making trouble here after dark. Come, I will take you to your car.'

We walked out of Mr Tivarekar's office and he let me take a photograph of him between a bougainvillaea bush and the dedication to those kind persons who had made sizeable donations towards the upkeep of the graveyard. He took off his glasses for the picture and stood very erect, next to a podgy-cheeked stone cherub blowing trumpet tunes of praise for those on the donation board. Another angel with a mournful expression and a pair of jet-black ravens on its shoulders rose behind Mr T's head. The angel watched over a grave. The ravens watched over a *mali* who was asleep on the stone slab beneath. The gardener's thin legs were twisted in sleep and his arms hung over either side of the

Mr T and his blue-eyed star on the shelf

stone. He could as easily have been a corpse. I took a picture of him as well.

'You will please not show this in public. It will cause me problems, this thing.' Mr T shouted at the *mali* and sent one of his assistants to tidy the sleeping man from under the angel. 'This is a place of eternal rest. It is not for a few winks,' he said, folding his hands together in prayer and raising his eyebrows at the scuttling *mali*.

At the gate Mr T and his assistants stood in a line to wave me away.

Mrs Kanwar knew all about Merle Oberon. She held her up as an example of the low morals and questionable mores of Hollywood, as against her pristine vision of the Hindi *filmi* industry. In fact she had had much to say on the matter during a previous conversation at La Belle.

121

That afternoon at the salon I had been across the room from Mrs Kanwar, my eyes closed in a state of ecstasy while almond oil was rubbed into my hair. My head lolled to one side as I made a concerted effort not to dribble in that drifting moment between sensual pleasure and sleep. Dolly Singh as usual was under the beautician's depilatory thread. She was not happy. Mrs Kanwar had assured her friend that rubbing coconut oil into her skin for a month would slow her prolific regrowth. But Dolly's undesired hair had come back just as rapidly and luxuriantly as ever. Mrs Kanwar, ensconced under the hair-dryer, obviously felt it was her duty to take Dolly's mind off her problem.

A young bride was sitting near Mrs Kanwar. Her hair was being coiled into a mass of layered curls around a *mang bindi*, the gold bridal headdress that runs down a bride's central parting and comes to rest in an explosion of carats on the forehead. One of the pedicurists was at her feet, a manicurist was gilding her fingernails to match her *mang bindi*, and the make-up artist was flicking brushes and fighting for space with the manicurist. The bride-to-be sat rigid and wide-eyed while her friend and comforter sat beside her, leafing through magazines and jiggling in the muted world of her stereo headphones.

I was almost asleep and missed the beginning of Mrs Kanwar's monologue, but when she began to flick the temperature control of her hair-dryer up and down I came to with a start. A Hollywood outburst seemed imminent.

'And that girl, that wicked girl who kept her mother as a slave. Pearl, that was her name, wicked Pearl.'

'Merle,' I blurted out from the depths of my head massage.

'Whatever. You know what she did to her mother?' Mrs Kanwar dismissed me and rolled her eyes at Dolly. Dolly rolled her eyes back in response, unable to make any other gesture as the threader dived and plucked.

'She was so ashamed that her mother was Indian that she kept her as her own servant. Can you imagine such a thing as keeping your very own mummy as a servant?' Mrs Kanwar shivered under the heat of her hair-dryer. 'Oh my God, just imagine my *bahu* . . .' She knocked her fist to her forehead at the thought of her daughter-in-law forcing her to swab floors and roll *chapatis*. 'These Anglos, they are not right in the head, you know.'

'Would you call Merle Oberon an Anglo?' I asked.

'*Yaar*, why not, half-Indian, half-whatever, better to call her Anglo than what is the other thing?'

'Half-caste?' I offered.

'This is not a nice thing to say but this is the case. But still it brings a kind of madness.' Mrs Kanwar folded her hands primly in her lap. 'To say it straight, their fairness has a strangeness to it, with those pale eyes and all. It's not right. Now, see this lovely girl here, she is fair in proper Indian way.' Mrs Kanwar waved her hand at the rigid bride whose almond skin was being powdered pale, making her dark brown eyes seem even wider and more terrified. 'Such a pretty girl. Such a lucky man who is getting you.' Mrs Kanwar smiled at the girl. 'Such a sweet girl would never think of any of these things, would you?'

The girl could not speak – her lips were being outlined in heavy plum. She wrinkled her forehead instead.

'Perhaps she does not understand me, poor sweet thing. See how frightened she is, terrible thing this is, marriage should make her so happy.' Mrs Kanwar spoke to the girl in Hindi and then translated in case I had not kept up. 'I am telling her that this is the most beautiful day of her life and she must try harder to be happy.' She nodded at the girl.

The pained furrowing across the girl's forehead deepened. Mrs Kanwar ignored her expression and addressed herself to Dolly, returning to her subject of maternal slavery.

'This wicked thing would never be happening here, such is family and love of family. Can you imagine such a thing, Dolly?'

Dolly rolled her eyes again.

'Could your *beti*, your daughter, ever do something like that?'

Dolly Singh had a painfully thin eighteen-year-old daughter with terrible astigmatism. It was unlikely that she would enslave her mother. Mrs Kanwar did not give Dolly a chance to reply.

'You believe me, this kind of betrayal of family and name would never happen here.'

If I had already met Mr Tivarekar I might have been able to contradict Mrs Kanwar. But I remained silent and just slid back under the hands of my masseur, leaving Dolly to roll her eyes in tacit agreement with Mrs Kanwar's argument.

I managed to get lost in the twilight and the traffic and did not have time to go home and change after tea with Mr Tivarekar before meeting Sophiya and Jules. Union Walk on Pali Hill was not easy to find, and when found it was hard to navigate. As the car climbed, the walls closed in. The driver stopped twice, sliding himself out of the door to peer at the road and shake his head at the decreasing clearance on either side of his gleaming car. He squeezed us out at the top into a dark clearing in the road. The colonnaded homes of the *filmi* stars lurked behind huge gates, looming out of the darkness like extra sets from *Gone With the Wind*. Their security guards were grouped together under a street light, engrossed in cards. A rank of expensive cars, mostly four-wheel drives with jacked-up suspension, pointed their bonnets at our destination, their drivers sleeping, eating or making desultory attempts to join the card game.

A very erect security guard stood at the entrance to Olive, silhouetted by the soft light that filtered from the restaurant out into the darkness of the walled-in neighbourhood. A froth of conversation erupted over Olive's walls, bubbling temptingly over the crowd outside who were trying to get in.

As I got out, a fleet of cars slid to the restaurant entrance. Doors opened and a range of long polished legs emerged. I had managed to turn up at the hottest new restaurant in town at the same time as twenty sleek models fresh from an international fashion show, all dressed up and hyped on catwalk adoration. I was in army fatigue trousers and a grey T-shirt that had been a very different colour before its life in the Indian *dhobi* system. The models were long and thin, their polished angles barely covered in shimmering triangles over spray-on hot-pants and handkerchief-size skirts. They were as lean and international as I was scruffy and grave-yard-soiled.

Olive's front-of-house was all about making an entrance. Each of the twenty catwalk sirens did their bit, striking a pose at the door before stalking in with the sensual corkscrewing stride of the fashionistas. I hung around the edges watching the show as all the men snapped to and took in every hip and thigh in stunned silence. I saw Sophiya and Jules smiling from a central table, watching the girls go by. I waved and Jules got up and came over to the door. He was very London, very shabby-crumpled cool with hair that looked as if it stayed at home a lot.

'Thanks, I need a bit of support. I'm still working on my ramp walk, haven't quite mastered the twist and slide thing yet.'

'You look great. Love the fatigues, very Soho.'

He led me across the restaurant to their table and introduced me. There was a director from London in the middle of making a series about Bombay for the BBC, a woman with short power hair and early-morning-call shadows under her eyes. A young man sat next to her, his fingers stroking his goatee beard.

Jules introduced us. 'This is Rajiv.'

'Love the combat gear, very punchy, very now,' Rajiv observed with fashion-house sibilance.

'Thank you.' I smiled and shook his soft hand.

Sophiya kissed him on the cheek with her puckered puff.

'Told you she was sassy,' and she went on kissing him.

'I was in a graveyard, it's not really a fashion thing.'

Rajiv looked up from Sophiya's kisses. 'Cool, you do combat and death.'

The models were all lined up just behind our table having their picture taken. The photographers were having difficulty getting all twenty into the shot and they were sweating as the girls waited, all angles and symmetry.

'How thin can a person be?' asked Sophiya as she leant on Rajiv's shoulder, stroking his orange silk shirt. 'It makes me want to wear maternity clothes for the rest of my life.' She plucked at her jutting collar bones.

'Babe, you're in a different league,' Rajiv pouted.

She laughed and most of the models turned round. They knew her laugh, she had compèred almost every other fashion show they had been in. They waved and blew kisses, and Sophiya waved and puckered the air back at them.

Jules came and sat down beside me.

'Half of them are trying to get into film at the moment. They all know Soph is doing her first feature.'

'Does that make her unpopular?' I asked.

'No way, it would be really dumb of them to piss Soph off. Not only does she host most of the shows but they also know that she can give them a good pump if they need it.'

'Have you seen the rushes for *Snip!*?'

'Bits and pieces, it's really great stuff, really great . . .' His voice trailed off as he watched a new batch of people coming into the restaurant.

'Do you think Sophiya will get her break with *Snip!*?'

'Of course I do.' Jules smiled at me. 'What do you want to drink?' He turned away and waved to one of the waiters. 'Have you seen that dance she did with Sanjay Dutt in *Khubsoorat?*'

'I have.'

'Wasn't she clever to make Sanjay's dancing look so hot?' He waved at someone behind me and started to talk to them over my shoulder.

Sanjay Dutt is famous for so many things, his physique, his famous mother, his wild lifestyle and his bad dancing. It was an achievement that Sophiya had somehow made his notorious two left feet look nimble.

Next door to us the models were arranging themselves, sinuous arms draping over the backs of chairs, long, long legs crossing and uncrossing. At the bar the puppy plutocracy of Pali Hill ordered drinks and checked each other out, the boys all short gelled hair and Hrithik-style torso-sucking T-shirts, the girls all beautiful naked shoulders and belly-button rings. They were watching each other but more than this they were watching Sophiya and the models.

A young man in a soft blue linen shirt leant down over Jules's head and hugged him. Jules grabbed his nose.

'Heya, big guy, meet Justine, fellow Brit and in town doing a bit of film-star chasing. Justine meet Martin, Mr Event Management and part-owner of this joint.'

Martin smiled up from Jules's shoulder, kissed my hand and sat down next to me. I was about to ask him a question when a girl who looked as if she was one of the models draped herself over him and ran her lips up his neck. He put his hand on her cheek for a moment, and smiled. She moved on.

'What do you do about these beautiful women?'

'She's my fiancée.' Martin smiled.

'So that's what you do, marry them.'

'Just the one will do me,' he laughed.

'And what happens to the rest of them, the ones who don't get to marry you?'

'Guess they'll just have to take to the screen.' He turned and ran a finger down the back of one of the models.

She whipped round, her hand raised, but she dropped it back into her lap when she realized that the finger belonged to Martin. He bent down as if to kiss me goodbye.

'Each and every one an Aishwarya Rai in the making. Question is, can they dance?' he whispered against my earlobe. 'Best get back to the punters. See you later.' And disappeared into the swelling crowd at the bar.

'Hope he wasn't being rude about me.' Sophiya reached across the table, fork in hand. 'You have to try this, it's sex on a plate.'

A piece of pink pepper-crusted tuna fell off her fork into my glass. 'Shit, sorry, let's try again. You have to taste it.' She waved at one of the waiters to get another glass. 'It's all these models making me shaky. They're all so bloody young.' She delivered another forkful of tuna to me and then turned to try and give some to Rajiv.

The models were young, young enough to be very thin and not look drawn or jaded, just underfed and gamin, long necks arching from backs unmarked by bra straps, smooth and tawny, the strings of their various twinkling triangles just resting on taut skin.

The photographers had finished and were leaving.

'*Main sabko katna chahta hoon*, I want to bite them all,' a stocky man in a journalist's safari jacket said as he passed our table.

Rajiv was talking to Sophiya. 'Can you get me into the *Fiza* première with you?'

I did not hear her answer. A crowd around the door was shouting and trying to push out on to the street. A small plump girl at the back was jumping up and down to try and see over everyone, pulling on the man in front of her each time she bounced up. He turned around and pushed her away. She started to cry. The pressure of the crowd was making it almost impossible for anyone to get in or out. The models at the next-door table seemed uncertain whether they should join the thrusting crowd, torn between trying to retain their graciousness or joining the scrum. In my graveyard gear I had nothing to lose and I began to wriggle my way to the door.

Two hopeful entrants to the restaurant had got bored of waiting and picked a fight, each backed by a gang of friends. On the edge of the scuffle, a sultry, bee-sting-lipped beauty, presumably the cause of the fight, hovered, her expression a mixture of surprise and excitement. Two boys, both in tight-fitting black jeans and equally tight T-shirts, were flinging abuse at each other. From my crouched position on the edge of the crowd it was hard to tell them apart. Then one of the boys let rip with a particularly profane insult involving the virtue of his opponent's mother. The other boy made as if to hit him and then retreated in the roar that came from the insulter's cronies. During my happy home-viewing of the previous night's classic movie, Amitabh Bachchan and Shashi Kapoor had shown no such qualms about getting in there with some swift kung fu. The boys outside Olive were still merely trading insults. At the same stage the movie boys had been flying through the air and flinging chairs around like Frisbees, blood flying in every direction. Olive's security man seemed to be making no effort to break up the fracas. The token policemen in the *filmi* fisticuffs had piled in like Sylvester Stallone, hurling furniture and bloodying noses with the best of them. The temptress outside Olive jumped up and down in a feverish state, transported by the almost-fight she had caused. The girl in the film had been crying and imploring the two pugilists to stop, tears glistening on her impossibly long eyelashes. The boys outside Olive had an audience of about fifty, a mixture of black-jeaned Pali puppies, excited drivers in crumpled uniforms, and an ineffectual handful of security guards. Amitabh and Shashi's noisy, gymnastic, prime-time punch-up had had an audience of millions, from the languid Parsi millionaire up on Malabar Hill in his wedding-cake palazzo, to Mrs Nirmal and the *bhelpuri* man in First Pasta Lane, crouched in front of a tiny set rigged up to a car battery.

Up on Pali Hill we were still to witness the first punch. In fact the heroes seemed to be happy just shouting and shuffling, with a few dramatic gestures thrown in for effect. Taking advantage of a lull in the proceedings I made a lunge through the crowd to where the cars were parked. My driver pulled me out of the mêlée with an expression of awe on his face.

'*Ap thik*, Madam? Are you okay?' he asked, wide-eyed and amazed, as if I had been at the centre of the commotion.

'*Bilkul thik*, absolutely fine.'

He touched his forehead and ears, and rolled his eyes heavenward, creating our very own little movie moment. If the boys in the brawl could not come up with the goods my driver at least had the style to rise to the occasion. He bundled me into the back of the car and sped away, with just one small hiccough as he was forced to come to a grinding halt to negotiate the narrow opening of Union Walk. I watched the fading crowd through the rear window. The fight was breaking up, the crowd were losing interest and the security guards were already back at their game of cards. Life had not mirrored *filmi* art on Pali Hill. Only my driver gave a highly creditable performance as the getaway guy. As the movie magazines would have said, he emoted with power.

There was a piece about the brawl in the Bombay section of the *Times of India* a couple of days later:

> Okay, movie lovers who love to dine in the hot spots, take this as a health warning. The catty fights of the *filmi* crowd seem to be spilling out on to the streets. Our reporter nearly had a touch of Pali Hill cosmetic surgery when he came face to face with a fist fight outside the golden gates of Olive, the coolest must-go joint of the moment. Apparently the two punchy heroes were cutting up rough over the lovely Urmila Sen, one of the catwalk queens riding high on the ramps of the moment. Our reporter reckons he was one of the few to get away without a bloody (whoops) nose, and took cover while the gorgeous Ms Sen was right in there, claws out. Who says real life can't be reel life and a catwalk queen can't be a cat fight queen – mia-owwww.

Apparently life had mirrored art while I was not looking.

The hype leading up to the release of *Fiza* needed no such exaggeration. Hrithik's second film role had a life of its own, a surreal power that began to burst at the seams as the opening day of the film approached.

I was back in Delhi and in the safe hands of Mrs Kanwar and the ministrations of the beauty salon set at La Belle. I went to have my hair cut on the day of the *Fiza* premières in Bombay and Delhi, the day before it was due to open in city cinemas all over India. Even as I took the long glass lift to the beauty salon, thousands of lovelorn teenagers were picketing the cinemas of metropolitan India, camping out to get their tickets for the opening night.

For the first time since I had known her Mrs Kanwar was a woman scorning Bollywood, dressed for the occasion in a bright yellow sari that made her look like a huge cross canary. Her middle grandchild, the fourteen-year-old daughter of her perfect son and his not-so-perfect wife, had been on hunger and homework strike. Mrs Kanwar was regaling the ever-quiescent Dolly Singh with the awful tale as I came in.

'This is the most terrible thing. She is not eating and has not done so since days. What day are we now?' Her voice was trembling.

Dolly gave a rare contribution. 'It is Wednesday, I believe.'

'Yes, you are right. So Sunday my *poti*, my granddaughter, is having just a little terrible pizza rubbish. What that woman is doing feeding my beautiful *poti* this junk when we have *desi khana*, proper home cooking, in such plentiful abundance and freshly made in our own kitchen, I do not know or understand.' She narrowed her eyes. 'Now three days since she is not touching so much as *adha puri*, my special deep-fried *chapati*, until she is allowed to go and sit with her friends in line at the cinema to get tickets for this film that is opening.' She rammed her hands into her bosom in grief.

Dolly wobbled in sympathy.

'Tickets for *Fiza*?' I asked.

'Of course, what else is there that is making my *poti* starve and throw her books around like so much of this confetti?'

I too wobbled in sympathy.

'What is it these *filmi* people want from our children? What

'Young girls have need of heroes'

example is this they set that makes them starve and throw their future away with their studies?'

I was supposed to have an answer. Uma, the manicurist, came to my aid.

'Madam*ji*, this has always been happening. This year it is Hrithik, last year it was Salman, ten years back it was Amitabh. Young girls have need of heroes.' She popped the tray of nail varnishes in front of Mrs Kanwar so that she could pick a colour.

Mrs Kanwar was not satisfied and gave us all a lecture on morals and the value of proper *ghee* in home cooking. Uma painted her nails a screen-shimmering silver and massaged her arms until the polish had dried. I chose not to tell tales of Mr T and the Anglo film stars who lie in Bombay's Christian Burial Ground.

Fiza opened and Mrs Kanwar's *poti*, my fifteen-year-old new best friend Mira and several million other budding fans were devastated.

CHAPTER 6

Passion

Cue big dance number

THE FEVERED FANS had reason to be devastated. Hrithik was not the star of *Fiza*. Worse, he was only on screen for about a third of the two-hour fifty-minute running time. This meant that the girls who loved him, the girls who had gone on homework and hunger strike to get tickets, were wriggling in their seats with indignation for almost two hours of Hrithikless screen time.

The plot was simple enough. Aman (Hrithik) and his sister Fiza (played by Karisma Kapoor) live with their mother in Bombay. Their father is dead though he has a nice cameo role in a devotional picture on the wall, often referred and deferred to in moments of drama. They are a Muslim family, and the story begins on the eve of the Bombay riots in December 1992. Aman is the golden boy.

'Aman, my brother, very innocent, very lovely': Fiza introduces him, as lovely innocent Aman smiles right into the hearts of teenage India. 'He is a bit naughty too': Fiza laughs as her baby brother obediently pulls faces for the camera, twitching his nose and sticking out his tongue in a movie-star way, not too far out, just sort of neat and cute.

The riots break out and Aman gets caught up in them. He goes missing, leaving his sister and mother waiting and longing and hoping, and the female audience checking their watches in horror at Hrithik's apparent departure just thirty-two minutes into the film. There follows much to-ing and fro-ing in Bombay as Fiza and Mummy search for news of Aman. Finally Fiza gets fed up with trying to extract information from a string of dodgy characters who blow smoke in her face over bowls of peanuts and glasses of whisky. She takes to the road in search of Aman, forsaking the respectable *salwar kameez* of a good Muslim Indian daughter and donning the independent wardrobe of back-pack, ponytail and jeans that are just a bit too tight. During a very sexy dance number, performed by a shipped-in screen siren, Fiza roams through the landscape of Rajasthan, looking for terrorist cells of the Taleban, in case her brother might be among them (not that the Taleban are renowned for hanging out in Rajasthan, but then the dancing siren's wardrobe would be deeply unacceptable in any bona-fide Taleban neck of the woods).

Sure enough Fiza finds her baby brother running around in full terrorist get-up – snug black jeans, torso-tight T-shirt and the standard-issue militant headdress, a long black scarf that can be flung across the face in tense moments, is effective as a bandanna and is generally menacing-looking. Aman has apparently taken part in a raid on a jewellery shop in Udaipur, though quite why is never fully explained. Fiza pounces on him, having recognized him in spite of his best efforts at militant bandanna-flicking. He gets a sisterly ticking-off for having deserted Mummy and Fiza during the riots. Now chastened and contrite, he returns to Bombay and settles back into family life. But not for long. As a result of his participation in the riots he is a wanted man on the streets of Bombay and cannot get work. In a flashback we see him being caught with a dead child in his arms. Naturally he has been comforting the dying girl. Naturally the bad guys assume he is her killer. Naturally when he returns to Bombay they come after him.

The film takes a big turn when Mummy drowns herself in the sea, unable to bear the news that her beloved son is a wanted terrorist and convinced that she has failed in her duty as a mother.

Aman now feels he has no choice other than to rejoin his unit. However, the terrorists will only take him back if he is prepared to die for the cause – there is to be no running home to big sis again. He re-enlists and is promptly ordered to assassinate two corrupt politicians. He does the job but gets seen in the act. Fiza chases after him. She has to save him from himself before the bad guys get to him. In the penultimate scene, holding the barrel of a gun to his chest, Aman begs Fiza to shoot him as the police close in.

'I'm not proud of my life, let me die with honour,' he entreats her. 'Mummy will be lonely, sis, I've got to go to Mummy. I want to put my head in her lap. I'm very tired, let me go, let me go.' As Aman pleads with Fiza, the sweet softness in his eyes drags the teen-dream fans to the very edges of their seats and their self-control.

Fiza pulls the trigger and we move into slow motion. Aman takes a long time to drop heavily to his knees, a very painful collapse that has us clutching our knee caps. Finally we see Aman peaceful in death, his pristine white T-shirt remarkably free of blood, given that he has just been shot point-blank in the chest. The wrap-up opens on Aman lying with his head in Mummy's lap at the Haji Ali mosque, out in the Arabian Sea beyond Breach Candy, and closes with poor little Fiza, back in Muslim mourning white, begging Allah to give her the courage to face the world as an orphan – swelling score, rolling credits.

Everyone seemed to have some complaint about *Fiza*. There was too much terrorism. There was not enough dancing. There was not enough of the shipped-in siren. There was not enough of Hrithik, and there was definitely not enough romance. Instead the audience had to make do with a brief flashback to happier times before the riots when Aman had a girlfriend and time to dance around Bombay's bridges and gardens.

But there were two things about *Fiza* that did make everyone happy – two particular dance numbers, neither relevant to the plot but both extremely relevant to the survival of the film.

Sushmita Sen, the shipped-in siren

Sushmita Sen, the siren who had been crowned Miss Universe in the same year that Aishwarya Rai teetered away with the Miss World tiara, burned up the screen for approximately four and a half of the one hundred and seventy minutes of the film. The audience, particularly the men and the boys, seemed happy to sit through the rest just to see Sush strut her stuff. And strut she did in magnificent, diaphanous, belly-swivelling, hip-grinding glory, thrusting herself at the camera and drawing in every man, woman and child watching. It was about as close to live sex as you can get on Indian celluloid. In those four and a half precious minutes Sushmita also worked her way through four costume changes and enough jewellery to clear a small country's World Bank debt. And according to the *filmi* press it was not just the *Fiza* audience that Sush was making out with. The nasty unsupported rumour doing the rounds was that she was having an affair with Sanjay Dutt and that his wife of just a year and a half had left their freshly refurbished house almost before the post-nuptial paint had dried. On screen and in the catty columns Sushmita was dynamite.

The other dance number, wisely added at the eleventh hour by the director, had the female audience back on the edges of their seats. Hrithik performed a *taandav*, normally the speciality of the god Shiva when he is working up to a spree of mass destruction. But Shiva had never performed like this. In *Fiza* Hrithik set a new standard.

The *taandav* started with an insistent and mesmeric voice-over from Aman's terrorist mentor: 'You have to become like steel. Do you understand?' Aman begins to caress his telescopic sniper rifle in long, slow, sensual movements. Then the pace hots up as he gets into his stride with a series of hard-core endurance tests that have his muscles rippling like a sack of pythons, and an ice-block-breaking routine of the Bruce Lee school. After a volley of high-flying kicks he hurls himself at the camera in a final heart-stopping dive. Then, slicked in sweat, every muscle pulsating, he snuffs out a candle-flame with a single, perfectly aimed shot from his rifle.

The audience were ecstatic, but the critics failed to see what very elaborately choreographed physical jerks had to do with preparation for shooting two corrupt ministers with a long-range rifle, complete with a minutely accurate telescopic sight. The audience did not agree. They were happy to dance with Hrithik every vicarious step of the way. The critics were just being picky. They hadn't said that Sushmita's dance routine was irrelevant to the plot. So why did they mind Hrithik being pumped up, Shiva-style, when he actually was going out on a killing mission that required him to 'be like steel'? One female columnist was brave enough to venture her opinion in print:

Just fine for all you men to drool over Sushmita Sen, but give the girls a bit of a look in with Hrithik doing the male version of the wet sari routine, and you get all hot under the collar and think it is unnecessary to the plot – and since when have our dance routines ever had anything to do with the plot? Come on you guys, stop being such insecure wimps.

In the good old days of the early movies the boys could improvise their dance moves as they went along. Down at Film City, the great dream factory built with millions of rupees' worth of government money twenty miles north of Bombay, the boys could get away with a wiggle here, a shimmy there, a head flick at just the right moment and lots of erotically suggestive hand movements up and down imaginary bodies. Film City had fifteen shooting stages spread over fourteen thousand acres, and it was as divorced from reality as the films it produced. Here directors could shut themselves away with their stars and their dreams, pull frothy concoctions out of the ether and slap them on to celluloid, complete with rinky-dink dance routines put in place by Pinky Ali, the queen of the wet-sari routine.

Things have changed. Now the great gates of Film City creak open to TV stars rather than movie stars. Big films have been replaced by soap operas. Bombay's soap matriarchs and their henpecked, pan-sticked TV husbands now wander the back lots where once disco divas and Hindi heroes ducked from set to set, sometimes shooting five films on five sets in the same day, running from stage to stage with a stream of dressers in tow, wriggling their way out of policemen's uniforms and *salwar kameez,* and into Hindu god costumes and ready-to-be-wetted saris as they ran. Now the slums are creeping in on what was once state-of-the-art. Film City has seen better times and the boys can no longer rely on Pinky Ali for their dance moves.

Soon after the opening of *Fiza*, at a cocktail party in Malabar Hill, I met a Pinky link. I had done my best to scrub up and felt unusually slick in a passable frock and a new pair of high heels. Even Severin had given me a surprised look of approval.

The heels were a mistake. Unable to keep my balance, I propped myself on a windowsill that curved around the whole of one side of the room. Bankers and brokers in blazers and wives in chiffon and silk were reflected in the glass, and beyond them I looked out on a panoramic view of Malabar Hill in the last sliding moments of twilight.

'Hullo, lovely lady,' said a reflection in the glass.

I stood up and turned to find a man smiling at me from above his cravat. He too was in a blazer, his baby Buddha belly resting on top of a belt pulled in about three notches too tight. His hair was dyed very dark and the roots were just beginning to show through. He was certainly not a banker or a broker.

'I know you . . .' I started.

'I would remember, I can assure you, but I do not believe I have had the pleasure.' And he kissed my hand.

But I did know him, in the *filmi* sense at least. He was an actor who had married a daughter of one of the big industrial houses.

'I loathe these parties, no one ever has anything interesting to say. My luck to have found you,' he went on, and he began to pick distractedly at a bowl of nuts.

'I've seen some of your films. I loved that one when you did the big classic dance number by the stream with all those doves flying out of your hands when you were trying to get in with the girl.' It was all coming back in a flood of flapping wings and daisy-covered riverbanks. 'What was it like at Film City then?'

His whiskey-sour expression melted into *filmi*-star joy, and he gripped my hand and hung on to it. 'How very right I was, it is my lucky night.'

He waved to one of the waiters. 'A whisky, no ice and this much water.' He pinched his index finger and thumb almost together.

'What will you have?' And then, without waiting for a reply, he started on his story.

'Bloody hell, we had so much fun at Film City in those days. No one expected you to turn up on time, to know your lines or to be able to act, and we certainly weren't expected to be able to dance. That was Pinky's job.'

'You mean Pinky Ali?'

'Of course, she was the battleaxe of the dance routines. You have to meet Pinky.'

'Is she still alive?'

He took his whisky from the butler. 'Do you know I'm not even sure she is. You will have to ask around. She had this marvellous idea that she was the great-great-great-something-or-other of some Mogul emperor.'

He laughed and drained his whisky at the second shot. 'Oh, she used to scare the hell out of us all. Either that or we would be laughing at her so much we would have to eat our hands. Don't tell Pinky that if you meet her. She would die of shock. She thought we all adored her.'

He waved to the butler to bring another whisky. 'You know there was one time when I was making eight pictures at the same time and, to tell you very frankly, if it had not been for Pinky I think I would have got fired from the lot of them. She used to write the dance moves she wanted me to make on great big cards and she'd hold them up so I could just look straight into camera and do the thing.'

I wobbled on my heels and reached for the windowsill again.

'So sorry, am I boring you?'

'No, no, absolutely not. I'm just not used to high heels.'

He looked confused for a moment but it did not put him off his stride.

'You know there was one time, so fabulous. I was doing the whole routine, same, same as usual, dancing around a tree, hopping side to side of some little stream running through the set.

And I'm worrying all the time about not pulling the crazy plastic tree down when I'm chasing . . . Who was it? I am forgetting, maybe Ritu Jaitly, maybe Hema. So there I am trying to keep the tree up. We were working in the most terrible conditions I have to say, half of the sets used to fall down on top of us. Bloody hell, it was fun though.' He paused as he took his fresh whisky from the waiter.

'You're running around the tree and . . .' I coaxed.

'God, yes, and I'm supposed to be getting all romantic with Hema or whoever, I am so sure it was Hema, no matter.' He took a big slug from his glass. 'And you know of course that we are not allowed to show anything that can be seen as being at all unsuitable by the censors. So we have to do it all in the dancing.'

He had to stop again for a moment to shake someone's hand. As he did so he gave a smile as wide as the belly that was quietly easing out over his belt, and then he turned it off as quickly as it had been put on. 'Silly bastard, thinks he's *Shivaji* because his grandfather started an inner-tube company. Not really something to give you so much of social class, wouldn't you say?' He pursed his lips.

'So you just had to put all the sex into the dancing?' I prompted.

'Sure, sure, that is why we were always running around in the rain. You know, a wet sari clinging to all the bits that you would see in a film in the West in a bedroom scene, or on a bathroom floor or a dining-room table, whatever, whatever.' He was laughing at his own joke.

'And Pinky Ali was helping you in this scene round the tree?'

'*Yaar*, and perhaps I am not doing such a good job because Pinky holds up a sign for me to read and it says "Grind your hips, make it like you are putting your kingsize in her".' He started to laugh again and people around us turned and looked and then raised the volume of their conversation as if trying to ignore us, the vulgar *filmi* element.

141

Pinky Ali no longer puts together wet-sari routines for the big stars. Now she takes a new generation through their paces in her studio in Colaba, just a few streets away from Leopold's Bar and Café. These days, however, it is not actors and actresses that Pinky teaches. Her unwilling pupils are more likely to be the daughters, and the occasional very reluctant son, of the nouveaux super-rich who are beginning to realize that super-rich and super-fat do not necessarily have to go together. Pinky Ali's Dance Academy is just one way of keeping the junk-food spare tyres at bay. Though for Pinky, each and every one of these little scions of the billionaire houses of software and tupperware is a potential dance star.

I went back to Colaba and found Pinky in her mirrored dance studio where she still reigns supreme. It was just towards the end of her afternoon dance class and Pinky had five pupils. Sonni Contractor was a thin eleven-year-old Parsi with pale blue eyes and a sly expression. Behind her was Anjuli Malhotra, a chubby thirteen-year-old who kept plucking at her underpants when she should have been dancing. Alice Penn, a very blonde ten-year-old American who was already giving off an aura of supreme confidence, stood next to Sonni. Alice wanted to be a star. Lurking behind her was Marcie Graham, her friend and satellite who seemed happy just to be in young Alice's orbit. Sonni Contractor's brother Feroz was sitting in a nine-year-old sulk in the corner in shorts, a white shirt and a very small bow tie.

I had arrived a little earlier than expected. Pinky Ali's assistant asked me to sit to the side of the studio, a chair away from Feroz. He seemed momentarily pleased to have a diversion. He looked up and was about to smile when he remembered that he was supposed to be sulking. He subsided back into his small cloud. On the other side of the room sat the various *ayahs* who had been sent along to the dancing class with their charges. They gossiped and giggled and paid no attention to the efforts on the dance floor.

Pinky stood proud among her pupils in a sea of startlingly pink chiffon. She was not tall but she stood as if she was. Her hair rose in a highly teased concoction of lacquered blue-black, and she had rings on her fleshy fingers and bright pink nail varnish on her toes. Her fine and prominent nose lent authenticity to her claim to Mogul ancestry.

Pinky had prepared a rather complicated routine for her pupils. The tape-recorder started and the warbling tones of a Hindi dance track joined the whirr of the air-conditioners, Pinky Ali's exhortations to her pupils and the thud of their feet on the floor. Pinky thumped her heavily ringed hand on the tape-recorder as she marked time, and the tape slurred with each blow.

'Swoop, drop, spin, turn. Sonni, you are not at the *dhobi ghats*. What is this with your whirling arms? Are you a washerwoman?' Pinky boomed. 'Marcie, your hair is very nice but let me see your face.' Marcie had her eyes firmly fixed on the floor. 'Ladies, let us imagine we are floating on air.' Pinky's free hand took flight. 'Air, ladies, air, not mud. Sonni, the arms, softly with the arms. Anjuli, can you leave your undergarments where they are? If they were supposed to be on the outside you would be Superman. Dip, dip, spin, spin, oh lovely, Alice, very pretty.'

Admittedly, smug Alice did have flashes of ability but the rest were shambolic. Pinky looked on with a fixed expression, her lower jaw slightly set and her hand continuing to thump the tape-recorder, pounding out the beat with grim determination. Then she hit the 'off' button and stood in front of the class with her hands on her hips.

'Really lovely, ladies, you are all doing so well.' The set of her jaw softened and she gave a cinematic smile.

The girls looked relieved and I was surprised.

'Feroz, you will join us for a short free dance. You will dance with Alice. Marcie will dance with Anjuli, and I am sure our guest

143

would like to dance with Sonni.' Pinky waved her hand graciously in my direction.

Feroz seemed to shrink in his chair. I got up with alacrity, the memory of years of ballet lessons flooding straight back in a sea of pink wrinkly tights and buttock-creeping leotards. I was eleven again and about to hit the floor for a dose of free dancing. Feroz was pulled off his chair by Alice, his lapdog eyes popping, his mouth tight as a zip. Pinky juggled some tapes and we were off to the sound of Abba's 'Dancing Queen'.

Alice swayed in front of her beau with a sensuality way beyond her years. Feroz stood his ground by looking determinedly at his shoes and shrugging his shoulders a bit. Anjuli and Marcie were having a great time just joining hands and spinning around at top speed, leaving Sonni and me jiggling in their wake in a somewhat desultory fashion. I had started out with great enthusiasm, but Sonni had been so horrified by my Olivia Newton-John *circa Grease* jive moves that I had rapidly edited myself down to a bit of shy school-dance wobbling.

As the music came to an end Pinky clapped her hands together. 'Thank you, ladies and gentleman. And now it is the end of class.'

My five fellow free-dancers were off the floor at speed, Marcie and Anjuli suddenly as fleet-footed as gazelles, Feroz charging as if on to a football field, with Sonni close behind. Only Alice dawdled. Sonni and Feroz's *ayah* tried to get both of them out of their dance shoes and into streetwear at the same time. They were arguing over a Gameboy, kicking and pushing, Sonni once again giving her *dhobi-wallah* impression, this time right in her *ayah*'s face.

'Mrs Ali thinks that I will probably be very successful if I go on dancing,' Alice confided in elaborately hushed tones.

'Madam Ali to you, Alice Penn, but please call me Pinky.' She held out her hand and took mine between both of hers in an affectionate clasp. 'So good of you to join the class, such spirit. You like to dance I think?' She held on to my hand.

'I love dancing.'

'Love is a strong thing to say. Many people say they love dancing when what they are really saying is they would love to be able to dance but lack the spirit.'

'I really do love dancing,' I assured her.

Pinky turned to her pupils. 'Come, come, *chalo*, let's go. Goodbye, everyone. I look forward to seeing you all next week. It was so nice to have you with us, Feroz. Your free dancing was very beautiful. I hope we will have the pleasure next week as well.' Pinky gave Feroz one of her melting smiles.

His eyes popped again and he nodded enthusiastically before realizing what he had agreed to.

'Now come to my special room.' With a graceful gesture Pinky motioned me towards the door of the studio, waving over her shoulder to her pupils as we left.

Pinky Ali's sitting-room was Bollywood's past in aspic and a tribute to its owner's name. Every over-stuffed satin cushion, each of the photographs that crowded most of the surfaces, every swathe of the fuchsia-velvet drapery in the windows echoed *filmi* fantasies of the past. In the centre stood a heart-shaped, raspberry-coloured occasional table next to a low armchair, its silk upholstery plumped with cushions that were shaped like slices of watermelon. Above the chair and the table hung a portrait of Bahadur Shah Zafar, the last of the Mogul emperors. It was framed in the same fuchsia velvet as the curtains.

'Such a lovely picture, don't you think?' Pinky asked.

'Yes.'

'You are wondering perhaps why it is there?'

'Yes,' I obliged.

Pinky settled herself beneath the portrait, sinking sweetly into her silken fruit bowl, pink on pink on pink.

'My *dadi*, my grandmother seven times, was a nautch-girl in his court. He was very fond of the way she danced and she became one of his most special concubines, one of his almost wives, so to say. He was so partial to her that she was one of the very few he took with him when he was exiled to Rangoon by you Britishers after the Mutiny.' She paused for a moment, taking her time to rearrange a single strand of hair.

'I thought he only took his wife and one servant.'

'This is so. He sent for my *dadi* some time later. She had a son and several daughters by him, and their son was my *dada* times six.' Pinky turned her head to show her profile beneath the portrait.

'It's hard to see the resemblance through his beard and moustache,' I said.

Pinky laughed, stroking her finger down her swooping profile.

'Some people say our noses and foreheads are identical. What do you think?'

'Your *dadi* times seven must have been some dancer.'

'Oh yes, it was an honour to be a nautch in those times, you know.'

'Wasn't it more like being a geisha, more of a craft?'

Pinky smiled. 'Correct, nothing like now. How dare they call those pathetic things on Falkland Road nautch girls.'

'I met one of them. She was a dancer, a film dancer.'

'*Acchha*, really, who, who?'

Immediately I regretted opening my mouth. 'I think maybe I've got it wrong, I think she was a dancer of some kind, I'm not really sure . . .' My voice trailed off.

Pinky eyed me with suspicion.

I shrugged and said no more. Pinky could easily have met Madam Deepa in her life before Falkland Road, in the great days of Film City. I was not going to try to explain what had happened to her since.

'So you are really just carrying on the family business?' I asked, steering her away from Falkland Road.

'Yes, I suppose.' She smiled again. 'You like my little studio?'

'Yes, especially the free dancing.' I was looking at the other

146

pictures that lined the alcoves and the shelves and that stood ranged on other tables. There were no pictures on the raspberry heart-shaped table. That was reserved for a large bowl of boiled sweets in every shade from tea rose to toxic hot blush.

'Is that who I think it is?' I pointed to a prominent picture of Pinky being hugged by a tall and familiar figure.

'Amitabh Bachchan, such a sweet man. Not such a very good dancer, however.'

'Isn't that sacrilege?' I asked.

'*Yaar*, to some people who are not dancers. They don't know the difference. But for me his dancing is painful to watch. He just is not enjoying it when he is dancing. He has had so many years of practice but he is not going to get any better.' Pinky paused for a moment, and then got up and touched the picture. 'Very, how can I say it, very bang, bang, bang.' She took three leaden steps, her upper body stiff. 'Not, la, la, la.' Again she took three steps, fluid strides with a matching shiver of movement through the rest of her body. It looked good.

'So you mean he's static?'

'Maybe this.' She settled back into her chair. 'Show me, make three steps like this,' she commanded.

I tried to copy what she had done. It felt quite sexy. I was pleased.

'Not bad, but not so good. You move your top and bottom separately. You have to keep them together or they fall apart.'

'Does Amitabh fall apart?'

'No, no, darling, he never moves enough to be able to fall apart.'

'What do you think of the dancers now?'

'What dancers?' Pinky picked up a tiny bell from beside the large bowl of boiled sweets and let it tinkle.

'The new crop of film stars, say Salman Khan, Shah Rukh Khan, Aishwarya Rai, Hrithik Roshan.'

Pinky counted them off on her fingers. 'Cannot dance, cannot dance, she dances quite well, and Hrithik is brilliant.'

'You think so?'

Aishwarya Rai: 'she dances quite well'

'Definitely.' She rang the little bell again with more insistence. 'Where is that girl? Yes, definitely, he is so good. Have you seen his films?'

'There have only been two so far and there wasn't much dancing in *Fiza*.'

Pinky Ali raised an eyebrow at me. 'Rubbish, that Sushmita Sen girl has so much talent and Hrithik's dance was so lovely.'

'I don't think I'd really classify his *taandav* as a dance. It was more a case of eye candy for the girls, wasn't it?'

Pinky started to laugh. 'Oh my God, this is too good, eye candy, I must remember this expression.'

A small woman and a tiny dog came into the sitting-room at the same time. The dog scrambled at Pinky's legs in an effort to climb up, its miniature ears flying and turning inside out in the excitement. Pinky swept it up in her arms, cooing and cuddling it. The girl waited by the door, her sari wrapped tightly around her, the end of it tucked into her waist in working style. She had enormous eyes and a dark, beautiful face.

'Lemonade,' Pinky said to the girl. 'What will you have, tea, coffee? The lemonade is very tasty, I make it myself.'

'Lovely.'

Pinky ordered again and the girl turned to go. She had frangipani flowers tucked into the twist of her long plait and there was just a hint of their scent as she left the room.

'Hrithik, yes, you know in a way you are right. As a scene it was not very much about dance. Much more about all that terrible blown-up muscle thing, so unnatural. But you know there was some dancing in there that was so, so impressive. Do you remember a section when he runs up a wall and flips over?'

I did.

'Gene Kelly, *Singing in the Rain*, the same move, exactly the same move, the same kind of talent.' Pinky took the tips of the dog's ears and flapped them up and down. 'See my little flying angel, so cute, so sweet.' The dog sat impassively.

'You see,' Pinky went on, 'he has really studied it like a craft and he has a lovely sense of rhythm too. To me he is the cleverest out there at this time because he has looked at dancing in the West, you know, all this stuff on MTV and whatever. He has found a way of dancing with the new very gymnastic style that is so much about the body and very much with a sexual tone, and he has wrapped this up with our Indian style. Sometimes he is really very classic and his *bhangra* movements are so lovely to watch. He does a bit of Madonna too. What a clever girl, really a fantastic dancer.'

'And you think Sushmita Sen was good as well?' I asked.

'Oh *yaar*, you know most girls are not really brave enough to dance like that.' Pinky got up and plopped the dog into my lap. Then she gave me a more-flesh-for-your-rupee version of Sushmita's signature dance step from *Fiza*.

Pinky is short and well-covered. Sush is long and very lean. Still Pinky managed to convey Sush's deep thigh dips with flowing arms and flashing eyes.

I clapped and the tiny dog barked. Pinky swooped him up again. 'Baby loves Mummy dancing, don't you?' she purred.

'Do you miss doing film dance now?'

'I am going to be sixty this year. It was getting too hard. My knees were paining me. I think I quit at the right time, unlike some of the people who think they can go on until they fall down dead on set. That is not possible in dance.'

'I know people miss you.'

'How sweet.' She looked out of the window. 'You know, that Hrithik boy really is something very special. You want to keep watching him. He is learning all the time. A few more films and he really might become one of the greats.'

'I'm hoping to meet him.'

'How nice. Tell him to eat more, he is getting too thin.'

The girl with the frangipani in her plait came back with a tray. The lemonade was pink.

'I have to tell you, I am really very proud of this recipe,' said

Pinky as she poured. 'It was given to my mother by a lovely English lady who used to live close by to our house when I was a child. Her husband was something quite big in the Indian Civil Service, I remember.' She passed me a glass.

'What a pretty girl,' I said.

'Who?'

I pointed to the door that was closing behind the girl with the flowers in her hair.

Pinky looked surprised. In India it is unusual to talk about a domestic servant.

'Yes, a bit dark perhaps. Part of her salary is paid in dance classes. I teach her with some street children on Sunday mornings. It is so important for them to have something to hope for, don't you think?'

I left Pinky still sitting in her chair, beneath the hooded one-eyed gaze of her grandfather times seven, her miniature dog on her lap.

'You should keep dancing,' she said as I left, 'it will keep you young, like me.'

'Please can I speak to Hrithik Roshan?'

'Who is calling?'

'Justine Hardy. I have left quite a few messages now, over quite a few months.'

'He is out of station.'

'When will he be back?'

'This information I am not at liberty to give you.'

Again I ran the gauntlet of the Film Kraft girls. Again I told them my story. Again I sat in the window in Carmichael Road while the telephone sirens in Santa Cruz put me on hold.

'You could talk to Rakesh*ji*,' the switchboard police suggested.

'What?'

Why had no one suggested this before?

'Could I speak to Rakesh Roshan please?'

'He is in a meeting. Who is calling?'

'It's still Justine Hardy.'

'Oh *yaar, yaar*.' She melted just a little. 'If you are calling back in one hour it may be possible to talk with Rakesh*ji*.'

'Thank you so much.'

Severin was about to plug in the Hoover. I grabbed her and gave her a taste of Pinky Ali's free-dancing style.

'God, what is this?' she gasped as I whirled her between two tables piled high with books, spinning past *The Seven Pillars of Wisdom, More Common Birds of India, Hobson-Jobson* and *The Autumn 2000 Newmarket Sales Guide*.

We headed out around the sofa and past the French windows.

'Stop this now, you are mad.' Severin finally managed to break free as I was about to cha-cha-cha her around the twelve-seater dining-room table.

'I'm almost there,' I said.

'Almost where?'

'Almost through to Hrithik Roshan.'

'You have spoken with him?' she asked.

'Not quite.'

'What is this then?'

'I am going to speak to his father in an hour.'

'This is not speaking with Hrithik Roshan, this is speaking with his daddy.' Severin readjusted her *chunni* and straightened her *kameez*, her tunic and her shawl.

'True, but it's progress.'

Severin rolled her eyes. 'Oh my God, too much of tension.' And she bustled away to the kitchen.

I rang, I held, I was put through.

'Mr Roshan?'

'Speaking.'

I explained my plight.

'It is not possible now. Hrithik is booked up until the end of 2003.'

Hrithik, booked up until the end of 2003

It was October 2000.

'I just want a short interview.'

'He is in Pune right now.'

'When is he coming back?'

'Tomorrow, maybe day after.'

'Might it be possible to arrange an interview when he gets back?'

'This is not possible. He has a very tight schedule for the next few months. His new film is about to come out. It is really just not possible. You can call again in February.'

'Are you joking?'

'No joke.'

'I have been trying to get an interview for eight months.'

Rakesh Roshan laughed. 'This is not possible.'

'I assure you it is. You try getting through your reception thought police.'

He laughed again. 'They are very fine girls, and we have had some problems.'

In the circumstances it was an unusually understated way of referring to an assassination attempt, not to mention the fact that the majority of India's female population would happily kidnap Hrithik.

'Yes, I am so sorry. Of course I understand.'

'So you can call back in February.'

Of course I could. What was another three and a half months when I had already waited for eight. I had his new film, *Mission Kashmir*, to keep me going. It was about to hit the screens in time for Diwali, the festival that kicks off the winter party season. Hrithik was going to play another terrorist, this time a high-kicking, gun-toting, Taleban card-carrying, disco-dancing Srinagar boy. It was going to be a sort of *Fiza*-on-the-lakes.

As I put down the receiver the ageing evening walkers were out on Carmichael Road. A much younger man in cycling shorts and a sinew-sculpting T-shirt pounded his way through the walkers. His haste amidst their sedate progress was unseemly. Of course I could wait until February.

CHAPTER 7

Romance

Boy gets girl

'YOUR HAIR LOOKS SO . . .' I searched for the word, 'chic.'

Mrs Sawan, the manageress of La Belle Hair and Beauty, smiled, running one hand through her new cut as she hid a cigarette under the lip of the salon reception desk.

'We have a French hair . . .' she paused, waving away the suspended smoke that hung between us, 'designer in the salon this week. But you will have to book in at the soonest. He is very full up even now.'

Thierry, the Parisian hair-designer, was wearing a grey suit with a deliberate rumple to it. He was shod in a pair of equally expensive bowling-alley themed shoes. A snug T-shirt and a lightly feathered haircut completed the picture of carefully studied nonchalance.

Nearly all the salon staff had been under Thierry's flying scissors and as they passed the many mirrors they checked their reflections, as if seeking reassurance that their new looks really were as chic as Thierry had promised they would be. Manoj, the master of my feet and toenails, knelt in front of me with a very snappy hair-do that had been quiffed up with gel and that gave him a look of permanent mild surprise. As he pumiced my toes, his gelled peak rubbed against my shins and made me laugh.

Mrs Kanwar was not laughing. She was ensconced in one of the larger floral chairs, her arms tightly folded across her bosom, her hair thin and flat, the grey showing at the roots of her parting. Thierry was trying to persuade her that a Paris-look coiffure was really all she needed to start a new and exciting phase in her life. She was clearly not happy, and as Thierry tried to sell her the idea of doing away with her usual lacquered helmet and replacing it with something neat, sharp and short, Mrs Kanwar was working on a deflecting tactic.

'I am telling you this once more. I never have anything different, never. See, this is my friend Dolly. She is so often saying that she would like something really lovely to happen with her hair.' She pointed to Dolly who was sitting in the corner, fingering the rather frazzled trails of hennaed hair that had escaped from her meagre bun.

Unsurprisingly, Mrs Kanwar ended up having just the same as usual while Dolly, who had innocently arrived with the intention of having her arms waxed, found herself being washed and primped. I kept my head down in case Thierry decided that I too needed to set out on a new and exciting phase in my life, but I need not have worried. He had his hands full trying to make something of Dolly's lank locks.

Mrs Kanwar went silently and smugly to be washed. Twenty minutes later she emerged from the basin after an especially long head massage given, under her close instructions, by a nervous assistant, and planted herself beside me. She was just far enough away from Dolly not to be able to see the fear in her friend's face.

I had not seen Mrs Kanwar since her granddaughter had been on hunger strike over a Hrithik ticket.

'Did your granddaughter get to see *Fiza?*' I asked.

Mrs Kanwar was engaged in a discussion about her rollers, the large pink variety with bottle-brush centres. She was giving a long explanation to the assistant about just how to put the rollers in around her ears.

'I have most sensitive ears. You must take the maximum care,' she insisted before turning to answer my question. '*Yaar*, and not just my *poti*. We all went.'

'What did you think?'

'Such a body, *naar*.' Mrs Kanwar scrunched her knees together like a little girl.

Thierry heard and looked up from his stance over Dolly's wet mane and preened.

Mrs Kanwar rolled her eyes and dropped her voice. 'These Frenchies, such amounts of ego.'

'You really like all those muscles?'

'Oh, lovely, lovely.'

'What about the rest of the film?'

Mrs Kanwar thought for a long moment.

'Not so bad, perhaps a bit boring for a time.'

'Which bit did you think was boring?'

'Oh, maybe some of it in the middle,' she replied evasively.

'When Hrithik was not in it?'

She ignored my question and turned to Dolly. 'You are looking very nice, Dolly.'

Thierry was teasing the sides of Dolly's hair forward around her face. 'You know in my salon I am always having to find more hair to push around the ladies' faces. So many of my ladies in France are doing this thing with surgery for their faces. So there are all these little scars around the edges that I am having to find hair to cover up.'

Dolly looked horrified. Thierry patted her shoulder. 'Oh please, excuse me, this is not why I do this for you. It will make you look younger, softer and what is it . . .' He waved his ringed hand in the air to catch the word. 'Fresher, yes, this is what I am saying, fresher. You like this?' He peered over Dolly's shoulder at their reflections in the mirror.

Dolly was not looking very fresh.

'I thought Karisma Kapoor was good,' I said to Mrs Kanwar.

'*Yaar, yaar,* for sure. But Hrithik, what super acting, really talented. I think he has all the critics confounded with his emoting.'

'He wasn't really in it that much . . .' I was stopped by Manoj.
He was waving his foot rasp in the air to make a point. 'Sushmita
Sen was very beautiful.' He smiled and bent down again over my
foot.

Mrs Kanwar's eyebrows met in a menacing line as she repulsed
the threat of another pink roller coming too close to her ear. Once
the roller was under control she relaxed and smiled sweetly. 'Oh
yaar, very pretty suits and such lovely jewellery.'

Thierry was running his hands through the back of Dolly's hair.
'You must always cut from the back. It is a crime to start at the front.
The little fronty piece is just decoration, the very last little thing
that you do.' He gave a little hip flick, very Hrithik, very chic.

'Really lovely, Dolly,' Mrs Kanwar shouted across to her friend.

Dolly stared rigidly at her reflection.

'What about Hrithik's *taandav,* the big war-dance number?'
I asked Manoj.

He thought for a moment too long and Mrs Kanwar jumped in.

'Fantastic, such gymnastics, *yaar.* What about that thing when
he ran up the wall?' She clutched her knees again.

'Did your granddaughter like it?'

'Sure, sure, very much except . . .' She stopped.

Dolly was waving mutely across the room, panic on her face.
Thierry was discussing a range of hair-colour samples with one of
the salon's own hairdressers. They flopped in his hand, a stable of
My Little Pony tails.

'Streaking, what is this?' Dolly managed to squeak.

'Oh lovely, how pretty,' Mrs Kanwar shouted back over the roar
of the hair-dryer that had just been lowered over her tightly curl-
ered hair.

'Really this will look so nice, very natural, very modern, very
how do you say?' Thierry waved the My Little Pony tails around.
'Girlish.' He patted Dolly's shoulder again.

'But this is not what I want. I am to be sixty this year. I do not wish for this "girlish".'

I had never heard Dolly say so much.

'Trust me, it will be totally natural. I promise you will be happy with this.' Thierry put his hand on his heart with a sincere expression.

Defeated, Dolly slumped down in her chair. The trolley of colours and foils was rolled over as she sat like a rabbit trapped in headlights. A flesh-tone swimming hat was snapped on to her head while the colourist put on a pair of rubber gloves. As the first hook went in to snatch a scrap of hair through one of the holes in the hat, Dolly looked as if she was about to cry.

'These lovely ladies will do such fine work for you.' Thierry floated past Dolly's falling face and then popped himself down beside me.

'Highlights and lowlights would be so pretty for you. What do you say?' he offered, palms outstretched.

'Have you seen Hrithik Roshan since you've been here?' I countered.

Thierry was momentarily thrown off course as I snatched *CinéBlitz* from Mrs Kanwar's hands and held it up. Hrithik smiled out from the cover, his biceps glistening, his eyes emoting under a *Fiza*-style bandanna.

'Of course, how could I not have seen him? He is everywhere. He would be huge in Paris if he came. I am told he does dance shows. It would be *énorme, absolument énorme*. You know, they really like this boy/girl look he has.'

'Boy/girl look-*shook*, what is this?' Mrs Kanwar rattled the controls of her hair-dryer at Thierry.

'See, look here. He has all these so huge muscles but he has a very pretty face, no?' He held the cover up for Mrs Kanwar to see.

'My *poti* would not feel so much for someone who is all girl-*shirl*.' She made a sound like a spoon being extracted from jelly.

'What do you think of his hair?' I asked.

Hrithik's hair-do had been puzzling me

Thierry flicked through the magazine. Mrs Kanwar sat under the dryer, fingers still twitching at the insult to Hrithik's masculinity but evidently curious to hear Thierry's professional opinion.

'Very blocky, very big.' Thierry pointed to a couple of pictures showing Hrithik with his hair indeed looking quite blocky and big, a sort of Bobby-Ewing-blowing-in-the-Southfork-terrace-wind look. 'I would take it much shorter and layer in some highlights.' Thierry held the cover shot away from him at arm's length and half closed his eyes. 'Yes, it is too solid on his head, you know, how do you say?'

'Like a helmet?' I suggested.

'*Absolument*, like a helmet, you are right.'

I was relieved. Hrithik's hair-do had been troubling me.

'What is this rubbish? He has such lovely hair.' Mrs Kanwar crossed her arms and jutted her lip.

By the time I left La Belle, Mrs Kanwar was almost freshly bouffed and was engrossed in an elaborate defence of Hrithik's hair. Thierry had wandered away, and Dolly was sitting disconsolately beneath her own helmet of twisted silver foil and skin-tone rubber.

Alarm and despondency spread among the beauty salons of India when Hrithik announced his engagement to Sussanne Khan at the end of November. No wonder he did not have time to see me before February. In addition to the films he had to make, he had a wife to take.

Madonna, the unquestioned queen of superstar spin and hype, was scheduled to marry Guy Ritchie in Scotland on 22 December. The rumour was that Hrithik and Sussanne were going to preempt them and get spliced on 20 December. But while everyone knew where the biggest pop star in the world was going to get married, the biggest star in India kept us all guessing. He was due to be on location in Australia at about that time. For a whole week the telephone lines hummed as the *filmi* journalists got on to their Australian contacts. Then Mauritius came into the running. After making his Charlie-Chaplin-by-the-sea Coca-Cola advertisement there, Hrithik had apparently said it would be a lovely place to get married.

I rang Meena, my magazine queen. If anyone knew, she would.

'Justine, hiya, how are you?'

'I'm fine, thank you.'

'Has our interview come out yet?'

'It comes out next week, at the beginning of December.'

'Great, great, can you get me a copy?'

I promised I would.

'Fantastic. What else?'

'Do you think Hrithik is going to get married in Australia, Mauritius, Ulan Bator or where?'

'No to Australia and no to Mauritius. What's this Yoolan Batter?' Meena turned big city Mongolia into New York Chinatown flying tonite.

'Nothing, I just wanted to know what you thought.'

'You are sure this is not some wedding thing I should know about?' she asked, a note of panic in her voice.

'Absolutely sure.'

'Okay, so he wouldn't be so crazy as to get married out of India.'

'Why not?'

'Oh so many reasons, but you know he is such a sweet boy, the thing that would really be troubling him would be the idea of all his family and friends having to fork out so much of money for the international tickets.'

'So where then?'

Meena laughed.

'You're not even going to give me a clue?' I persisted.

'Okay, so not Bombay.'

'Why not?'

'Too close to the bad boys for comfort. Don't forget it's not really so long since they shot at Daddy. Security would be just a joke and it would be totally impossible to keep the location a secret.'

'Wouldn't they just like to run away somewhere really quiet?' I asked.

'Oh nice dream, *yaar*,' she said sarcastically. 'If you're the hottest thing in India you can't just run away and get married under a pretty tree like those druggy Hollywood types. He's too smart for that. His fans would feel, you know, really ripped off.'

'So, if not Bombay?'

'Let's say it's no more than an overnight train journey from Bombay,' purred Meena. 'But then trains go in so many different directions, don't they?' she added.

'Thanks, Meena.'

'No problem, just send the article.'

I looked at Bombay on the map. Most overnight train journeys in India cover a distance of between 1,000 and 1,200 kilometres. It was unlikely that they would head for anywhere quiet and remote. Bollywood weddings require flower arrangements and garlands by the ton, fancy tinkling water features, elaborate constructions for the bride and groom to sit on in trussed-up agony, and hot and happening live bands that are allergic to the idea of being more than thirty kilometres from a major city centre. I began to draw up a list of cities within likely striking distance.

Goa was at the top, a whole state of seaside hedonism and hippy flip-flops, and thick with five-star resorts that could be transformed into living, breathing Bollywood nuptial fairylands at the ring of a mobile. Potential, about 9 out of 10. Then there was Bangalore, capital of Karnataka and Indian yuppy heaven, a booming town that still manages to hang on to some of the airs and graces that Delhi and Bombay have long since lost. Potential, 7 out of 10. Hyderabad was in with a chance, Urdu-speaking, Mogul-monumented, erstwhile Nizam-residing, twin capital of

Andhra Pradesh, though the enervating heat and proliferation of dusty bazaars marked it down. Potential, unlikely. Bhopal, the unfortunate capital of Madhya Pradesh and the victim of a toxic gas tragedy in 1984, the world's worst industrial disaster, was even less likely. As for Ahmedabad, another Manchester of the East, Gujurat's teeming textile capital, where chaos reigns and the skies never do except when they can cause the utmost monsoon damage, forget it.

It had to be Goa but could I get there? Could I find a reason to hang out in the land of loose living for weeks on end just in case the Roshan marriage procession rolled past? I had a friend who had a house. He was away. I could house-sit and wedding-wait. But no, the house was miles from anywhere and news travelled there at about the same speed as hippies paying their rent. And even if I did hear news of the wedding, what would I achieve? At best a tan and perhaps a glimpse of a passing star, safely tucked away behind the darkened windows of a limousine.

As the wedding approached I was still in Delhi. At last the evenings were cool. No fans turned, no air-conditioners roared into the twilight. Even the mosquitoes had curled up and died. I sat in the fading light on the balcony of my apartment, bundled up in a shawl, swaying in a rocking-chair under a money plant, juggling my stalking plans for the Asian wedding of the year. In the quiet residential street below, the *pheri-wallah*, the walking toy man, jangled past, pushing his miniature Ferris wheel, its four bucket seats swinging empty. He has few customers now in the middle-class residential areas. He rolls by unheeded as the children of affluent India huddle in front of computers, boggle-eyed as Tomb Raider Lara clamps another victim between her vixen thighs. Still the *pheri-wallah* makes his rounds, hoping perhaps to find a straying sweeperess's child who would be happy to have a ride. He talks to people on verandas and balconies to pass the time.

He called up in Hindi to the balcony above him.

'Hey, auntie, like a trip to the stars?'

I laughed and waved at his clanking Ferris wheel. 'I'm too big and too old.'

'Never too old to take a ride to the stars, auntie*ji*,' he called back. 'Have a fine Christmas. That is your festival, *naar?*'

It was three days before Hrithik's wedding, a week until Christmas. I would take a trip to the stars, to Rajasthan, to Udaipur, a beautiful city by a lake. That was where, in *Fiza*, Hrithik had strutted his bandanna and his stuff as Aman the terrorist. I would find the well where Sushmita had dipped and ground in her hot little dance number. I would find the jewellery shop that Aman had raided. I shimmied, Sushmita-like, from my rocking-chair and took a turn around the balcony, among the fig trees and the money plants, with footwork that would have made Pinky Ali smile. The *pheri-wallah* disappeared down the road, his empty Ferris wheel clanking in the dusk.

A few days before I left Delhi it was announced that Hrithik and Sussanne were going to get married in Bangalore at her father's brand-new, all-singing, all-dancing, super-deluxe resort, Golden Palms. While I packed my bags for the lake city Sussanne was being spiralled with *mehendi*, the snaking henna patterning worn by a bride-to-be. We were reliably informed that she giggled right through the ceremony. As I took the first taxi ride of my journey, Sussanne's parents, Sanjay and Zarine Khan, were apparently telling a *filmi* magazine all about Golden Palms.

Oh darlings, now we all know where to go when we are washed out and whipped. Sanjay and Zarine Khan have built just the perfect piece of paradise for Hrithik to marry his Sussanne! And no wonder he chose it, pussycats, because Golden Palms is just the very last word in Utopian comfort.

Zarine has just taken all those Bollywood movies to heart and created a little piece of *filmi* magic with Spanish and Moorish interiors, cascading fountains, rolling greens, ballrooms, banquet rooms, a disco, a nostalgia bar, even an Italian restaurant . . . This side of heaven it is the only place to be. Did I say little, darlings? Forgive me, Golden Palms is spread over 14 verdant acres and the pool, oh me, oh my, the pool is a positive lake, all 135 metres of it. Sanjay whispered to me that this bijou spa was unparalleled anywhere in the world. And to think that THE wedding is just the dress rehearsal, and that we can all flood in after 25 February when it will be officially open to us mere mortals. Just hope they don't clean the room where Hrithik changes too thoroughly, darlings . . . rrrrrrrrr.

As I stepped out on to the airport tarmac on the edge of the Thar Desert, bridges to a little island in the middle of a lake-sized pool at Golden Palms were being bound with great garlands of roses, lengths of strung marigolds and ribbons of jasmine. As I drove past the Shiva temples of Udaipur, their dark, erect *lingams* glowing with the patina created by millions of devoted hands, Sussanne was speeding around in a golf buggy, checking the preparations for her big night. Hrithik's tiny granny was in the back, pinned in place by a gaggle of Sussanne's shrieking handmaidens.

Udaipur rests at the feet of the ancient Aravalli hills. Here, for twenty-two generations, its Rajput rulers built their fortressed palaces in a bid for architectural immortality. The Rajputs believed themselves to be descended from the sun, and among the marble courtyards and corridors of their palaces, the same sun still beats down at midday, throwing into intense relief every arabesque and fretted alcove. The light on the lake changes with the late afternoon, washing the palace that floats there with the colour of ripening pomegranates. The city itself is a cake shop, an icing decorator's dream of crenellations and frills, set amidst all the usual paraphernalia of dusty, chicken-scratched back-street desert city life.

As I stepped off the plane I thought of bougainvillaea cascading down white walls, the sound of ankle bells crossing still courtyards, and the liquid dance of fountains under hibiscus trees. Instead I found myself surrounded by scenes more in tune with the worst excesses of the office Christmas party and rush hour at Santa's Grotto. My palace courtyard tableau fell away in the face of a festive pantomime set from Holiday-on-Ice with bells on. A huge tree stood in one corner laden with a collection of decorations apparently straight from Woolworth's Christmas counter, and beneath its groaning branches a strange gathering of gnomes peered out from thick cotton-wool landscaping. There were no ankle bells either. The entrance to an exquisite drawing-room in an inner courtyard was flanked with over-sized speakers pumping out 'Rudolf the Red-nosed Reindeer' on a continuous loop.

As the first point of pilgrimage it was disappointing. Closing my door on the enforced merriment I sat down and wondered which room Hrithik had stayed in during the filming of *Fiza*, and at some point between 'Little Drummer Boy' and 'Ol' Blue Eyes' rumbling 'White Christmas', I fell asleep.

Waking up in the knowledge that you are missing something vitally important is not a good feeling. I snapped back into the Udaipur evening realizing I had been snoozing through Hrithik and Sussanne's wedding vows.

At Golden Palms, Hrithik rode across a garlanded bridge on a white horse to meet his bride. She shimmered in red and gold. He wore a turban of drifted snow, a layered *angarakha*, a flowing shirt, waistcoat and topcoat the colour of pale doves' wings, picked out in soft gold. While I staggered around looking for a light switch, peering mole-like through horribly tinted glass at the Lake Palace Hotel, afloat on another man-made lake Hrithik dismounted and took the hand of his wife-to-be. He had been learning his lines. As the women of India held their breath, just in case he changed his mind, Hrithik turned to his *mehendi*-spiralled bride and looked deep into her eyes.

'I, Hrithik Roshan, take you, Sussanne, to be my lawfully wedded wife, to have and to hold, for richer or poorer, in sickness and in health, until death do us part.'

A stunned audience of family and friends looked on. Sussanne was equally surprised. She had not expected to hear Christian altar vows. Fiddling with the garland of roses around her neck she replied, 'Whatever you have said, I agree with and more.'

The audience sighed and her father, Sanjay Khan, stopped holding his breath. 'She's a clever kid, my girl,' he told his son and wife, wiping his eyes as the bride and groom laughed and smiled at each other.

Most of the audience were in tears. The bride joined them, and her mother had to tickle her. 'Stop crying, baby, or your make-up will be ruined.'

But there was no stemming the tears. They flowed full and free into the 135-metre lake-pool as the new Mr and Mrs Hrithik Roshan signed on the dotted line of the register. It was not a conventional wedding.

'I have always loved the seriousness of church weddings. I would really like to have something small and dignified like that,' Hrithik had said in an interview when his wedding plans had first come out. Small perhaps by Indian standards, just a few hundred.

'If we had the wedding in Bombay we would have to call more than 10,000 people,' Rakesh Roshan had told one journalist who had insisted that the wedding must surely be held in *filmi* city.

'How many guests will you have to the wedding?' another journalist had asked the bride's mother.

'Not as many as we would have liked to have. Ideally we would have liked to ask around 4,000 people, but we have had to restrict the guest list for security reasons.'

A combined guest list of 14,000 people was on the high side, even by Indian standards, and it was not what the bridegroom had in mind. Luckily for him, his instant stratospheric celebrity and the resulting security headaches had given Hrithik his wish – a drastically pruned guest list and the chance to marry Sussanne without all the ritual fire-walking paraphernalia of a traditional Hindu wedding.

In Udaipur I headed out with a sinking heart and a weak appetite for the pre-Christmas buffet by the pool. Several thousand kilometres away, Hrithik and Sussanne were taking to the floor beside their pool to the sound of the hip-hop *bhangra* boy of the moment. Their light dinner was tastefully served at the table among delicate flower arrangements, very specially created by Mrs Neeta Parekh, the floral diva to the stars, and flown in from Bombay for the big event.

'In the absence of photographers and outsiders, everybody was so relaxed that they had a great time,' Rakesh Roshan told a journalist a few days after the wedding. 'Everybody was dancing. In fact this must have been one of the weddings where the bride and bridegroom danced the most.'

No one was dancing in the courtyard in Udaipur. Instead a random selection of guests were toying with plates in front of the buffet, a sad landscape of cultural confusion: desert-dry turkey, lumps of grey stuffing, mounds of mushrooms piled high like so many shiny bunions, watery cabbage, congealed brown *dhal*, tired rice, limp salads, deep-fried fish and a strangely pallid Christmas pudding. Then the reception manager appeared as Father Christmas in oversized gum-boots and a cotton-wool beard that looked as if it had been swiped from around the gnomes under the Christmas tree. He strode among us with giant gumboot-sized strides, ho-hoing as he handed out lollipops to diners great and small, and now and then giving a little sideways jig. It was almost dancing.

The following day at Golden Palms Mr and Mrs Hrithik Roshan spent time with their families and friends, and Sussanne's

They Could've Danced All Night

Mr and Mrs Hrithik Roshan, featured film-mag style

father gave her some private advice, a moment that he later apparently shared with the readership of *CinéBlitz*.

> I just said the same thing to her that I had said when we were talking the night before the wedding. 'Be like your mother has been with me. If Hrithik is angry, don't get angry too. Always support him. If he is wrong, though, have the courage to tell him so.' My wife did that. After three days I would realize that she was right! Some wives have a tendency to agree with their husbands like sycophants and unwittingly destroy their marriages. Families break up and the kids suffer. I could see Sussanne taking this in, like a camera taking pictures.

The morning after the night of the long buffet in Udaipur I tackled the manager who was now back at reception, minus the cotton-wool and the gum-boots.

'Did you enjoy having part of *Fiza* filmed here?' I asked casually.

He narrowed his eyes for a moment, checked that there was no one else listening, and then leant towards me. 'This is not official information.' He stood back and gave me a professional smile.

'But everyone knows that they stayed here while they were shooting,' I persisted.

'It was only Mr Mohammed and Mr Roshan who were staying here. The rest of the persons were not at these premises.'

'Did they enjoy themselves?' I asked.

'They seemed most satisfied with the facilities.'

A gushing member of the hotel staff had let slip further information as she had chattered away to me over my breakfast by the pool.

'Hrithik stayed on for a couple more days at the end of shooting, you know. Poor boy, they went off with his bags and he had nothing, nothing. We had to rush out and find him everything from toothbrush to sleeping suit. He was so happy and grateful with all the things that we gathered for him.' Rumour had it that someone had pinched the toothbrush and some shaving things and had tried to sell them over the Internet.

'Who is saying this thing?' demanded the manager when I told him.

I could not shop my poolside source, so I shrugged.

'Madam, it is with sincere apologies that I must say I cannot assist you further with this matter.' He was furious, but decorum had to be maintained. I was after all a paying guest.

'He got married yesterday,' I offered peaceably.

'This is very happy news and I know that I can speak for all my staff here in extending our greatest good wishes to him and the lovely lady.'

That source had dried up. I returned to the plot of the film. When sister Fiza tracks down her baby brother he is mid-raid on a fancy shop, bandanna flying. On screen the shop sign was clearly visible. The raid had happened right in the middle of the main courtyard of the palace complex.

As I entered the shop an elegant woman in a rich golden sari was politely convincing a German shopper of the luxurious pleasures of owning a pashmina shawl. The customer was picky and her husband was bored. He sat to one side, ripping open the Velcro pockets on his safari waistcoat in noisy rotation. Both his wife and the woman in gold were ignoring his petulance. I went to sit in the corner beside a pile of small silk carpets with big price tags. Just as the German shopper seemed finally to be distracted by her husband's fiddling, the golden sari floated another pile of shawls in front of her, rippling them out with a jangle of bangles. Even the husband was momentarily entranced. Then he took a stand with a Teutonic command. His wife gave an apologetic smile over her shoulder as she was herded out of the shop. The golden sari turned to me, her poise unruffled.

'Can I help?' she asked in mellifluous tones.

'I am looking for Hrithik Roshan.'

'I am not sure I can help you in this, though it would be more than good for our business if I could.'

She smiled but she was also confused. I explained my *filmi* mission. She had only worked in the shop for a couple of months. *Fiza* had been filmed six months earlier. But she was polite and interested, and she went to find her manager. He was as poised and golden as she, and almost as feminine. I admired the shop. He thanked me and asked me what kind of shawl I was looking for.

'She is looking for Hrithik Roshan, not pashmina,' the golden sari explained patiently.

Her manager was momentarily flustered and then he laughed, a boyish, embarrassed sort of laugh. He led the way to the door of the shop and out into the hard midday light of the courtyard. He was older than I had at first thought, his hair carefully dyed and arranged to cover a meagre patch at the front, and his skin had a slightly papery quality.

'He was standing right here when I came to open the shop.' He pointed to the ground beside a tub of wilting plants. 'They had got all the days and dates mixed up. You know how it is with these *filmi* people,' he said with a note of admiration in his voice, and he raised one hand to his ear in a flutter. 'We had all been told that they would like to use the premises on . . . I think it was a Wednesday and Thursday.' He stopped for a moment. 'Maybe it was Thursday and Friday. No matter. I came the next day and they were still here. Hrithik was standing just there, just in this place.' He waved towards the tub of plants again.

'But I thought the scene was shot at night in the film.'

'They did more than just that one shot here.'

He led me around the corner of the shop to an outside staircase. 'Do you remember there is a little bit at the end of that big dance scene with Sushmita when Hrithik is standing at the bottom of a staircase?'

'Yes.'

'That was just here.' He posed at the bottom of the staircase, pulling the lapel of his jacket up over his mouth as if it was a black bandanna, and peered at me over the top with narrowed eyes.

I clapped. He bowed.

'Obviously you have seen the film,' I said.

'Of course, and more than once.'

'Do you think he is a good actor?'

'Does it matter?' His hand flew to his ear again. 'He is so much finer-looking than some of the other big stars who have not so much talent. And his thumb, you know his double thumb, very sexy.'

Hrithik has a double thumb on his right hand, the twin digits webbed together. Nearly everyone I had spoken to saw it as a lucky omen, and only a few dared murmur that they thought it odd.

The shop manager paused for a moment. 'Lovely boy,' he said wistfully.

We left the plant pot and the sacred spot and walked back to the shop. It was filling up with a tour group. The manager apologized.

'I will have to take my leave.'

I thanked him.

'No problem, a pleasure talking with you. You know I think he is very lonely, poor boy. Who can he trust now? Everyone wants to take a little bite from him.'

He started into the crowd of pashmina-seekers with a flutter, then stopped and turned back to me. 'If you see him you must tell him how important he is to so many of us.' And he disappeared into the crowd in his shop before I had a chance to answer.

Millions of people now loved Hrithik but out there, beyond Udaipur's lake quivering in the heat of the day, beyond the Golden Palms' own shimmering 135-metre water feature, the piranhas were gathering.

The feeding frenzy began as Hrithik and Sussanne were packing away their wedding clothes, and the first attack came from a curious quarter.

The *Chitwan Post* is a weekly vernacular newspaper with a tiny circulation. It is published out of Narayanghat in central Nepal, a town that does not even feature on large-scale maps of the kingdom. It is not a pretty place and it owes its inclusion in guide books to the fact that it lies at the junction of two of Nepal's major roads, the Mahenda Highway and the Prithvi Highway. Narayanghat is simply a *chai* and pee stopover on the road to Kathmandu.

Nepal is an important buffer zone between India and what the Chinese refer to as the Tibet Autonomous Region, and as such it has become a target for terrorists. A destabilized Nepal threatens India's north-eastern frontier. For this reason, small and remote towns such as Narayanghat, far from the eyes of the central authorities, are favoured by insurgent elements from China or Pakistan – the locals are gentler and more easily bullied than city folk. Even so, there seemed no obvious connection between a small-town weekly paper and a Bollywood star.

A week before his wedding, on 14 December, Hrithik's first television interview was shown on Star Plus, the most popular channel in India. The interview appeared on *Rendezvous with Simi Garewal*, a sort of flower-filled walking, talking *Hello!* magazine-on-screen. The lovely Simi herself was once a Bollywood actress. Her interview technique is as smooth and polished as her make-up, and her fingers trail through her perfectly groomed hair as she asks the latest beauty queen, *tabla* player, politician or *filmi* star the perennial question: 'So what does it feel like to be the most famous person on the planet?'

Hrithik sat with his parents in the studio, the three of them framed in a lattice-work bower of lilies and roses. Seated on a sofa, Simi leant towards her guests in a caring, sharing way. Papa Roshan did most of the talking while his son sat motionless and erect. After many platitudes from Simi and speeches from Rakesh Roshan there was a star-studded commercial break. First Shah Rukh Khan coaxed the nation into believing that anti-dandruff shampoo is cool. Then Salman Khan enticed the youth of today into drinking Thumbs-Up, India's even sicklier version of Coca-Cola and Pepsi. A not quite so starry ad for VIP underwear followed, offering the wearer 'hands free comfort'.

After the break Simi got Hrithik on his own. By now, in the space of one and a half minutes, viewers had seen all three top Bollywood box-office stars – Mr Pepsi Shah Rukh Khan, Mr Thumbs-Up Salman Khan and now, back in the flowery bower, Mr Coca-Cola Hrithik Roshan. All that and 'hands free comfort' too. It was enough to send anyone into an advertising tailspin. As the nation sat wondering whether they should be flipping open a Pepsi, a Thumbs-Up or a Coke, or throwing out all their old underwear for the 'hands free variety', Hrithik faced the nation. He was charming and graceful, a mixture of innocent abroad and frightened young man, worn down by his first year of super-stardom. Not a vicious word crossed his lips.

Having just recovered from the first commercial break, the viewers were then thrown into another, this time for snacks, sweets and chocolate. As Hrithik began to talk of his aims and dreams, the beauty salon brigade dutifully tucked into snacks, sweets and chocolate, and Simi simpered on her sofa, sighing along with the vulnerable young man's every syllable.

At about the same time as Hrithik was trying not to discuss his forthcoming wedding with sighing Simi, two youths broke into the office of the editor of the *Chitwan Post* in Narayanghat. They were carrying guns barely concealed under their shirts. They shouted at the other people in the office, first to bring them tea and then to get out. Once they had their tea they told the editor that Hrithik Roshan had just been making anti-Nepalese statements on a television programme being broadcast across the Subcontinent. The editor suggested that he try and see the interview so that he could judge for himself. The youths produced their barely concealed guns and threatened the editor until he agreed to run the story on the front page of the following day's issue.

It took a week for the story to be picked up by the more widely read *Himalayan Times*. The 23 December edition reported that effigies of Hrithik had been publicly burnt by youths in the streets of Chitwan a few days earlier. The agitation moved from small-town cardboard cut-out burnings to capital city unrest in Kathmandu. After hearing about the article in the *Himalayan Times* the general secretary of the All Nepal National Free Students Union decided to launch an agitation. He had apparently not even seen Hrithik's interview on *Rendezvous with Simi Garewal*.

This was not a spontaneous outburst of misplaced patriotic student energy but a planned campaign using a famous face that had the power to trigger riots in another country. Five students were killed in the riots and millions of pounds' worth of damage was wreaked on private and commercial property across Nepal. Effigies of Hrithik were reported to have been burned even in tiny villages that had only radio contact with the outside world.

An Indian intelligence report compiled after the riots pointed to Karachi-based Dawood Ibrahim, the king of the Bombay underworld dons, as the instigator of the civil unrest in Nepal. He was the same man who was thought to have been behind the attempt on Rakesh Roshan's life. The report stated that Ibrahim was probably working in conjunction with the Pakistan intelligence service, ISI. The man who was trying to milk money out of Hrithik's box-office value in India was apparently also using him as a political weapon.

On Boxing Day, the Nepalese Minister of Information and Communications poured verbal petrol on the rioting by making a public announcement. Hrithik's most recent film, *Mission Kashmir*, then being shown in cinemas all over Kathmandu, was to be banned. Like the leader of the students' union, the minister had apparently not seen the *Rendezvous with Simi Garewal* interview. The minister's order, referred to by some of the Indian press as a *fatwa*, incited further violence in the Nepalese capital.

In India a columnist on one of the more serious papers reflected on the events in Nepal.

Does it not amuse and sadden readers as much as it amuses and depresses me that our latter-day hero of screen and dance has been turned into the ultimate puppet of them all? Not only does this son of our soil have to play terrorists of the crescent moon in the suspended reality of *filmi* land, under the ever-present watch and grasp of our dear home-grown but off-shore Muslim mafia (let us not forget, dear reader, that in two out of three of our dewy fresh star's films to date he has portrayed Taleban-linked terrorists) but he has now also been cast in our apparently real world as an agent acting unintentionally for those with a vested interest in causing a rift between our good Himalayan neighbour [Nepal] and our good selves. Surely the line between *filmi* fiction and fuzzy reality has become a little too blurred . . . ?

The *filmi* magazines indulged in a flurry of conspiracy theories as extravagant as the language in which they were written.

The Roshan family had just flown back to Bombay from Bangalore, the scent of wedding flowers still fresh in their memories, the *mehendi* patterns still spiralling all the girls' hands and feet.

Rakesh Roshan was woken early the following morning, the first morning of his son's life as a married man. He saw the papers as he was getting ready to leave for a shoot in Tamil Nadu. He woke the young bridegroom and asked him if he had said anything against Nepal in his interviews. The bleary-eyed young star insisted that he had said nothing of the kind. His father flew off feeling reassured. When he saw the news reports on television later in the day he realized that the riots were being attributed to his son.

'I told him not to call a press conference,' Rakesh Roshan said later in an interview with *Movie* magazine. 'But I told him to just clarify his position to any TV channel or newspaper that would call him up. We don't think there is anyone out to get Hrithik. We don't want to believe any of that. When he asked me whether he should put off his trip to Australia I told him not to let all this come in the way of him trying to lead his life normally. There was no need to cancel his honeymoon or put off the shooting schedule because of what happened. Of course we are sad about this incident. But otherwise we are prepared for all kinds of controversies. They have to happen because Hrithik's success has been so phenomenal. His kind of phenomenal success will have its phenomenal backlash.'

Hrithik did what his father had advised. He made a televised statement pointing out that he had not even mentioned Nepal during the interview and that he had only affection for the country. He encouraged any doubters to watch the interview again to back up his statement. Initially the statement was blacked out by channel operators across Nepal. The Indian government put pressure on the Nepalese prime minister to insist that Hrithik's statement be aired. The riots continued across Nepal. Only after the statement was finally broadcast did order begin to return to the streets of the Himalayan kingdom.

'Nobody was even wanting proof. It was as if the whole thing had its own momentum and the truth was irrelevant to that thing. What I had or had not really said was not important,' Hrithik stated in another television interview several months after the riots.

As he talked about the events that had followed so soon after his marriage his usual easy smile faded. 'It had been such a happy time and then suddenly it was terrible. It was so like when *Kaho Naa . . . Pyaar Hai* opened. One day everything was the best, the next my father was in the hospital with a bullet wound next to his heart.' Hrithik looked fragile, his eyes wide and lonely as he turned away from the camera.

The director of the interview was brave enough to stay with the silence that followed. Hrithik continued to stare into space off camera.

'I will forever be conscious that there are four or five families in Nepal who will always associate me with the death of their children.' He paused again, looking down at his lap. 'That bothers me, it really bothers me.'

There was a cut to another subject. Then the smile was back in place and the interview went on. But the backlash against Hrithik's first meteoric year was only just gathering momentum.

CHAPTER 8

Betrayal

Boy gets another girl (apparently)

WHEN, AT THE beginning of December, Hrithik had announced to the world that Sussanne and he were engaged, there had been a couple of ugly little rumours doing the rounds.

Hrithik had been on location in England for a few weeks in October, shooting *Yaadein* (*Memories*), a film directed by Subhash Ghai, one of the kings of the fluffier-than-froth *masala* movie genre and famous for his crowd-pleasing skills: 'I do not make films for my clever friends. I make them for my maid. If she likes them then I know I am hitting my audience.'

Playing opposite Hrithik was another rising star, Kareena Kapoor, one of the junior members of one more Bollywood acting dynasty. As the Nehru line has dominated modern Indian politics, so the Kapoors have become movie royalty to a nation longing for heroes and heroines. Kareena and Hrithik had known each other since they were children, growing up together in the same *filmi* backyard.

Yaadein was going to be a typical Subhash Ghai film, the story of two Indian families living in England who love and dance their way from Bombay back-lots to high-speed motor-boats on the Thames.

During the fortnight's stint in England rumours started to leak back to Bombay that Kareena and Hrithik were spending a lot of time together outside working hours. *Filmi* headlines squawked that Kareena had set her designer baseball cap at Hrithik and that she was trying to win him away from the lovely Sussanne. One of the grubbier stories even put it about that the lovebirds had holed up together in a London hotel room for at least twelve hours.

At first both parties were too far away from the scratchings of the poison pens to respond. Friends spoke out defiantly on their behalf, claiming that Hrithik and Kareena had known each other all their lives and that to suggest any kind of dalliance was as good as accusing them of incest. It did not matter what they said. The magazine-reading world fell on the story as flies fall on rotting flesh, fascinated to see a potential chink in the armour of the disco-dancing, iron-pumping white knight of the silver screen.

Meanwhile the victims were busy making *filmi* magic along the Thames and up and down the very long drive of a very large house, supposedly the home counties home-from-home of Hrithik's film family, and on a curious bicycle trip to Malaysia. Possibly the finest scene involved our hero warning our tricky heroine not to go on an island trip during said bicycling venture. Naturally she ignores him, obviously she gets attacked by crocodiles, and naturally our hero rescues her in a dinghy, the engine of which fails, meaning that our hero has to swim to safety, pulling the dinghy by a rope through crocodile-infested waters while our heroine lies looking faint and beautiful across the rubbery bows. *Yaadein* was going to be a movie of infinite parts.

By the end of October Hrithik and Kareena had finished dancing under Tower Bridge, on big flashy boats along the Thames, and up and down the various long drives of various large houses. They packed their bags and headed home to face the filth.

Kareena strutted and pouted but did not emphatically deny the rumours. Sussanne said nothing. Hrithik said nothing for a while, though at a later date, after his wedding, he gave an interview to *Filmfare* magazine.

A movie of infinite twinkle

'And what about the story in the papers on the day of your wedding?' asked the interviewer.

On the day Hrithik and Sussanne were married, a newspaper columnist had reported that Hrithik and Kareena had apparently been seen snuggling up together on a flight.

'I was very upset when I read the article about Kareena and me coochie-cooing in an aircraft,' replied Hrithik. 'Some air-hostesses were even supposed to have seen us. If I was having an affair with Kareena would I really be so stupid as to coochie-coo with her on a plane?'

The interviewer had no answer to that.

'When I'm on a plane,' Hrithik went on, 'people from the economy class form a queue for my autograph. I spend my time standing in the cabin-crew area giving autographs and having my picture taken with others on board. How stupid to think I'd cosy up with anyone when hundreds of people were demanding attention.'

The interviewer changed tack.

'Would you go anywhere close to an affair on the eve of your marriage?'

'That isn't impossible. Human beings are capable of any kind of behaviour. I'm not perfect. But please don't fabricate stories. I never hide anything.'

Hrithik's frankness did nothing to stop the gossip. Some said he had rushed into the marriage with Sussanne as a way of killing off rumours that might hurt his image. Others spread the story that the affair had not ended, hence the hasty marriage to bring Hrithik to his senses. The fact that Hrithik and Kareena were part way through making three films together, back-to-back, only helped to keep the rumour mill humming.

'You know, I don't feel bad for myself,' Hrithik went on. 'I only feel bad for Kareena because she is such a sweet girl. She's been completely misunderstood and misrepresented in the media. That's partly because she just says anything that comes to mind. She's brutally honest. At heart she's a very clean girl. Kareena has a pure heart.'

The media loved that. Hrithik was defending his lady love. They settled down to wait for the next instalment, and every time it seemed likely that Kareena and Hrithik might be at the same party or event they swarmed, waiting for a tell-tale sign, a flicker, a spark.

In the lull between Christmas and the New Year, La Belle was a source of seasonal comfort. Frilly golden balls resembling festive fairy undergarments were pinned all around the reception desk, framing Mrs Sawan, the manageress, in a glowing haze of tiny can-can knickers. Dolly was not in a festive mood. Thierry had somehow managed to make her look like Ziggy Stardust caught in front of a wind machine, and as she made her way across the room to her usual corner for a quiet round of familiar and safe waxing she was trying not to be there at all.

Mrs Kanwar seemed determined to look on the bright side. As she was rolled over to the basin for the first stage of helmet creation, with the latest edition of *CinéBlitz* firmly clasped to her bosom, she caught sight of the tip-toeing Dolly.

'Still looking lovely, I see.'

Dolly winced.

'How is your daughter?' I asked Dolly, to take her mind off her hair.

'So thin and so tired. Why will she not eat more?' she sighed. Women of Dolly's and Mrs Kanwar's generation are appalled by the thought that a girl, particularly one to whom they are related, should actually strive to be thin. Thin means sick. Thin is a reason for constant worry.

'I have been making her *gajari halwa* fresh every day and she will not have even one spoon.' *Gajari halwa*, carrot pudding made with lashings of *ghee*, sugar and handfuls of dried fruit, is every Punjabi mother's way of trying to fatten up her children.

Mrs Kanwar emerged from the basin. 'I will have to give you my recipe. She will not be able to stop herself. My son cannot keep his spoon still for even one minute when I have made it fresh.'

Mrs Kanwar's son was amply covered – proof, if proof were needed, of the quality of her *gajari halwa*, though she omitted to mention her husband, a mere wisp of a man. Doubtless his lack of amplitude was due to his liver dysfunctionality rather than his wife's recipes.

'Perhaps your son is greedier than Dolly's daughter,' I said, keen to defend Dolly in her time of trial.

'Are you wife and mother that you know so much of all this?'

'No, no, of course not, just making an observation.'

Mrs Kanwar huffed at me as she was popped into a chair and the assistant began to insert the usual huge pink hair-rollers.

'Obviously Mrs Roshan is not a good mother, then. Look how thin Hrithik is.' I pointed to the cover of Mrs Kanwar's copy of *CinéBlitz*.

Hrithik was gazing out from the cover in a silver leather jacket, its collar up, its short sleeves rolled back to reveal his biceps. The whole look was completed with tinted yellow sunglasses and gold leather trousers that seemed to hang off his narrow hips. He looked beautifully chiselled to me, but to the ladies of the school of *gajari halwa* he was a shining example in leather of motherly neglect.

'Too much of kissing-*wissing*.' Mrs Kanwar pursed her lips and hissed.

'What?'

We all stared at the oracle. For the first time in our long salon relationship Mrs Kanwar looked embarrassed.

'You know this thing, you know.' She waved her magazine at me. 'This, this . . .' She puffed and stabbed her fingers at Hrithik's leather trousers. 'You remember I was saying, how many months ago now?'

Dolly and I were lost.

'Saying what?' I asked.

'You know, how it was very nice and all for him having a pretty girlfriend but what would happen if he started doing men's thing-ies and then getting caught. And see, see how right I was.'

'Oh, you mean Kareena Kapoor.'

'*Yaar*, and who all else we are not knowing as yet.'

'So you think he is having an affair?' I asked.

Mrs Kanwar shuddered and so did all her curlers.

To the ladies of the school of gajari halwa he was a shining example in leather of motherly neglect

'It is saying this is so in all the papers and magazines, so what else are we to think? Of course this is so. See, this is why he is so thin. What more proof are you requiring on this?'

'Don't you think perhaps he is just naturally thin and now even thinner because he has been working so hard?'

Mrs Kanwar looked at me.

'Maybe this is it. Maybe you are right.' She looked at the cover shot again. '*Gajari halwa*, he needs some of my *gajari halwa*. Is this not so, Dolly?' She waved the picture of Hrithik at Dolly.

Dolly gave a wobbled yes.

'See, Dolly thinks this is the case as well. Such a sweet, lovely boy.'

Mrs Kanwar loved Hrithik as a *filmi* mag reader, as a Bollywood fan and as a Punjabi matriarch who worried about his weight, but she also loved gossip. The question was, how long could Hrithik command her unconditional love?

'You must be from Delhi,' the driver declared as we swung on to the flyover, heading for town from Bombay's Sahar International Airport.

'I am. How did you know?' I pandered – my bags were liberally tagged with 'Del' flight labels.

'See how you are taking all your bits and pieces of clothing off? That is how I know this fact,' he said proudly.

I was. There had been a New Year nip in the air in Delhi, and I had left home in a jersey and shawl. My taxi-driver on the way to the airport that morning had also been wearing a thick shawl, only his was wrapped around his head, chin to crown, Crimean War-wounded fashion, and I had watched his breath hanging in the air as he exhaled a mixture of *paan* and tobacco. Bombay was about fifteen degrees hotter than Delhi and I was shedding layers as we drove past a huge hoarding of Shah Rukh Khan in scuba-diving gear. He had an inscrutable expression on his face and it was not clear what he was advertising. By the time I had taken off another layer we had moved on to the next great hoarding.

Hrithik stood tall, lean and tough in front of a motorbike. His expression was as inscrutable as Shah Rukh Khan's had been, and again I could not see what he was advertising.

'Have you seen *Fiza*?' I asked the taxi-driver.

'Super film. Hrithik and Sushmita are number one stars.'

'And what about Shah Rukh's latest film?' *Mohabattein* was an epic designer-label family saga starring both Shah Rukh and the mighty Amitabh Bachchan.

'I did not see.' He sounded unimpressed.

'Why not? It was the biggest film of the season.'

'My wife was making me go to *Mission Kashmir*.'

Mohabattein had been released at exactly the same time as *Mission Kashmir*. Here now was more proof of the extent of Hrithik's appeal. *Mission Kashmir* was not traditional fare for your average taxi-driver's wife, but she had chosen it rather than *Mohabattein*, a classic popcorn-and-pack-'em-in *masala* Hindi movie.

'So she likes Hrithik,' I said with glee.

'No, Sanjay Dutt,' he snorted.

Sanjay Dutt, the man with the criminal record, had played a high-ranking Kashmiri police officer in the film. In spite of dalliances with the underworld, and despite the fact that he was over forty, Sanjay was clearly still housewife crumpet.

'Did you enjoy *Mission Kashmir*?' I asked.

'Preity Zinta was very nice.'

Preity had been Hrithik's love interest in the film. She had also been one of Shah Rukh Khan's girls in *Dil Se*, the film in which the hero and heroine blow themselves up at the end, much to the audience's disgust. Do you follow? Warp speed – Bollywood-speed.

I tried to keep count of whose face flashed past more often on the hundreds of hoardings lining the route into town. I lost count when Shah Rukh was fourteen to nine up on Hrithik, but then maybe Hrithik is more choosy about what he advertises.

Delhi had been dry and cold. Bombay was hot and humid, but

the evening walkers on Carmichael Road were determined to cast the season as winter. They were out and about as we arrived, the women's billowing *salwar kameez* of the summer months now topped with a fine cross-section of cardigans, the men tightly zipped into tracksuits, striding out next to their cardigan and *salwar kameez* of choice or long habit. I had stripped down to a T-shirt by the time the taxi-driver pulled up.

Severin was waiting for me. She looked morose. My flight had been delayed by two hours. Her mood indicated that she had better things to do than hang around the house waiting for me to turn up on the whim of domestic airline rescheduling. But her spirits lifted a little when I admired a newly acquired wooden carving of St Anthony, her favourite saint. He was ensconced on a chest right outside my bedroom door with fresh jasmine flowers reverently placed at his feet.

'How lovely.'

Severin beamed.

'Is he here to encourage me not to lose the house keys?' I asked.

Severin scowled. I was committing harassy again.

By the following afternoon I was back on Breach Candy Road. I had swum around India eight times at the Breach Candy Club and now I was ready for a carrot and orange juice, freshly squeezed. A young boy in the earliest and worst stage of moustache growth was minding the stall and it took him four times longer than the juice-*wallah* to get the whole thing from fruit and vegetable to glass. He was the juice-*wallah*'s nephew.

'Where is your uncle?'

'It is Friday. He is at Haji Ali,' the boy replied.

Haji Ali is the great white mosque that swims in the bay. The name means 'Ali who went on the *Haj* pilgrimage to Mecca'. The devout say that Ali was a local nineteenth-century business-man who gave up the material life, *haji*ed off to Mecca, came home and meditated on a headland where his eponymous mosque was then built by devotees. The less devout say that he was a *Haji*-to-be who died *en route*. Ali's body was then thrown overboard with a sign around his neck saying he was to be buried 'wheresoever he be ashore'. However it came about, Ali's mosque stands cool, white and proud at the end of a causeway poking out into the Arabian Sea, just down the road from Breach Candy and not far from the Mahalaxmi Racecourse where I go to run damply and half-heartedly. The causeway is always a flurry of headscarves, *burqas* and *topis*, a bobbing sea of worshippers making their way to prayer. At high tide Haji Ali becomes an island, but it is not such a bad thing to be stranded on the rocks below the mosque in the softness of a sea breeze, waiting for the tide to ebb, looking back on the city shivering in ferment.

Haji Ali of course had had a starring role in *Fiza*. Here, in the final dream sequence, in the shade of the mosque's pillars and domes, Aman had laid his head in his mother's lap.

Waiting beside the great grinder and thinking of the juice-*wallah* at the mosque, I realized that I had not paid much attention to his religious bent.

'He doesn't wear the *topi*,' I said to his nephew.

'All the time, he wears all the time.'

I started to argue and then remembered that I had only seen him recently in the hot season when he wore a towel over his head to absorb the sweat. Perhaps the *topi* was perched underneath.

For some reason I was surprised that he was a devout Muslim. He seemed too garrulous, too media- and movie-conscious. I could not remember him making a single reference to the Koran and he had never *salaam alekum*ed or *inshallah*ed me. His nephew was apparently reading my thoughts.

'*Mamaji*, my uncle, is not so usual for Mussulman.'

The term was an old-fashioned one and carried with it a note of respect. In *filmi* terms Shah Rukh Khan is referred to as a

Mussulman. The religion of Salman Khan, on the other hand, who is so often seen bare-chested and rippling, is rarely mentioned. The shedding of clothes in public is not something that a good Mussulman does.

'When will Uncle*ji* be back from Haji Ali?' I asked.

As it was Friday, the big prayer day, he could be hours.

'Soon,' he assured me, then he paused. 'Maybe not so soon.'

I settled down to wait beside the juice stand. Nearby a cow was holding up the traffic as she meandered from a blue plastic bag to an abandoned flip-flop with a broken thong. High up above us rose the hoardings on which Shah Rukh and Hrithik had fought out their fizzy pop wars. Now they were at it again, Shah Rukh slicked up and ready to dive, Hrithik leaning against his motorbike. I stared long and hard and still could not work out who they were posing for and being paid by.

The juice-*wallah* came down the road with a spring in his stride and a wide smile. He waved when he saw that a regular customer was back in town, and as he did so his other hand went to his head and slipped his *topi* off and into his pocket. His nephew shrugged and secured his own *topi* more firmly in place.

'So long away from the benefits of fresh juice,' the juice-*wallah* said as he approached. 'Is it any wonder you are looking so wheatish?'

'How was Haji Ali?' I asked.

'Decent.'

'Have you seen *Fiza*?'

The juice-*wallah* looked at me, trying to find a clue to this apparent non sequitur.

'I was telling you some time back that I do not go to films. Not for so many years now since . . .' His voice trailed off.

Madam Deepa's face came back to me, across the table at the Delhi Darbar Café on Falkland Road, her sad, sunken features the reason why the juice-*wallah* had lost his faith in *filmi* magic.

'I'm sorry, I forgot. It was just that there was quite a lot of Haji

Ali in *Fiza*. Hrithik played a Muslim in it, a young man caught up in the Bombay riots,' I explained.

'What would he know of this?' The juice-*wallah*'s mood and tone had changed.

'Were you here during the riots?' I asked.

'I was, and not moving from my house with my family.' He began to pick rotten carrots out of the pile on the front of his stall and lay them on the road for the cow who was nonchalantly chewing on the broken flip-flop.

'I have well-known Muslim neighbour with three small childrens. Me and my family are taking these peoples in for their protections. Three places of brother Muslims in my street were being burnt, four Hindu places also.'

The cow spotted the pile of rotten carrots and ambled across the road, sending a Mercedes and a rickshaw into near collision. She blinked slowly, let go of the flip-flop and began on the carrots.

'I heard that one of the Shiv Sena gangs poisoned milk lorries delivering to schools in Muslim areas.'

The juice-*wallah* sniffed and shot a jet of snot on to the pavement.

'Hindus sending bad milk to Muslim babies, Muslims sending bad milk to Hindus, same, same. I am starting my business in Bombay after Partition. This thing was same, same for us again, so we are hiding with our families and praying night and day.'

'Hrithik was living in Bombay too at the time of the riots,' I said.

'Really not so much of rioting up in the *filmi* areas of town.' He smiled again.

'You know out of his three films so far he has played a Muslim terrorist twice. It seems a strange role model to choose.' I watched the painful progress of an ancient and very lame woman crossing the road. The juice-*wallah* sent his nephew to help her. She was unimpressed by the offer and shooed the boy away.

193

'Role model?' he asked, shrugging at his nephew.

'This idea of Bollywood being secular, a Hindu playing a Muslim, Muslims playing Hindus. It just seems strange that they chose to cast Hrithik as a Muslim terrorist twice.'

The juice-*wallah* wiped his hands thoughtfully on a towel and then folded it carefully. His nephew in turn folded it into an even smaller square and placed it tidily between the grinder and a pile of oranges. Once the towel was stowed the juice-*wallah* started to laugh.

'You mean big *filmi* director *sahibs* are trying to solve all of my country's problems by making a boy who is advertising Coca-Cola a . . . a what?' He rubbed his already clean hands up and down the front of his *kurta*. 'A, a . . .' He rubbed his hands faster and more furiously. 'You tell me, *naar*. What is he, this *sunder larka*, this pretty boy? A *filmi-wallah*, a soft-drink-*wallah*, a political-*wallah*, husband, son? *Kya hogiya*? What is going on?'

'Did you hear about the riots up in Nepal?' I asked.

'How is it possible not to know? Every paper for days has only this story. And what are we thinking? That some bottom-soft face of a boy is going to cause a war between India and our good neighbour Nepal? Why will any persons want to buy any of the soft drinks or whatever if this is so?' He waved towards the great hoardings above us. 'You say you are going to see him. You be sure to ask him these things when you are talking with him.'

Satisfied that he had made his point the juice-*wallah* returned to his rhythm of vegetable piling and peeling, and I stood watching his methodical movements.

'You will be seeing him?' he asked after a long pause.

'I have a date in a couple of weeks when I can call him and then see if he will be able to see me.'

The juice-*wallah* rolled his eyes. 'See how mad this is. *Arre*, he is just a man like me or you. Yet someone with experience such as your good self has to have appointment to even so much as call him. This is madness.' He was shaking his head. 'He is just a boy, just a boy,' he finished, almost in a whisper, and he gave his nephew a playful sideswipe. 'Young persons like my family here are looking up to this boy.' He gently took hold of his nephew's ear. 'So what person is he looking to for guidance with half the world wanting to take a piece from him?' He shook his head and released his nephew's ear.

The cow beside us had finished the carrots, and the flip-flop was dangling from her lips again. She looked uncomfortable. Then she raised her tail and her eyes softened. A green jet shot over the bonnet of a parked car behind her and slid down over one of its gleaming hubcaps. No one took any notice.

I had left a few messages for Sunil, the director of the hairdressing film, but he seemed to have disappeared since *Snip!* had been released a month before. He had been licking his wounds. Sunil and *Snip!* had been chewed up and spat out.

When, eventually, he did ring, we agreed to meet at Olive on Pali Hill. It was on the opposite side of town and the traffic was going to be at its worst, but it was convenient for Sunil. Still, the drive was not something that I minded. It would be the Bombay version of the Beverly Hills star homes tour and it would take me almost to Hrithik's front door. I was not sure whether he was still filming in Australia or if he was back in Bombay, and I was feeling out of touch – not that I had ever really been in touch.

'Will there be more of fighting?' asked the driver when I told him where we were heading.

'Well, there wasn't much last time round,' I said as I got into the car.

The fact that I was not in army fatigues but was wearing a dress seemed to reassure him. 'Very brave madam, but maybe today not so ready for fighting?'

'I'm not planning on any.'

We sped away down Carmichael Road, putting the wind up a few ambling *salwar kameez*-wearing strollers.

It was not a starry night downtown. The sky was overcast and it was too early for the movie variety to be putting in an evening appearance. We moved on up into the *filmi* hills and my driver became my guide to the homes of the stars.

'You must pay attention in these streets. This is where you will find many residences of stars.' He waved vaguely at some high walls and high gates.

'Who?'

He sucked his bottom lip and continued to wave. I looked out for hints of *filmi* stars: low-slung cars, sunglasses behind tinted windows, heavily armed security guards in front of gold-leafed gates or sweeping façades of pillars and porticos. All I could really see was a horizon of satellite dishes and television aerials above tightly closed gates. The driver turned to look at me.

'Aamir Khan, this is exact location of his house,' he said triumphantly, still waving at the hermetically sealed row of gates.

'Oh, thank you.'

I kept looking, and perhaps I did see Aamir Khan's security guard in his sentry box, but then there was one in front of every house. The stars were just not out and about. We drove on.

The finest performance *en route* was given by a pi-dog as we sat gridlocked outside Bandra Station. A barrel-chested office-*wallah* was having his shoes cleaned just beside the entrance. His safari-suit was over-starched and he carried a highly polished briefcase that seemed almost an extension of his right arm. He shouted for *chai* as he settled down, and a glass was promptly delivered by a boy on the run, his full wire *chai*-carrier swooping past with just a dip in the flow of movement to give the office-*wallah* time to take the tea. As he did so, a pi-dog sidled up to the briefcase, mounted it and began thrusting energetically. With the *chai* in one hand, his briefcase attached to the other and one foot fixed under the *motchi-wallah*'s ministrations, the office-*wallah* was helpless in the face of this amorous advance. Too late, the *motchi* rallied and let fly at the animal with a newly cut rubber sole. The pi-dog slunk away, his tail and more between his legs. The briefcase was then dusted down and polished with great vigour while the office-*wallah* shrieked at the retreating dog. The traffic moved on before I could catch the closing scene. The mongrel and I had missed out on the climax, but he was a good-looking lad. His briefcase moment would come.

In spite of the traffic I arrived early. Except for waiters, waitresses and Sunil, Olive was empty. Sunil was sitting at the end of the restaurant's long bar with an equally long face and hunched shoulders. I waved from the door, and he straightened up and smiled.

'You look good. You've . . .' I trailed off.

He had lost weight, but I am never quite sure with Indian men whether it is a compliment or an insult to point it out.

'Reduced,' he laughed.

'And you look much less tired.'

'*Yaar*, I was just half dead when I saw you last. My God, I really don't know how I lived through that. But it's all change now. I'm getting fit and I drink this instead of the hard stuff.' He held up a glass of white wine. 'But I drink it by the gallon so maybe nothing has really changed. You know, it really is good, the only Indian wine that I have found to date that's not piss.'

'I'll try it, thank you. What do you mean, you don't know how you lived through it?'

'The film.' He waved to the waitress. 'Another of these, please, and some snacks.'

The waitress was at the other end of the bar with her back to us. She did not seem to hear. Sunil called out again. She turned to us, a mobile pressed to her ear, and waved to indicate that she would come over when she had finished her call.

'God, this town. Can you imagine that in London, a waitress

Sunil Sippy directing Sophiya in Snip!

telling you to chill out while she finishes her call? You know it's like a sex aid here. So many of my friends use it as a device for fooling around outside of marriage, no more having to call from public phones, no more running down to the market, pretending to just be out for a quick *paan* fix. It's like a mobile adultery tool.' He glared at the waitress.

She finished her call and Sunil politely repeated his order.

'Did you see the reviews?'

'Some of them,' I replied.

'Bullshit.'

'A few of them weren't so bad.'

'Oh sure, the ones in newspapers read by one man and a dog. "*Snip!*: another brave new addition to the brave new cinema that dares to approach the box office through untrodden pathways . . ." Did you see the film?'

'I did, twice.'

'How come?'

'I saw it once on my own and then I took some friends.'

'Thanks for that, you probably doubled the box office.'

'What was the opening like?'

'Opening?'

'Of the film.'

'Oh God, I couldn't do it, I couldn't go. I just drove around town from the minute that I knew it was starting until the end. Then I called up Sangeeta, hung up before she answered because I felt sick, then called her back again. You remember Sangeeta, don't you, my producer?'

The glass of wine appeared with two small bowls, one of cashew nuts, the other full of carrot sticks and celery. Sunil eyed the raw vegetables and his hand moved towards them before wavering and then plunging into the cashews.

'Bullshit, I'm trying, but I can't deal with all this horse-food. Cashew nuts aren't bad, are they?'

'The worst.'

'But nuts are healthy.' He was selecting some carefully.

'Fattening and healthy. And when you called Sangeeta back?'

'She said they loved it.' He popped the nuts into his mouth one by one.

I must have looked unconvinced. Sunil stopped eating.

'Really, they did. It was a press preview and I had only asked guys who I thought would get it. They did, you know, they really laughed. They liked it.' He was shaking his head. 'I was so high I just went in and, God it was so great, everyone was just like, oh I don't know, I just felt really good, really clever.' He rolled his eyes. 'That didn't last.'

The waitress was hovering, listening. Sunil had finished his glass and ordered another.

'Are you a director?' she asked.

'*Yaar*, I suppose.' Sunil shrugged.

'You did *Snip!*?'

'I did.'

'I saw it, you know, I saw it.'

Now she was really interested. Sunil thanked her, straightening up, his shoulders opening out.

'Are you making anything right now?' She filled his glass very promptly and very full.

'Not right now, I mean not a film, I'm doing some advertising shoots.'

'Oh.' She lost interest and went back down the bar to make another call.

'God, can you believe this stuff, mobiles and rude too.' He dived back into the comfort of the cashew bowl. 'So, *yaar*, after that preview it was all bullshit. The next preview they hated it, just total silence in all the places where they were supposed to laugh. It was like being eaten alive in public.' He took one of the carrot sticks and snapped it into little pieces. 'I need a cigarette. That's something else I haven't managed to kick yet. I will at some point, just not right now.' He lit one, closing his eyes as he took the first long drag. 'Then this whole Bharat Shah *tamasha* started and that kind of blew it all out of the water.'

Bharat Shah, an absurdly wealthy diamond merchant and exporter, was one of the biggest film backers in the industry, either financing or distributing half of the films in production or on release. Sunil had signed a distribution deal with his company, but Bharat Shah had been arrested the week after *Snip!* opened on the evidence of a tapped conversation seemingly linking him with the offshore underworld dons. Films in production went on hold as Shah was imprisoned. From Pali Hill to Juhu, celluloid city held its collective breath.

'Maybe this wasn't such a bad thing.' Sunil snapped some more carrots in half. 'I can use it as a reason for the film not exactly breaking any box-office records.' He tried to snap a celery stick in half, then abandoned it and returned to the carrots. 'In fact we probably did break a record – for being the shortest running film ever.' He examined the various pieces of carrot in his hand and then emptied them into an ashtray. 'At some point I'll be eating the carrots and throwing away the cigarettes, but not yet.' He inhaled again and closed his eyes. 'You know they murdered us on all the dildo stuff?'

'I realized.'

'Of course, you've seen it, haven't you? Were there many people in the cinema?'

'It was almost full the first time, a couple of days after it opened, not quite so full the second time.'

'You mean empty?'

I hesitated.

'How many do you think?'

'I didn't count, a few rows maybe. I think you should stop this. It's masochistic.'

'I bet more people would have gone if we had been able to keep the dildo in.'

'It was fairly inevitable that it was going to be cut.'

Sunil looked at me with a sad expression. 'How can anyone work in an industry that is so uptight that it cuts the best jokes? Can you imagine *Pulp Fiction* being shown here? It would have been censored down to a five-minute film, the beginning and end credits and that would have been about it.'

'Does it make you wary about doing another film?' I asked.

The waitress pricked up her ears again and moved back down the bar towards us.

Sunil leant towards me.

'Yes, it's called *Blood Bar* and it's about the hideous murder of a waitress, you know a kind of *Snip! II* with a cocktail twist.' He narrowed his eyes at the waitress.

She flared her nostrils and snatched the ashtray away from Sunil just as he was about to put out his cigarette.

'She gets blown up by exploding raw vegetables planted in an apparently innocent ashtray.' He leant over and dropped his cigarette into the sink in front of her, then lit another one.

Giving the people fantasy

'You know this industry makes about 800 films a year and grosses the equivalent of about a hundred and thirty-five million pounds. You'd think that our apparently intelligent metro audience was ready for something that didn't involve dancing around trees in wet saris, wouldn't you?'

'Apparently not.'

'I understand all this bullshit about giving the people fantasy, but look at the messages, *yaar*: boy, girl, kissy-*wissy*, big guys with guns and if in doubt let's dance. "Only the morally courageous are worthy of speaking to their fellow men for two hours in the dark. And only the artistically incorrupt will earn and keep the people's trust." You know who said that?'

'Frank Capra.'

Sunil looked slightly annoyed.

'Do you mean that all the films being made now are immoral?' I asked.

'No, no, not at all. For Christ's sake, I can't even get an innocent little dildo in. I don't mean immoral, what I mean is . . .' Sunil stopped for a moment. 'What do I mean?' He examined his cigarette. 'I mean we are selling this great big bullshit glamour lie to millions of people every day and I'm not sure if we really make their lives any better.' He stared at the end of his cigarette even more intently. 'I think I better have another glass of wine.' Then he peered at his watch. 'You're in the wrong city on the wrong date, you know.'

'What?'

'Are you still chasing Hrithik Roshan?'

'Chasing is rather a strong way of putting it.' I cleared my throat. 'I like to think of it more as a case of following his career in my role as a chronicler of the anatomy of modern stardom.'

'Well, you're most definitely in the wrong place. He's doing his great big show in Delhi tonight.'

'I know.'

'So?' Sunil was still trying to get the waitress's attention.

'I've got it covered.'

And on cue my very small grey phone began to vibrate fondly in my pocket. There was a text message from my man on the ground in the thick of the crowd at the Jawaharlal Nehru Stadium in Delhi.

'H 1 hr late! 25k pepl losing cool. Sn Coke ad 20 tms but can I buy Ck!?!?' read the text.

I passed the information on to Sunil.

'You really have got someone there?'

'Of course, directly linked by the joy of text.'

My pocket throbbed again.

'Playbck sngrs v v dull – peple r stackng chrs 4 bttr vu – man in frnt hs pile of 20.'

Sunil was snapping more carrot sticks.

'So have you met him yet?'

'Not yet.'

He laughed. 'How long have you been trying?'

'Nine months. I could have had a baby in the interim and he wouldn't even know.'

'What, you and Kareena Kapoor?' Sunil rolled his eyes.

My phone bounced and buzzed on the bar again.

'V v borng – big puff on flppng flmi fmly – granpa – unc – dad – at lst hr's Wndr Boy – wearng slvr astronaut drs/suit thng – audnce gng mad – 2 cool'

'He's wearing a silver astronaut suit,' I told Sunil.

He groaned. 'I bet you he'll be saying something cute to the audience right now.' He took out another cigarette, holding a lit match next to the tip. 'I'm being mean, I'm better off being me than being that poor tortured guy.' He sucked, pulling the small flame on to the end of the cigarette. 'Mind you, at least he doesn't have to fight for backing now. How cool not to have to even think about money.' He turned his cigarette round and examined the glowing tip. 'How is he going to keep the show going for more than half an hour? He's only got six dance numbers to date. There are only so many times you can go on doing *Kaho Naa . . . Pyaar Hai.*'

It was now just late enough for the party people to venture out on Pali Hill. They were coming into the bar around us, distractingly bright and shiny. A girl in a tiny turquoise-sequinned

T-shirt, her nails matching the sequins, her arms long, thin, dark and circled in gold, made a bee-line for us. She cuddled Sunil and he laughed.

'Justine, this is Gita. We met at a party yesterday. Gita is very friendly. She says she liked *Snip!* Gita wants to be an actress.'

Gita smiled through vampire lips, a study of ambition in blood red.

As I drove away from Olive the audience at the Nehru Stadium were still stacking seats in bakers' dozens to try and get a better view. The chairs were the type that are used at thousands of Indian weddings and party-*sharties* every day of the year, small, plastic and wobbly, definitely not adhering to any particular safety standard, definitely not safe to stand on in piles.

The audience had been getting agitated before the arrival of the superstar in his silver suit, the crowd moving around and chattering rather than focusing on the hastily assembled stage at the far end of the stadium. It was like a *mela*, a great religious fair. Policemen wandered in packs among the crowd, half-heartedly tapping the plastic chairs to check for bombs. The heaving mass was hungry and thirsty but was informed that there were 'no eatables and drinkables for reasons of security'. And all the while the advertisements beamed down their message: 'Coca-Cola: your generous and happy sponsor for the night'.

As with most live shows in India the audience was made up of young, over-excited boys. They were restless and ready to dance, all uniformly dressed in very tight jeans, an even tighter T-shirt, and wrap-around sunglasses. The majority of young girls are banned from such public expressions of teenage wildness by their nervous parents. That is just the way it is. The boys get to dance and scream without having to worry about seeming a bit girly in front of the girls. There were gangs of these boys in the audience, big gangs, and they had been drinking before the show.

Hrithik arrived.

The crowd froze. Then it screamed with one voice. The restless boys had become hysterical fans in full cry.

As Hrithik spun out over the audience in a builder's cage suspended from a crane, floating in glittering Lurex, thousands yanked their heads back to take in every detail. Hrithik reached his arms out in front of him and cocked his wrists. Then the hips began to flick. The audience exploded. This is what they had come to see. Hrithik laughed in his cage. 'I love you, Delhi. I'm going to open your hearts.' And the audience below throbbed like hundreds of thousands of vibrating mobile phones, wriggling and gyrating on their plastic stacks.

As the star hung over the crowd a boy of twelve was crushed under a tumble of chairs. He had been trying to get one of the cuddly, heart-shaped toys that had been thrown into the audience as the crowd had flipped out of control with every flick of Hrithik's hips. The boy survived with two broken ribs and a broken collar bone. A couple of others did not. The newspaper headlines on the following day stuck to the fact that the show had raised millions of rupees for the victims of a horrifying earthquake in Gujarat on India's Republic Day.

Hrithik was a hero. He was untouchable.

As far as I was concerned, he was also uncontactable.

CHAPTER 9

Seduction

Sub-plot

'I CAN GET you a meeting with Hrithik,' said a film star. He was sitting beside me in a hotel lobby, busy being famous. My new best friend.

'*Yaar*, this will not be a problem.' He squirted tomato ketchup all over a toasted cheese sandwich that had just been brought by a waiter. The waiter had been so awed by the star he was serving that he'd dropped the chips that went with the sandwich into Anupam's lap.

Anupam Kher has been making films since he was twenty-four, though he has never really made it to romantic lead. From the first he was cast as a character actor and to date he has appeared in 275 films over a period of nineteen years. That works out at about fifteen films a year. He is still in his early forties and he still plays a constant round of fathers and wicked uncles. Bollywood has no place for love stories about real early-middle-aged people.

When I had first called him he had been far more helpful than any of the other stars I had been in touch with. He was in the middle of directing his first film, but yes, sure, he would have time to meet me. When, where, how? My suggestions had been too low-key, cafés and street-level restaurants were too, too . . .

'Too what?' I'd asked.

'Justine, you know what it is like for stars. We cannot really be out in these places you have mentioned. People just do not leave us alone,' he'd replied.

Movie stars and magazine queens are all the same when it comes to fixing a rendezvous – it has to be five-star. We settled on the nearest big hotel to where he was filming, the Regent in Bandra, one of those great monuments to the modern business-man at ease on someone else's money. Its sweeping lobby has more glass than is sensible and a collection of chandeliers that would put Trump Tower to shame.

We had agreed to meet in the coffee shop which opens on to the lobby and is set up above it like a stage, and I arrived early.

'I'm at the Regent, baby. *Yaar*, me and the girls had our kitty here. Love you, see you later.' A girl in black, sunglasses nestling in her glossy hair, snapped shut a tiny mobile. She was sitting on a leather sofa in the lobby. I sat down opposite her.

Kitty parties are the Indian equivalent of Tupperware parties, except that instead of buying strange sandwich containers or bad taste *faux* jewellery, the Indian girls give each other money. As a concept it was once a good way of providing newly-weds with a bit of spare cash. Now it is more about women saving up for dia-monds, especially when the sipping, nibbling and swapping takes place in a spot like the Regent. But the woman on the tiny mobile phone opposite me was not with a bunch of her kitty friends. She was with a young man who did not look like her brother or her husband.

The girl saw me watching and narrowed her eyes. I scuttled away to the coffee shop to find a good place from which to follow Anupam's approach, to be relaxed and prepared, to appear non-chalant and in the habit of taking tea with stars. There was a deep sofa at one end of the raised 'tea with the famous' area, and a nice low table that did not restrict my view back down into the lobby. From my vantage point I could watch without being obvious.

The non-kitty-party girl was on her phone again. Her friend was on his. She finished her conversation, he continued his. She made another call. It was a curious meeting, endless conversations with other people without talking to each other. They moved a little closer together on the leather sofa and they watched each other as they talked. She licked the tip of one of her fingers and smoothed her eyebrow. He followed her finger. She crossed her legs very slowly and he watched the same finger journey down her thigh and start tapping her knee as she chatted. And he went on chatting and watching while I went on lolling on my sofa.

'Do you think they are married?' a voice said in my ear.

I bumped my head on the edge of the sofa, dropped my note-book, scrambled around to retrieve it and found myself at the feet of the voice. They were sporting very new, very unused, state-of-the-art pumped-up trainers.

'Hello, I'm Anupam Kher and you must be Justine. And you are . . . researching?'

'No, no, just snooping.' I looked up from the trainers and came face-to-logo with a designer belt buckle.

'Good, I like honesty. I'm starving.'

He bent down as I looked up and I blushed.

'Hello,' I said, holding out my hand.

We shook hands, Anupam bending over and me on my knees. Waiters were hovering and so the grilled cheese sandwich was ordered.

Anupam sat down carefully. As with all actors of ordinary stature he looked much smaller and neater in the flesh than on screen. He was neither flabby nor firm, just lightly layered in good living. His face reflected the light, as if regularly buffed, and his hooded eyes darted about, unable to keep still for more than an instant. A pair of glasses rested on his nose, looped around his head on a gold chain, the kind of glasses a university don with designer pretensions might choose, all tortoiseshell and gilt.

Like most of the big stars Anupam has that highly sought-after 'wheatish' complexion, a soft shade of caramel. And in the middle of it all sits the standardized Indian moustache, underlining his long nose and riding his slightly down-turned mouth. He is attractive, though not conventionally good-looking.

'Now what can I tell you?' he asked, switching off his mobile phone, putting it on the table and sliding his glasses down his nose. But as soon as he had settled he was up again. Someone waved from across the room. Anupam waved back and got up to go and meet the older man, a tall, good-looking figure with sad stooped shoulders. His face was familiar.

As he got up Anupam switched his mobile back on and put it in my hand, much as you might give a toy to a child when it is starting to whine. A smiley face appeared on the screen as the phone came to life and then it melted back into the liquid crystal and was replaced by a message: 'Life is beautiful'. Anupam looked back briefly over his shoulder at exactly the moment the words appeared.

I obediently wrote in my notebook that Anupam Kher's mobile phone comes on with the words 'Life is beautiful'. Then I crossed the words out. Every interview I had read about him had made some reference to the cuteness of the message on his mobile phone. Ha, not me.

Anupam came back and sat down.

'You know who that was?' he asked.

'He looks very familiar.'

'Not the thing you say to an actor.' He peered at me over his glasses. 'We are all very vain and do not want to be confused with anyone else. Good idea not to forget that.' But he was smiling as he said it. 'What are the lovers down there up to now?'

It was the first time he had looked directly at me. I looked over my shoulder quickly and down into the lobby. Yet again I was blushing and I could feel him watching me and smiling. I blushed more.

The girl in black had gone. The man was still on the sofa talking on his phone. He looked like a man talking to a woman, or rather a man talking a woman into something.

'She's gone and he's on the make again,' I said, my back still turned.

'I am sorry, I did not quite catch that.' He leant closer.

I took a deep breath and turned back to face him.

'You are all pink, oh how lovely, how pretty.'

I flushed a deeper, darker red and fanned my face. 'It's rather hot in here.'

'Perhaps you could take off your shawl.'

Now he really was flirting.

'So who was the gentleman you were talking to?' I asked.

'Oh *yaar*, of course.' He was laughing.

At me.

'It was Sunil Dutt, Sanjay Dutt's father. He's been an actor, a director and an MP, but the thing that's making him look old is the worry on his son's account. Not a good story. Where is that cheese sandwich? I really am about to starve.' He waved at one of the waiters who was beside us immediately, bending low. The waiter was chastised and dispatched, and Anupam's eyes began to roam again.

I gave in to the obvious. 'Why do you have "Life is beautiful" on your telephone?'

'Because it is.' He was waving at someone else down in the lobby.

'It's the name of an Italian film,' I said, trying to get his attention.

'I know, such a beautiful film. I hope to get some of that into my new film.'

'Is it set in a concentration camp?' I was trying to get away from the formulaic *filmi* magazine interview.

He focused again. 'No, it's about a family.'

'So was *Life is Beautiful*.'

Anupam laughed. 'Okay, so you have my full attention. I see I am going to learn from you. What is the lesson?'

I probably blushed again but by now I was past caring.

'Was directing part of the plan?'

'I have not planned anything in life. I remember reading this line: "If you want God to laugh, tell him your plans".' Anupam laughed too.

I had read that in another interview of his. I was about to say so but then I stopped. Anupam had made 275 films and he must have given at least 5,000 interviews during his professional career. He had the right to tell the same story a few times.

He was looking at me.

'What happened?' His highly arched eyebrows arched up even more.

'Nothing.' I smiled.

'So you are going to be nice to me?'

I shrugged.

'I knew you would be. I liked your voice on the telephone. I do not have the time to talk to just anyone. I knew you would be as you are. Now, how can I help? Who have you seen so far and where is my sandwich?' He waved at another waiter who rushed away immediately in pursuit of the sandwich.

'I haven't come for help but I did want to meet you because you buck most of the trends here.'

I listed the good, the bad and the glittery, everyone I had met, and I told him of my attempts to meet Hrithik. The sandwich arrived. The waiter dropped the chips into Anupam's lap. Anupam was annoyed. This time it was the waiter who blushed. The chips were delicately picked out of Anupam's crotch. Everyone was embarrassed except the man with the chips in his lap. He was just hungry and irritated.

Then he turned the charm back on and let fall quite casually that he could arrange a meeting with Hrithik. No problem. Anupam Kher had me round his little finger.

He bit into the sandwich and smiled, then he looked straight at me again.

'Next?' He ate quickly and carefully brushed his moustache

212

after each mouthful. He kept missing a tiny dab of ketchup. I wanted to reach out and wipe it off.

'Do you think Hrithik will survive?'

Anupam looked up from his sandwich in surprise. 'What, you think he is going to be shot too?' He swallowed his mouthful.

'No, no, I mean do you think he has the staying power to outlast the hype?'

He lost interest even as I was asking the question. He was looking around for a waiter, looking around to see if the other people around us were watching. He pushed the plate away from him.

'No more, enough of that or I will get fat. Do you think I am fat?'

'You look much slimmer than you do on film but then that is the same with everyone, we're all shorter and slimmer in the flesh.'

'Am I not so tall as you thought?'

I did not have to answer. He was waving at the waiters to remove the remaining chips. He called out in Hindi to them. He wanted his cigarettes from his car. He told them to go down to the car park and get his cigarettes from his driver. His phone rang. He picked it up and started to talk. It was a long conversation. I drew flowers all around the edge of the things I had been writing in my notebook. I added leaves to the stalks of the flowers. Then I drew bees buzzing about the flowers. And then Anupam's conversation ended.

'Now, you tell me how else I can help you. I would like to help you. I don't understand why you did not call me earlier. I could have helped you meet whoever you wanted to meet. This is my town. Where are my cigarettes?' He waved at another waiter who was then sent off in pursuit of the first one he had dispatched.

'I think I'm okay, thank you.'

'Come on, I am telling you, this is my town.' He waved at two girls who were on one of the internal landing balconies above us, watching him.

They waved back, smiling and laughing.

'Well, anything you can do to help me see Hrithik would be wonderful.' I was confused by the sudden charm offensive.

'Done.' He was beckoning to the girls above. 'Next?'

'Why have you started directing now?'

The girls above us began to run along the balcony, making for the big glass lift that would bring them down to Anupam.

The waiter returned with the cigarettes, his pursuer in tow. Both of them were out of breath and gasping apologies. Anupam waved them away, lit a cigarette, inhaled and finally relaxed back into his chair. His eyes settled on a point just beyond my ear.

'Oh, I was just cruising with the acting. I needed a challenge.'

'And you are not worried about failing?'

'My grandfather was a Kashmiri pandit, you know? He had this thing he used to say.'

The girls had made it to the lobby. They ran halfway across, clacking in heels too high to be safe at speed on the great stretch of marble. Then they got stage-fright, freezing in their tracks. Anupam waved them on. They came cautiously up the stairs and then faltered as Anupam got up, shy and wary now they were so close.

'Ladies, such a pleasure.' He held out his hands to them.

There was an awkward moment when the two girls thought he was reaching out to shake their hands and Anupam thought he was offering to sign autographs. The girls did not have pens or anything to write on. I tore two pages out of my notebook and handed them to Anupam. Irritation marched across the arch of his eyebrows. The girls were still standing in front of us. Anupam gestured to them. Embarrassed, they remained silent. Anupam coaxed them and they gave their names in breathy whispers. Anupam signed and they scuttled away.

'What was it your grandfather used to say?' I asked as Anupam watched his fans retreating in haste.

He sat down again, looking confused for a moment, and then he remembered where he had left off.

'You asked me about whether I minded if the directing did not work out.'

'In a way.'

'My grandfather used to say "Never do a thing twice".'

'So this is not your first time directing, then?'

Now I was lost. We both looked at each other blankly for a moment and then laughed.

'Not twice, no, not in that way. What he meant was, do not do a thing twice as in worrying about it and then doing it. So I am not worrying so much, I am just directing. Then we will see.' He lit another cigarette. 'You know the acting was not a challenge any more. Same roles, same lines, same expressions. I wanted to smell danger again.'

He talked about his film and invited me to go and watch the rushes of the first few weeks of shooting. He was in the process of watching them himself. He was animated and precise.

I asked him whether he felt threatened by the underworld's control of the industry and whether his film might be affected by it.

'You know everyone in this industry says they have nothing to do with the underworld. So how do they get their films made, I ask. The industry has almost stopped working now that Bharat*ji* is inside.'

He was talking about the same Bharat Shah whose recent imprisonment, resulting from his underworld connections, had pulled Sunil's film *Snip!* out of the cinemas.

'Everyone would like not to be involved in it, but they are.' He looked at me very directly and then his eyes flickered away. 'I am more than sure that everyone you have talked to has said that they have no dealings with the dons. Am I right?'

I nodded.

'Bullshit, *yaar*. Believe me, this is total, complete bullshit. We are all in this. India is half dark, half light.' He paused and inhaled. 'We all have our dark side.' He looked at me, his eyes half-closed, as he exhaled ribbons of cigarette smoke. 'What is yours?'

'I do chocolate.'

He laughed and his eyes opened up again.

'You should come with some kind of warning, you know. You are quite dangerous in this place. Honesty needs to have security guards with it. Good luck and I hope you will be safe.'

'Thank you.'

It was flattering but it was also a closing line. We walked out of the hotel together. Anupam seemed happy to do so, unconcerned that people were staring at us, watching our every move. The manager I had talked to at the front desk on the way in, when I had been just another foreign face, was now seeing me in a new light. Out on the steps at the front people steered around us, leaving more space than was really necessary, smiling at Anupam and peering quizzically at me. I was a friend of the famous. I was temporarily covered in stardust.

Anupam's car appeared almost as soon as we did but he did not go straight down to it. Instead he waited with me.

'You know that woman I was asking you about while we were inside?' He meant the girl in black on the tiny phone on the sofa.

'Yes.'

'You should not judge Indian women by her. That is not the usual way.'

'I am a very big fan of Indian womanhood,' I replied. 'I live here most of the time. I know it's not like that . . .' I trailed off.

'Good, I am glad. Indian women are better than this.' He smiled right into my eyes. 'You know something else?'

'About Indian women?' I asked.

'No, no, I mean the whole set-up here.' He paused for a moment. 'All the *bagwas* you hear about drugs and so forth. It really is not like that at all.' He took a deep breath and looked away over my shoulder. 'I have never worked with anyone who was taking drugs and I have worked with just about everyone.' He swung the other way to wave his driver closer, avoiding eye contact with me.

Sanjay Dutt

'But you've worked with Sanjay Dutt. He has openly admitted to taking drugs.'

My own car rolled up the slope to the hotel entrance. Anupam kissed me goodbye and set off down the steps, my question left hanging in the air.

'I really would like to see your rushes,' I called after him.

'Sure, sure, call me and we can sort out the Hrithik thing too.' He jumped into the back of his car and was on his phone again even before the car valet had shut the door. The same valet moved to open my car door without quite the *filmi*-star attention he had just shown, but he smiled deeply and richly as if he had logged me away in the file of faces to remember, somewhere between the giggling fans in teetering high heels and the women who talk into very small phones.

It was just beginning to get dark as we drove away. The lights along the shore were throwing handfuls of colour on to the water. I could see the driver watching me in the mirror. He had been with me all day and had treated me with polite indifference until now. The farewell kiss on the stairs of the Regent made me worth closer scrutiny.

As we drove in silence through pools of light I thought back to Anupam's comments about the girl in the hotel lobby and drug use in the film industry. His insistence on the purity of Indian women is borne out by hundreds of millions of women in threadbare saris who make their daily round to and from countless village wells. But there are also an increasing number of women like the one in the black dress in the lobby. Then, too, while he'd not denied the power of the underworld in Bollywood, his views on drug use among the *filmi* set were self-deluding. Class A drugs, particularly cocaine, are the latest toy in a burgeoning industry that is putting increasing pressure on its players to perform beyond the working hours of the day, to sparkle from dawn through to the late party hours. The white powder has become the latest little friend of many a young star trying to carry on through to sunrise. Nor does Bollywood now have room for the plump stars who once filled the screen in every sense. The star system that used to run on *desi khana* and plenty of *ghee* now pushes vulnerable stars towards the heavenly sand, the fairy dust of the twilight dealers. Thin is in, and cocaine suppresses appetites that were brought up on too many square meals a day.

Bollywood needs to believe its own dreams. It ignores the increasing numbers of women now playing the same extramarital games that the men of India have always played, and it continues to turn a blind eye to the drug-pushers who make late-night visits to *filmi* apartment buildings to peddle fairy dust. The fantasy formula blurs all the lines, just as the cameraman greases the lens. In Bollywood the world is seen in soft focus.

Severin was in no mood for philosophizing. The afternoon after my meeting with Anupam she was flapping over her tea-making ritual. Water was splashed into the pan and *chai* was spilt. She sighed over the shortage of milk in the fridge and grumbled that this was the second time I had asked for tea that day. As she added spoon after spoon of sugar to the mix and listed my tea-drinking crimes, it was clear that she was not remotely interested in my attempts to separate fantasy from fact in Bollywood.

'Do you think your son models himself on any of the film stars?' I asked.

'He is thirteen years old and is weighing less than thirty kilos. Who is he like in Bollywood? He is so small, what can I do?' She waved the tea-strainer at me.

'I am sure he will grow and put on weight. The big spurt usually seems to be around fourteen or fifteen. Surely he must have some *filmi* heroes?' I passed her a cup to fend off the menace of the tea-strainer.

'For what are you asking this and what is this big spurt?' Severin looked at me suspiciously, the tea-strainer still held aloft.

'The fast-growing stage, you know, when teenage boys suddenly shoot up and become all arms and legs.'

'Arms and legs?' Severin looked at me wide-eyed in horror.

'It's just a way of saying that the limbs seem to be so long when they are growing quickly. And I was asking about heroes because I'm trying to work out who appeals to someone of his age.'

The tea-strainer was lowered and put to work. Severin presented me with my tea.

'I could ask him myself if you're not sure,' I suggested.

Severin pulled the proffered cup back.

'This thing you are not doing. You will be putting bad thoughts in his head. I will tell you, I will think.' She held the tea out to me once more.

'Why do you think it would put bad ideas in his head?' Tea in hand, I retreated across the kitchen to the relative safety of the ironing corner. It is not Severin's favourite spot because it is where very large cockroaches come out to play. Severin hates cockroaches and she hates the fact that they do not seem to worry me even more.

'These people, they are taking drugs and what all. You know they have not respect for their Mummy/Daddy and families, they have no faith in God.' She crossed herself. 'They have no care for any of the commandments.' She crossed herself again.

'But they're not Christians,' I pointed out.

'See, this is thing, not Christians, they cannot be such good people.' Severin glared at me in bug corner. It was always hard to get her away from her saints and sensibilities.

'I do not want him thinking of these people.'

'What about you, Severin, who do you like?'

'Oh Sanjay Dutt, always him.' The name popped out before she had time to think. Severin had taken a shine to the lush-living, dope-smoking, ex-convict Sanjay.

Realizing that she'd been caught out, she stuck her head in a cupboard on urgent business while I drank my tea quietly among the cockroaches.

'You must stop all of this now,' she said as she re-emerged carrying a large bag of rice.

'Stop what?'

'All this asking of questions on these things. It is making too much tension in my head.'

'Okay.' I took my cup to the sink and a pair of very large cockroaches scuttled away. Severin hissed at them.

'Just one thing, though – you never told me what you think of Hrithik Roshan.'

Severin banged the bag of rice on the table.

'Are you going to be writing these things?' she asked.

'I think so.'

'Then I am not saying any of these things that you want me to talk on.'

With that she picked up a load of wet washing and stalked out of the kitchen, muttering to herself as she clanked the laundry bucket across the elegant collection of silk carpets in the sitting-room.

'I'm not the CIA, Severin,' I called after her. 'I was simply asking whether you thought he was cute.'

The front door banged as I finished. The coast was clear for me to make a call without Severin listening in.

It was late February. Rakesh Roshan had told me that I could try and get hold of Hrithik in February. I called. The reception police at Film Kraft were on form.

'Mr Rakesh Roshan is out of station.'

'Could I speak to Mr Ashok then, please?'

'He too is out of station.'

'So Hrithik Roshan must also be out of station?' I asked.

'Yes.'

'I was told to call back now.'

'Call back next week.'

Next week was going to be March. I would have been trying to get hold of Hrithik for a year.

Anupam had asked me to call him to see the rushes. He had also said that he was going to call Hrithik. His message service was on when I rang. He had asked me for a few film contacts in London and Australia so I left them on his answerphone with my numbers. I called again later and once more I listened to the answerphone. I noticed Severin smiling as she walked past. It was not the most generous of expressions. I flared my nostrils at her, and she pursed her lips right back at me.

Anupam did not call back that day, the day after or the day after that. On day four I left a slightly dry message saying that I hoped he'd got the information that I'd left. So ended my membership of the Anupam Kher fan club.

Every door that had been offered to me so far had opened into smoke and mirrors. Severin was right to mistrust Bollywood. The closer I came to the stars the more the stardust turned to just dust. It is the distance that creates the sparkle, the remoteness that feeds the fantasy.

A few months after my meeting with Anupam, a rising young actor was arrested for possession of cocaine. Fardeen Khan had been perceived as a nice clean boy. Some claimed that he had just been framed because his most recent film had not paid its dues to the dons. Others said that he had never got over the strain of his parents' divorce when he was thirteen – his cocaine abuse was understandable. Since the young actor had a sixteen-year history of drug use, that was quite a lot of strain.

Someone else pointed out that if every child of divorced parents became a cocaine addict then the net annual profit from global cocaine sales would be greater than the combined defence budgets of Europe, America and Asia. Whether China was included in this wild equation was not specified.

The star himself shrugged off his confinement in a cell after his arrest: 'I slept in a dormitory for four years while studying at Massachusetts University in the US. I'm not a softie. It was just more of the same.'

Even so he cried when his father, another Bollywood star of the older generation, came to see him in prison, and he made up the shooting days lost within a month of the incident. Fardeen was offered more film parts directly after his arrest than at any other time in his career. 'I understand now that I cannot take things for

Fardeen Khan

granted, my work, the law, my family, my everyday life or the people I love,' he told the press as he signed up for a string of post-arrest film offers. Two of the films were to co-star Anupam Kher. Though future interviews with Fardeen would undoubtedly refer back to the drug bust, his arrest seemed more of an advertisement for coke with a small 'c' than a warning to other users in the industry.

The young and ambitious talked about the post-arrest rise of Fardeen's star in breathy voices. Cocaine abuse was said to be on the increase.

*

'It's all just about selling sex without showing any tongues or nipples,' said the young man next to me, as he looked into his long, thin glass of beer. 'When you really look at all those dance scenes closely and break them down they are just constant sex, bang, bang, bang, all the way through.'

I was back in Bar Indigo – white-hot Mumbai-Bombay, right back in the place where I had first seen Hrithik Roshan almost exactly a year before, standing at the top of the steps, stunned by his instant fame, unsure how to make his entrance.

I had come full circle. I was full of information and I had been down a lot of blind alleys but I was still no closer to Hrithik. I'd had my *wadas* eaten by a magazine queen with spiky heels and a matching tongue. I'd swapped *filmi* moments with the girls from Milton Keynes outside the Millennium Dome. I'd watched a dildo being used to stir soup by a fat man in an afro wig. I had been to graveyards and cocktail parties, I'd thumbed a thousand *filmi* magazines, I'd drunk tea with a prostitute in Kamathipura, I'd tried *bhangra* free dance with a sulky young Parsi, and I had come close to a new and exciting phase in my life at La Belle. The young man beside me at the bar was yet another avenue.

Raf was a director's assistant and he had the kind of industry lineage that made the girl on the next-door stool at the bar quiver. He had also just been working with Hrithik. The girl beside us had been crossing and uncrossing her long, thin legs and trying to get Raf's attention. She had also asked him for a light, twice, and she was listening to our conversation with so much attention that he was going to have to notice her at some point. However, she had two disadvantages. Raf had his back to her and Raf had a boyfriend.

He had told me in the car on the way to Colaba, just before the turning to First Pasta Lane where Mrs Nirmal's husband's *bhelpuri* cart stands under a rain tree. We had been talking about a couple of stars and he'd laughed when I'd referred to their quick-fire succession of girlfriends, a new one for each month's edition of the *filmi* mags.

'Why are you laughing?'

'Because they're both gay. That's why they change companions as fast as those bloody little magazine parasites take the bait of the latest glamorous co-star plant hanging off their arm.'

'How do you know?'

'Because I am too. Takes one to know one. In case you hadn't noticed, homosexuality does not apparently exist in India.'

Raf was right. In my thirteen years in India only one other person I knew had openly admitted to being gay.

'I know. I'm still waiting for the first government AIDS awareness campaign to mention the phrase "homosexual activity" in passing.'

Raf laughed.

'And why are you so open about it?' I asked.

'I went to grad school in the States, and so I got over the whole thing. You know, Mummy's precious little man who is going to father a thousand sons. I had boyfriends all through my time in the US.' He looked so happy as he talked, his smooth face cracking with pleasure. 'When the first guy hit on me at school it was like, oh, I don't think I can even find the right word.' His hand hammered excitedly on the steering-wheel. 'Like, like . . .' He started to hum an old Queen song, 'I Want to Break Free'. 'That was what it had felt like until I got to the States, just one big jail sentence, all my life until that guy hit on me.'

'Oh, how I want to be free.' We had belted out the chorus into the traffic around us. People wound up their windows and stared at us from behind the safety of glass.

'Farrokh Bulsara, the singing Parsi queen from Zanzibar, what a great combination,' and he rewound Freddie Mercury again.

225

Raf's skin was Indian but his vocabulary and his sex life were American. He was boy bait of the highest calibre, beautiful to look at but not too beautiful to be taken seriously. When he laughed he managed to make it sound as if he was having sex at the same time. It was impossible not to laugh with him.

As we drew up to the kerb in front of Bar Indigo, Raf waved the parking valet over imperiously, but then he thanked the uniformed man so profusely that the valet climbed into the driving-seat of the jeep with an expression of total bewilderment on his face.

Just outside the pool of light that spilled out of Bar Indigo on to Battery Road, a man sat crouched over a sheet of newspaper on which a small array of old pens and broken children's toys were laid out for sale or barter. He was squatting in a way that made his shins look longer than his thighs, the skin lying so close to the bone that every ligament and tendon was visible. His matted hair had been wound up under a deep violet-blue turban and he was staring into the middle distance, his gaze opaque and empty, his beautiful long fingers trailing through his beard. He looked part holy man, part beggar. Raf crossed the road and squatted down in the same way beside him. I do not know what he said to the raggedy man, and he did not give him any money, but the opaque veil lifted from the old man's face and he laughed loudly with Raf, the sound bouncing out into the darkness. Then Raf came back across the road and took my hand, leading me up the steps and into the bar as if he had known me all his life. He said nothing about the raggedy man but laughed instead at the crush of people at the front of Bar Indigo, all pushing against each other, bare midriff to tight T-shirt, head to shoulder. People looked at him as he walked in and I watched them trying to work out who he was. It was like being with a movie star. When we found our place at the back of the bar, out of the front-of-house crush, the girl next to us on the bar stool thought so too, hence all her attempts to grab his attention.

Over his long, cold beer Raf warmed to his subject.

'You know you only have to watch those dances carefully and you can see the whole sex act being played out right in front of you. It's how they get around our crazy censorship and still get the guys hard and the girls hot.'

He smiled at me. He had taken in the girl on the next-door stool and her efforts to grab his attention, and the hot and hard line had been for her benefit.

'Played out metaphorically speaking?' I asked as a small girl with a beautiful diamond stud in her belly button came and stood very close to Raf, her tiny stiletto kitten heels right up against his shoes. In a bar in London or Los Angeles such toe-to-toe proximity would have been described as an invasion of space. In Bombay, body to body, it was okay. Raf smiled at her but turned back to me as she was about to try and speak to him.

'Metaphorically speaking, yes. Say you have Salman Khan doing the whole no-shirt routine, pumping up those biceps and twirling around whoever it is, let's say Aishwarya Rai.' Raf laughed his orgasmic laugh. 'No, that doesn't work, does it? They really are having sex so they don't get to be in films together. So who else? Okay, let's say Sushmita Sen, she's so fabulous at all that almost-intercourse revved-up *bhangra*. So Salman is all pumped up and running his lips up her neck each time he twirls her into his arms. Sush is giving us all that woman-in-ecstasy stuff, heavy on the curves squirming under whatever diamond-studded flimsy thing they've put her into. We get Salman giving her that big long look, then zap, cut to Sush flipping the top off a Coke bottle and all that frothy stuff bursting out all over her face. It's just fucking with a bit of clever product placement thrown in and no tongues or nipples.'

The small girl up against Raf's shoes giggled and the girl on the other side perked up.

'Why is it taking so long to get even a kiss on the screens?' I asked.

Raf was looking over my shoulder. I did not turn around. I had seen the barman when we arrived. He was all angles, symmetry and cat-like eyes.

The small girl parked beside Raf's shoes had stopped giggling. She was obviously trying to work out why Raf would possibly want to hang out with something as old and pale as me. I gave her that 'I'm not really with him, we're just friends' smile and she moved away. I had obviously done drunk and sad, rather than knowing and sophisticated.

'What was that about kissing?' Raf was back from his short exchange with the sculpted barman.

'Oh, the censorship thing and why it's taking so long to get proper snogging into a script.'

Raf's laugh popped along the bar, all the way down to the beautiful boy who was playing around with ice at the other end. Angles and Symmetry looked up towards the ripple of erotica bubbling his way. Another electric charge passed up and down the polished wood and around the thin glasses of icy, smoking beer. I felt I was in the way. Then Raf smiled at me again.

'There have been a couple of big-screen kisses.' He paused, looking closely at me. 'You know that is the first time you have sounded really *desi farangi*, really foreign. "Snogging" is so cucumber sandwiches, so Ascot.'

I blushed. It was becoming my Bollywood habit.

'You must have heard about all that fuss over Madhuri Dixit in her *choli*.'

'I know but there weren't any tongues. It wasn't snogging,' I replied.

Raf laughed again. 'I guess we have yet to have our first fully fledged snog, as you would call it.' Then he thought for a moment. 'We've had quite a lot of shots from behind, you know, so that they are head to head and you just get the impression that they are in a big clinch.'

'It's got to be tongues for it to be the real McCoy,' I insisted.

'It won't happen for a while. We still have a censorship law drawn up in the Seventies. Everyone was so scared of the dreadful Mrs Gandhi. Snogging just wasn't patriotic. Imagine what it would have done to the moral fibre of *Mera Bharat Mahan*, My Great India, if kissing with tongues had been permitted when we were not even allowed out on the streets after dark.'

Raf was referring to the crippling months of Mrs Gandhi's Emergency from June 1975 to March 1977, a period in India's recent history that left sores that still fester.

As he talked Raf's mood changed. In anger his face simply lost all expression. It was no longer beautiful, just an arrangement of smooth skin over bones.

'How old are you?' I asked.

'Twenty-eight,' he replied.

'So you were only two when the Emergency started. What are you so angry about?'

'Isn't the whole of India?' he said, and the skin on his bones became lovely again as he smiled.

'But you don't really think Mrs Gandhi is single-handedly responsible for the fact that there is still no kissing with tongues in Bollywood, do you?'

Raf shrugged but his expression was serious again. 'You know the thing about this industry here? It's about stars, not actors. An actor is a professional who does a job. A star is someone who is trying to find adoration because they have a warped view of love and have this uncontrollable need to overdose.' He looked at me for a moment, still serious, and then the skin around his eyes crumpled back into laughter. 'A therapist in New York told me that. That's a pretty expensive definition, about $5,000 for that moment of truth. I don't know about your parents fucking you up but Bollywood certainly does.' His laughter was tumbling about us again and the barman was smiling.

The girl sitting beside us had given up. Raf had not responded to her legs in motion, and I was clearly not worth talking to. She

collected her drink from the bar and looked over our shoulders to
see what lay beyond.

'Do you think Hrithik would do a screen kiss, a proper one,
really full on, tongues, the lot?' I asked Raf.

'Tongues, the lot?'

'Yup, with tongues.'

The girl moving away from the bar slid right back up on to her
stool and the barman leant forward.

Raf was laughing again. It began in the usual erogenous bubble
and then it exploded out all around us, bouncing over the crush
of the crowd. He paused to breathe.

'Why is that so funny?'

'I'm not really sure but I just got this image in my mind of sitting
in Hollywood having the same conversation with oh, I don't
know, Brad Pitt, say. "Mr Pitt, do you kiss with or without
tongues?" "I'm not at liberty to answer that question, Raf."' He
gave a lovely little sketch of himself and Brad doing boy's talk.
The barman and I clapped. 'I just have times when the whole
shtick of the industry becomes too absurd for me to do anything
except laugh.' He looked back into his long, cold beer. 'You should
ask Hrithik yourself. It would be interesting to see what he says.
My take is that he won't be the first one to do it. Just wouldn't
really fit the newly married, Mr Clean image.' Raf looked straight
at me with those big barman-melting eyes. 'You are going to meet
him, aren't you?'

'Sure.'

Sure I was going to meet him.

CHAPTER 10

Happy Ever After?

The End

'CHOPPED RIGHT OFF. And so much of blood everywhere as only to be imagined in fearful dreams. Can you envisage this much of blood?' The juice-*wallah* crashed his great cutting blade through a raw beetroot. Half of the beetroot fell into the road and we both watched it settle next to a monsoon drain. One of the juice-*wallah*'s dreamy-eyed regulars saw it as well.

'Have it, *mataji*.' The juice-*wallah* waved his blade at the cow.

'But what was cut off?' I asked.

'His head, bloody hell, his whole head!'

The accident had happened several months before, while Aishwarya Rai had been making her latest film, *Devdas, The Slave of God*.

It was just an average filming day. A cast of hundreds of dancers were done up in their spangly best and were ready to roll. Almost as many technicians were running around trying to set things up that should have been set up already. A lot of people were telling other people what to do, a lot of people were sitting around drinking tea, and a few people were throwing tantrums.

Aishwarya Rai was being given her final steps by the choreographer. Everything was nearly ready. Since this was to be a big dance number, it naturally required large amounts of artificial rain. The lovely Ash and her dancers needed wet, clinging saris.

While the dancers got into position two huge storm fans, each ten feet by twelve, were rolled on to the set, hoisted up on wooden stands and switched on. As the giant fans began to turn and the artificial rain began to fall, one of the wooden stands collapsed. The two technicians manning the fans were sucked into the blades. One was beheaded, the other seriously injured, and Ash and the dancers were splattered in blood. A subsequent report of the accident stated that the set suddenly became 'a gruesome scene of carnage, confusion and hysteria with loud shocked screams reverberating to the ceiling, blood everywhere and people running helter-skelter'.

But it was not the accident that disgusted the juice-*wallah*.

'Accidents are happening each and every day to every person. Allah gives and Allah takes back.' The juice-*wallah* rarely spoke of his god. That he did so now meant that I was in for some high-grade moralizing.

'You know the thing that is the most shaming of all?' He waved his great blade at me.

I shook my head.

'These bloody bastard people, only thing they are interested in is how is big star in all of this.' He took the remaining half of the beetroot and dropped it in the grinder. Some juice splattered on to my arm and I winced.

'In paper all big lines are only about poor big star having all of blood on her person, and how big brave Salman boyfriend was oh, so lucky to be on set seeing his lady love that he could be so much of help and support to her at this most terrible time.'

The coverage in one of the *filmi* magazines had made much of Salman Khan's presence on the set at the time of the accident:

He was 'a pillar of strength and support', Ash later confided to friends and colleagues. Ash was won over by her man all over again when Salman rose to the need of the hour, and did all he could, during the time of dire need and dreadful crisis, to be of assistance. He used his celebrity status and star-power to cut through red tape and get the second worker to Nanavati Hospital, plus he dealt with the police with great charm and grace.

'And what of family of dead and stricken persons? This I ask. It is my belief that this is what all of India asks.' The juice-*wallah* dropped his head dramatically into his hands until he realized that he was getting beetroot juice all over himself. His towel was in its usual spot beside the grinder. He grabbed it and dabbed at his face and hair.

'What importance is it having to my life as to what Rai is thinking and feeling when she is covered in blood of dead and dying persons?' He shook the towel, now stained red, at me.

'What happens to Mummy/Daddy of dead boy now when Rai is on to next big *filmi* party, and perhaps not even remembering name of their son whose blood was all over her?'

Ash and the rest of the cast had been seen visiting the surviving technician at Nanavati Hospital. Their visit was referred to in *filmi* parlance as 'a touching sidelight in the dark tragedy'. All the reports assured the public that the film's production company would pick up the hospital bills for the young man. He had a fractured skull, a broken jaw and deep lacerations all over his body. Shortly after the accident the producer of the film was arrested for negligence and taken to the police station. He was then immediately released. It had just been a formality. The director of the film held a *graha-shanti pooja*, a large Hindu prayer ceremony, a few days later on the set. No shooting days were lost. It was unclear whether any support was offered to the family of the dead technician. As a title, *Slave of God* seemed apposite.

There is no union that protects technicians. As individuals they are not insured on the sets where they work and they seldom start out with any formal training – they simply learn on the job. Nor is there any recognized set of safety standards. India's film industry has more fatal and disabling accidents each year than that of any other country.

The juice-*wallah* had lost patience with the cow. He picked up the split root vegetable and bowled it at her, the cleft to the cloven.

'Bloody good spin, *yaar*?' He smiled and wiped his hands on the towel again.

The cow eyed the beetroot and then ambled off up the road. The juice-*wallah* shrugged and refolded his towel. The lightness fell away.

'No one has this right to play God with persons. No one has this right. Who is this Bollywood? They think they are God?'

He picked up his large blade and started on a carrot.

'They think it is all okey-dokey because it was not big star who ended up like . . .' He hacked the carrot to pieces. 'They think it is okey-dokey to do things that make lovely dancing lady end up in filthy place living as if she is a dog.'

The juice-*wallah* had not spoken of Madam Deepa for a long time, not since he had asked me whether I had found her after my visit to Falkland Road, but his anger was fuelled by Madam Deepa's fall from the celluloid heights. He was an ex-movie fan, a broken-hearted *filmi* lover.

A customer came to the juice stand. He was a small elderly man dressed in a linen suit, a solar *topi* and a pristine pair of lace-up canvas Oxfords. He was leading a Yorkshire terrier, the dog as trim as his master. He looked like a Parsi of the old school, a sartorial anachronism in canvas and linen. He asked for a small glass of carrot and spinach juice, and he and his dog waited patiently while the juice-*wallah* went to work. There was a short conversation about the weather warming up. The juice-*wallah* mopped himself down again after handing over the glass of juice. The Parsi stood cool and contained under his solar *topi*. The juice-*wallah* introduced me.

'This is Mr Taraporewala. He is one of my most regular customers.'

Mr Taraporewala shook my hand. 'Every day for fifteen years I have been coming for carrot and spinach juice. Seven days a week. Is this not so?' He paused with a finger to his lips. 'No, I must correct that error. I have missed two weeks in that time. The week when my fine lady wife was taken from me, and then last year when poor Johnny had terrible canine flu.'

Mr Taraporewala's English was pure and softly spoken, bringing back memories of BBC radio plays filtering up the stairs during enforced childhood afternoon rests.

'And what is it that keeps you in this dirty city of ours?'

'I'm chasing a Bollywood star.'

'A very dangerous occupation,' said Mr Taraporewala.

'*Acchha*, I am telling her of the badness of this Bollywood on a daily basis,' said the juice-*wallah* with a wag of his head.

Mr Taraporewala drank his juice, then pulled a handkerchief from his top pocket, dabbed lightly at his mouth and returned the still unmarked handkerchief to its pocket.

'My dear young lady, I would not even presume to warn you against the dangers of chasing a movie star. I myself can see the attractions of that occupation, and I can also imagine some success for someone as pretty as your good self.' He patted my hand and I felt blessed. 'But it must not be forgotten by any of us that these are people who have very little regard for their fellow humanity. They are cruel people, but it is we who have made them this way. We put them up on such high pedestals that it is impossible for them to see any longer what life is like for us down here.'

The juice-*wallah* nodded along with enthusiastic approval. Mr Taraporewala handed over a five-rupee coin for his juice, thanked the juice-*wallah* for his good services and then turned back to me.

'I wish you every success in your pursuit, but I must add that it gives me the gravest of concerns. You are moving in a pit of vipers.' He patted my hand again. 'But perhaps I see in you a bit of the snake-charmer.'

Mr Taraporewala smiled and pulled the front of his jacket

straight to smooth away any creases caused by the consumption of one small glass of juice. He looked down to check that Johnny was ready to go and they set off. Then he stopped and turned back.

'You ask your film star when you catch him if he would have started at all if he had known what it really was going to be like high up on the pedestal.'

'I will.'

Mr Taraporewala waved, and Johnny and he walked on.

'Very fine man,' the juice-*wallah* said as the pair strolled away, neat and erect. 'His family are from among main Parsi families of our city. They were making the fish house on Marine Drive. Very good family.'

The Taraporewala Aquarium near Chowpatty Beach was once a source of pride but now it has an air of neglect, its dank rooms displaying only a motley collection of fish and shells. Even so, it is a tribute to the impartiality of the Parsis, for among the exhibits are a Quran fish, believed to have verses of the great book upon its tail, and a Christ crab with the sign of the cross on its shell.

I asked the juice-*wallah* whether he had seen the Quran fish but he chose not to hear the question.

'His good lady was very fine woman.'

'Did you meet her?' I asked.

'No, no, not suitable for such a lady to be walking about like *Sahib*.'

'So how do you know she was a fine lady then?' I asked.

'*Sahib* was not on such good terms with his family for taking her for his wife,' he explained, flicking some flecks of mould off a carrot with his thumbnail. 'She was not Parsi lady.'

'So he married outside his religion. That was brave. Where was she from?'

'She was actress, very lovely actress. You could not believe her eyes, so huge, so dark. I have many, many memories of those great huge pools of eyes. You will know her picture if you see it, you cannot make a mistake on those eyes. She was in oh so many films, I am thinking it was around time not so long from Partition. I was not more than small boy.' The juice-*wallah* tilted his head and he was suddenly young again, gazing up at the big silver screen of his childhood. 'It was very big love marriage and all kinds of drama, drama.'

It would have been. The Parsis of Bombay seldom marry outside their community.

'He is wise man on *filmi* matters. You must take great notice of his words. And it is important that you ask his question to Mr Hrithik Roshan when you see him. You can ask this from my side also. I would be most interested to hear the answer to this question.' Then the juice-*wallah* turned his attention back to his great Sunbrite Grinder of Calcutta.

Mr Taraporewala and the juice-*wallah* wanted me to ask the biggest star of the day if he regretted his meteoric rise to stardom. The shop manager in Udaipur wanted me to tell him how important he was to his audience. All the ladies from La Belle beauty salon wanted me to tell him that they thought he was the most beautiful man in the world but that they were worried he was getting too thin. In addition Dolly wanted me to ask him for some diet tips that might help her wafer-thin daughter put on weight. Pinky Ali, the dancing queen, wanted me to tell him that he danced like Gene Kelly and, in agreement with the ladies of La Belle, that he should eat more. And I wanted to know whether he would kiss with tongues.

It was now the very end of February. A week had passed since I had last called and been told to call back in a week.

It was the usual late afternoon at Carmichael Road. Severin was shouting at somebody about something, and the last of the hot sun was still pushing through the trees and throwing patches of light on the balcony and the steps below the front door. I picked up the telephone and put it on the window ledge, then went to ask for a cup of tea. Severin was so enraged with something beyond the kitchen window that she made *chai* on automatic pilot with hardly a glance in my direction. I took my cup of tea out on to the steps just as the first early evening breeze rustled the trees, and I picked up the telephone. The guard was not outside the Belgian Consulate. It didn't really matter. The early evening was nice enough for it not to matter very much whether I spoke to anyone or not.

'Who is calling?' asked the Film Kraft police when I got through first go.

'Justine Hardy.'

Before I could even start to elaborate I was transferred.

'Hello,' said a new voice.

'Please could I speak to Rakesh Roshan?' I asked.

'Speaking.'

'Oh, hello, we spoke several months ago. I am the English writer who was trying to get hold of Hrithik, and you told me to call back in February.'

'You are late, it is almost March.'

'When I called last week your receptionists told me that you were all out of station.'

Rakesh Roshan was laughing. 'You are a very persistent lady. This is to be admired. You are lucky to catch me now. I leave for London tonight.'

As we spoke I could visualize the *filmi* director in his office. I could see him behind his big smoked-glass desk, his body sunk low in a high-backed, leather-padded swivel chair. There would be a row of telephones in front of him, all of them covered in buttons and flashing lights. There would be glass along one wall of his office, naturally in the same smoky shade as the executive desk. Beyond the glass, the reception police would be sitting in serried ranks behind their switchboards, screening, editing and evicting callers. Then I realized that from behind his big desk and his bank of phones, Rakesh Roshan was asking me something.

'Do you know anyone at Channel 4?'

I sat up. For a second I had a chance. I was no longer begging.

'Yes, I do have some contacts.'

'Do you think they would buy *Kaho Naa . . . Pyaar Hai*? You know it really has been such a very huge success here. I think it should be seen in UK. You have seen this movie?'

Kaho Naa . . . Pyaar Hai, Hrithik's first film, the big one, the rocket-launcher. How could I not have seen it?

'You enjoyed this movie?'

'Very, very much.'

'You think it would be a hit in UK?'

To my left Severin was trying to evict a small cat that had been straining behind one of the flower pots that lined the steps. She had got some of what the cat had shat on her sandal. She was squawking.

'What is this noise?' Rakesh Roshan asked.

'A cat.'

'Oh.' He seemed satisfied.

'The Non-Resident Indian community will love it. Everyone wants to see Hrithik and what he is doing. Why have you picked Channel 4?' I asked.

Severin was now beside me on the step, her sandal in one hand, the garden hose in the other. She dropped the hose among the flower pots and went to turn on the water. It was one of those rare days when the pressure was high. The hose writhed and then shot into action, leaping off the step, dousing the sandal and firing water straight into my face.

'Shit!' I shouted.

'What?' exclaimed Rakesh Roshan.

'I was asking why you had picked Channel 4.' I glared at Severin.

'I have been told that Channel 4 has a good affection for Indian material. Is this the case?'

'Yes. I'll try and get a contact name for you. When do you leave for London?' I asked.

'Tonight.'

'Oh.'

Severin was halfheartedly trying to regain control of the thrashing hose. Another jet of water hit me smack in the face.

'Is it raining on your side?' Rakesh Roshan asked.

'No, our garden hose is a little out of control.' I gathered up the phone and marched inside, leaving Severin hosing down her sandal with a beneficent smile on her face.

'Can you call me again with the contact's number? I will be speaking with Hrithik after some time and I will fix up something. So you will call me back?'

'I will, as soon as possible.'

'Good.'

The line went dead. I stood with the receiver in my hand for a few moments, waiting for my heart to slow down. Out on the steps Severin was still hosing with relish, her smile a little more demonic now. I looked again. She had pinned the bewildered cat in a corner and was water-gunning it. I chose not to interfere. Severin was in a mean mood.

I was out on Peddar Road buying tuberoses to sweeten Severin and the sitting-room when my Channel 4 contact called me back. It was six-thirty. Rakesh Roshan was leaving for the airport at seven. With no time to get back to Carmichael Road, I looked around for somewhere to make a quiet call away from the twilight pandemonium on the street. Beneath a huge poster of Hrithik as the hero of *Mission Kashmir*, black bandanna flying, eyes on fire, there was a low wall. I clambered up, mobile phone in hand, and started to make the call. As the line connected, a man walked up to the wall a few feet away and began to urinate.

Rakesh Roshan answered the phone straightaway and I gave him the contact.

'I hope this will work,' he said. 'Call Ashok*ji*, Hrithik's assistant, in the morning. Hrithik will find time for you.'

'Thank you, and good luck with Channel 4.'

'They will love this film. I am sure on this.'

And he was gone.

The man beside me was still urinating. The wall was a regular haunt for those needing to pee, and it stank. I buried my face in the tuberoses and walked away.

Ashok*ji* seemed a new man when I managed to get him the next morning, though he was still not quite the charm-school model.

'Tomorrow afternoon you will go to Madland,' he instructed.

'Madland? Is that part of Film City?' I asked.

It sounded so appropriate.

'No, listen to what I am saying, Mad Island.'

'Where is that?'

'Not so far from Film City. You tell your driver. He can find this. Take road and you come to Beach House. This is where filming is. You say what is your name and you meet Hrithik.'

'Just Beach House, no other details?'

'Yes, and no camera, you must not have camera.'

'Okay, no camera, thank you.'

And he too was gone.

Severin was in a gentler mood. Her sister was coming over to Carmichael Road, and bringing her daughter with her. It would be a family day of endless *gup marna*, endless gossip, and a day of endless eating.

Severin was wearing a turquoise *salwar kameez* for the occasion. A frangipani flower was tucked into her coconut oil-slicked bun, and she had a fresh *bindi* mark of blood-red *sindoor* powder perfectly placed between her fine eyebrows. Severin wears the Hindu marriage mark on her forehead despite her love for the Madonna and her celestial pantechnicon of saints. Whoever she prays to Severin is still an Indian woman, and the *bindi* mark is the badge of traditional womanhood, saints or no saints. She looked soft and pretty and not at all the feline bully of the previous day.

I hovered in the kitchen doorway. Already there was a stack of *chapatis* several inches high on a plate beside the stove and now Severin was brewing up *masala* prawns, her signature dish. Chillies were frying and the acrid fumes made me choke.

'Where is Mad Island?' I asked her with my hand over my mouth.

'Mad Island, what is this?'

'It's quite near Film City, so I guess it's out beyond Andheri somewhere.'

'Oh, this is Madh Island.' She pronounced it Mud Island. 'It is very far.'

'How far?'

'Maybe two plus hours, maybe three, time of day depending.' She popped another small handful of chillies into the pan and smiled as I retreated, coughing, into the hallway.

'You like my *masala* prawns? You must try some, it is ready soon. You want *chai*?'

'*Chai* would be nice,' I called as I retreated further.

'*Chai* coming,' she called sweetly after me.

I stood in the sitting-room and pondered. Two things were troubling me. I had somewhat casual directions to Madh Island, and Severin's niceness was unnerving me. I still had the image of the cat spread-eagled under her water-cannon in my mind.

I was working out the distance to Madh Island on a bad map when she came in with the *chai*. It was a perfect cup, sweet, rich and laced with cardamom, ginger, cloves and black pepper. I thanked her, but instead of heading back to the kitchen she stood watching me. She was thinking.

'This day you are really to have meeting with Hrithik Roshan?' she asked, one of her eyebrows rising in disbelief.

'Yes, Severin, I really am going to meet him today.' I could not help sounding triumphant. 'This is such good *chai*, thank you.' I attempted to sound more humble.

'And what are you wearing?' Severin asked.

'What do you mean?'

'What are you to wear for meeting with Hrithik Roshan, biggest *filmi* star?'

'I'm going like this.'

'Oh my God, what is this? You are meeting biggest *filmi* star outside of Amitabh and you are going dressed as man?' Severin clutched the sides of her head.

I knew what was going to come next.

'Too much of tension, this is too much of tension for me. What is he to think of this?'

Severin was all dressed up for her sister and niece with a flower in her hair. I was all dressed down to see Hrithik in a pink T-shirt and army fatigue trousers. I was also wearing my favourite beaded flip-flops. I thought I looked fine, but Severin did not.

'This is what they all wear,' I assured her. 'Hrithik wears combat trousers in every other photograph you see. This is very Bollywood, very now.'

'But he is man,' said Severin, her brows knitted in gender confusion.

'Severin, this will be fine.'

'More *chai*?' she asked, still looking worried.

'That would be lovely.'

She bumbled back into the kitchen and the *masala* fog.

I had dreamt about Hrithik the night before. It had been a charmingly romantic thing in which we had been starring opposite one another in a schlockbuster. I had been trussed up in a fantastic sari, and we had done a great dance number together through trees, across hillsides and over streams. Naturally there had been an unexpected rain shower that made my sari cling to every curve. Hrithik had been there doing his thing, dancing like Gene Kelly with a tan, twirling me through the trees and across the streams. When we finished the number, apparently in a single take, as can only happen in the world of upgrade dreams, the crew applauded.

The final dream sequence had been Hrithik and me drinking fresh lime sodas in a downtown Parsi café, talking about buying a beach house. I had woken up feeling happy. Then I had a sudden panic attack and rang a good friend in Bangalore who is a psychiatrist. Was my dream an early sign of Clérambault's Syndrome? Was I becoming obsessed to the point of believing that I was actually having an erotic relationship with Hrithik? I worry about erotomania. My friend told me that I was over-reacting and that I had obviously been reading too many dark edgy novels. I said it had never happened to me before, and I had interviewed loads of famous people. He pointed out that the dream was hardly surprising. I had spent a year trying to interview Hrithik and the idea had simply become a subconscious desire. But he warned me not to let my subconscious dictate my dress sense. I paused for a moment. Okay, that meant no black, his favourite colour, no Ferrero Rocher chocolates ready to whip out of my bag, and definitely no pizza. I just caught myself before the daydream got out of control and then told my friend that I thought he was taking his psychiatry too seriously.

Severin might not have approved of my outfit but I was wearing it on doctor's advice. Even so, it annoyed me that I had passed over a flippy summer dress in the cupboard in favour of faintly butch trousers and a slightly less butch T-shirt.

Severin came back with a second cup of *chai* and gave it to me with another generous smile.

'You are really sure you will be meeting with him?'

'I hope so.'

'Will you have him sign this to my boy?' She produced an Easter card of some daffodils surrounding a crucifix, a little painted Easter egg nestling at its foot and a bunny rabbit peeking around the side.

244

My heart sank. I already had young Mira's T-shirt for Hrithik to sign. Now I had the Easter card too. Severin was holding it out towards me.

'Of course I will. Do you want me to get it signed to him by name?'

'No, no, this is not necessary, no name is fine,' Severin replied very quickly.

I took the card and put it in my notebook, thanked Severin for the second cup of tea, wished her a happy day with her family and reassured her that I would do my best to get Hrithik to sign the card for her son. I think she blushed. I think she thought that maybe I knew that the card was not really going to be for her son.

I had a new driver. He had a bored expression on his face and was as unimpressed by my androgynous outfit as Severin had been.

We set off in silence. He had the air-conditioning on at its highest level and it was too cold. I asked him to turn it down a bit. We were less than five minutes into the journey and already I had made a bad impression. All foreigners of any importance like to have the air-conditioning on at full throttle at all times.

We passed the Mahalaxmi Racecourse. The beggar who sits under a blanket, regardless of the temperature or time of day, was in the place where he always is, upright and tented in thick wool. Though I knew he could not see me I waved. I felt like royalty, I wanted to wave at everyone.

From the edge of the sea we rose up on to the Mahim Causeway, the great flyover that crosses Mahim Bay and the creek, the area reclaimed from the sea to make Bombay the fingered sprawl that it is, reaching out into the Arabian Sea. The city spread out around us, shimmering in the burn of the early afternoon. The driver remained silent. I watched the great *filmi* hoardings flash

Hyped to the hoarding heavens

past: Hrithik, Shah Rukh, Hrithik, Hrithik, Shah Rukh, Amitabh for a change, Shah Rukh, Hrithik, constant, omnipresent, gargantuan, hyped to the hoarding heavens.

We were forced to stop at a point equidistant between a huge Hrithik and another giant Shah Rukh. They were not *filmi* posters but the strange advertisements of Shah Rukh doing his Jacques Cousteau thing, and Hrithik by his motorbike. An over-stuffed three-wheeler had scattered its load of yellow paint cans right across the highway. Various people were wandering in and out of the sea of paint, leaving a growing trail of yellow footprints around the scene of the accident. No one of any authority had arrived. It was going to take some time.

The driver was more interested in the posters above us than in the scene of the yellow footprints.

'Do you like Hrithik or Shah Rukh more?' I asked him, attempting to break the icy silence.

'Hrithik is hero number one,' he replied, with a smile that changed the temperature in the car.

'You really like him that much?'

'No one is better, no one, not Amitabh, nothing. I am liking this man too much.' He rolled his eyes in awe at the skinny young man above us, standing next to a huge, shiny motorbike, machine and boy frozen and branded.

'That is who we are going to see today.'

The driver turned his whole body to face me.

'Bullshit, *yaar*?'

'No bullshit, we really are.'

'*Hari Om*.' He touched his ears and face in a gesture of reverential gratitude and then held out his hand over the back of the seat. 'Sanjay is my name. Very happy to meet this way.' He shook my hand vigorously.

'Thank you.'

A small boy, yellow paint all over his hands, was scuttling around the car, chasing an even smaller girl and hand-printing her raggedy blue dress whenever he got close enough. Sanjay opened the car door and yelled at the boy to stay away from the car or he would beat him. The boy laughed and stuck his hand over his face, then he laughed even louder through the yellow print he had left there. Sanjay snorted and got back in the car.

'The only thing is, if we are stuck in this for much longer I'm not sure if we will get to see Hrithik at all,' I said.

Sanjay settled himself calmly behind the wheel and reversed back through the traffic, apparently oblivious to the mayhem he was causing. I put on a pair of dark glasses and tried to behave like a star. We reached an exit point and Sanjay became a man possessed at the wheel.

'Sanjay, could we slow down a little perhaps?'

'*Hari Om.*' Sanjay slowed a little, just enough for him to turn to me again. 'Mummy saying to me this very morning that great good thing to happen this day. *Hari Om.*' Sanjay turned back to face the traffic with a smile of serene ecstasy.

'You live with your parents?' I asked, trying to move on to a less passionate topic.

'Yes, yes, Mummy/Daddy, bigger brother, his children, my children, two boys is of brother, and one boy is mine,' he told me proudly.

'No daughters?'

'We have daughters, three of them.' He was perfunctory.

'And do you have wives?'

'Yes, we have wives.' Again he was offhand.

'Good, I'm glad all your children have mothers.'

'Yes, thanking God, and thanking for this day too.' Sanjay was grinning.

'I'm not sure how much God has to do with it,' I said, more to the window than to Sanjay.

'What is this?' He turned to face me again.

I felt compelled to answer very quickly.

'It's just that I have spent quite a long time arranging this meeting.'

Sanjay took both his hands off the wheel and touched his ears and face again.

'*Hari Om.*'

I gave up arguing about God's role in my pursuit of Hrithik and settled in for the ride, my arms up, spread across the top of the seat, just in case there was any chance that I might sweat into my pretty pink T-shirt. I checked my reflection in Sanjay's mirror now and then too. I did not want to look shiny.

We sped in silence through Santa Cruz where Papa Roshan had been shot outside the Film Kraft offices. We hurtled up into Juhu, on the route to the stars, Roshan Villas to the left of us, Amitabh and the Bachchan family clan to the right, sequestered behind the high walls of celebrity.

'I think that's where Madhuri Dixit lived,' I offered, as we drove past one particularly chic-looking street.

At the mention of the temptress who had caused the young men of India to riot in the streets, the brakes went on.

'Is this so?' Sanjay turned to me again.

'I think so, though I am not sure if she still lives there now.'

Sanjay lost interest and accelerated away.

From the heady heights we dropped down to Malad, a network of roads, railways, factories and the city's rubbish mountains. At a traffic light not far from Andheri Station we stopped next to one of the larger dumps. There was a big sign between the road and the rubbish. 'There is no better thing for health than a walk in our clean fresh air,' said the sign in big green letters. A hand-painted picture of a happy family out on a tree-lined stroll backed the bold statement. Long metal legs held up the sign and framed a section of the dump beyond, its surface shivering where the internal heat of fermentation met the glare of the afternoon sun. Groups of rag-pickers were moving in their strange dance across the steaming rubbish, plucking what they could from the filth, their arms swinging with an elegance of their own through the manmade mound of city waste.

Madh Island is a peninsula that juts out into the Arabian Sea from Malad Creek and it feels like the seaside, rather than just an extension of the sprawling seaboard metropolis. Madh Island is Bombay's Long Island. It is where the stars have houses to get away from the smog and the hustle. There are also a lot of empty houses with boards that look like 'For Sale' signs, until you get up close and see that they actually say 'For Shooting'. Many of these houses were built with illegal money and now their owners have been forced off-shore. Some were dreams that became too expensive after the underworld dons had called in their dues. The pools are empty, the sunken bars have a weathered look to them, the furniture is reminiscent of Barbie's bedroom suite set in white and gold *circa* 1976, and the gardens that stretch down to the beach are dusty and untended.

Each time we drove past one of the signs, Sanjay slowed and turned to check with me. When we came to one offering 'Deluxe luxury shootings in lush surround', he braked hard. But it was not the one.

Eventually, in a place called Ringal, just off the main road, Sanjay stopped to ask a man who was stacking a pile of bricks. He turned to us, sat down on his freshly ordered pile, thought carefully and then pointed to a driveway ten yards ahead.

The house had no name plaque but the drive was jammed with lighting lorries, camera equipment vans and overgrown three-wheelers packed to their limit with spools of cabling, enormous arrangements of grubby fake flowers and great arc-light heads. Jammed on top of one of them was a huge white, fluffy, droopy-eyed toy dog, its red tongue hanging out. A little red velvet heart with the words 'Squeeze me sexy' on it hung around its neck.

Sanjay parked and I got out into the heat. It was three o'clock in the afternoon. The smell of rotting fish blew in from the sea beyond the house, and great crows circled just above us, eyeing the remains of the crew's lunch which were scattered across a couple of tables in the driveway. A large aluminium tea kettle sat on a rock beside the tables. Small groups of film crew were lolling on furniture that seemed to have been turfed out of the house for the shoot, great puffed-up sofas with gold detailing and heavily embroidered floral cushions, and matching chairs with fancy legs and gold-clawed feet.

I was on the set of *Yaadein*, directed by Subhash Ghai, the showman and master of the *masala* movie at its frothy, shimmering and shimmying best.

I walked past the lolling groups and out on to the dusty lawn in front of the house. A stray dog was looking down into an empty swimming-pool. Hrithik Roshan was sitting on the other side of the pool with two girls. They were all wearing sunglasses. The rest of the crew and cast were keeping away from them. I called out and waved. No one seemed to notice. I called out again. An assistant appeared beside me holding a roll of masking tape.

'What is it?' he asked, as he tore small strips of tape off and stuck them on his arm.

'I have an appointment to interview Hrithik Roshan. It was arranged with Mr Ashok.' I was speaking too quickly. 'He knows I'm coming.'

'Sure, sure, no problem, just hang on.' He had a faint American accent and he smiled at me. 'I'll go and check.' He walked around the pool and leant over Hrithik's shoulder. Hrithik turned to look at me. I half raised my hand. He got up and hurried away towards the house, past the empty pool and the stray dog, a thin boy in a tight see-through T-shirt and the same tuff-on-terrain shoes that he had worn in *Kaho Naa . . . Pyaar Hai*.

The two girls who had been sitting with him also got up and walked back to the house without apparently noticing that I was there. I recognized one of them as Kareena Kapoor, the young actress who had supposedly been holed up in a hotel room in London with Hrithik during the early shooting of *Yaadein*. She looked beautiful but irritated.

I waited for the assistant to come back.

'So sorry, Hrithik has to shoot now. You will have to wait for some time. I have to go, excuse me.' And he too ran back on to the set.

The sandblasted garden stretched right down to the sea. I went and sat on the wall above the beach, and the stray dog came over and sat beside me. Beyond the empty swimming-pool men were hauling arc-lights into position. Inside the house someone was standing right in front of Hrithik holding a mirror, another man was checking his make-up, and a thin boy was adjusting his T-shirt and brushing down his trousers. Hrithik stood very still. On the beach a group of women were bent over the sand, their thin, frayed saris tucked up into their petticoats. With their conical baskets on their backs they were like a gathering of hermit crabs silhouetted against the heavy glare of the mid-afternoon sun.

In the garden another man had come to sit by the pool. He was alone. The stray and I went to him. The dog was shooed away, I was allowed to approach.

I introduced myself to Subhash Ghai. He was playing with his mobile phone.

'I'm sorry, I don't want to interrupt you,' I said.

'No, no, it is no problem. The monkeys are getting too much for me in there.' He waved his phone towards the house. 'I am just taking some air while they set up.' He turned to me. 'Stay, you are not a monkey, it is fine to stay.' Subhash Ghai smiled his showman's smile.

'Are you enjoying *Yaadein*, working with this brand-new generation of big stars?' I asked.

Subhash Ghai is one of the few directors in the industry who can call the shots in a star-controlled system. Even so he had been forced to divide *Yaadein* into four filming chunks over a period of nine months to fit around the commitments of his stars.

'They're great kids. You know for me every time I feel like a kid too. Every film I make I feel excited again.' He was still fiddling with his telephone as he spoke. 'The audience is changing now and I can make films that will work for my friends instead of my maid.'

There it was, the making of his films for his maid, the phrase that I had read in every interview. He told me about his favourite foreign films. He was polite but distracted.

'I have a film to shoot,' he said and got up to go.

He sent one of his assistants out to invite me to watch the next scene being shot. I followed him in obediently and crouched down beside a pillar, close to where Hrithik was rehearsing.

He paced through his sequence over and over again, pausing only to check himself in the mirror that was still being held up for him. Each time he paced away from the camera he was coming straight towards me. I gave him a warm supportive smile every time just in case he might look my way. I was beginning to get cramp in one of my legs but I had no intention of moving. I was sweating with excitement, occasionally flapping my arms slightly to try and get a bit of air moving around me, and the arc-lights were adding to the heat. Hrithik's make-up was being attended to with such diligence that it was hard to tell whether he was sweating or not.

As Subhash Ghai moved behind the camera for the final rehearsal Hrithik tightened up, his whole body wound and ready. The shot involved Hrithik walking into a room with a jacket slung over his shoulder. He had to give the jacket back to a girl who had left it behind at a party, a very simple three-line scene. The girl was already in the room, balanced on a pair of four-inch suede platforms, sucked into a very short clingy skirt, and wearing a wig straight out of a Doris Day film, all big and bouncy. In spite of all these drawbacks she seemed much more at ease about the shot than Hrithik. He rushed through two more rehearsals and the first take. Subhash Ghai cut and the make-up assistant ran to Hrithik with a mirror. He in turn ran across the set with the make-up assistant trailing behind him. He stopped beside the camera to watch the playback, squinting at the screen with a nervous expression. He watched it several times over and asked Subhash Ghai's opinion as he watched. They talked. Subhash called one of his assistant directors over and talked to him as well. The assistant director then came over to where I was crouched by the pillar.

'I am Sourabh, assistant director on this shoot. Subhashji has a message for you,' he said, standing over me.

By now the cramp had taken hold and I had to stay crouched down.

'He says that you referred to the industry as Bollywood.'

I nodded, trying to remember if I had.

'He would like to correct you on this.'

'Okay.'

'Come.'

Limping, I followed Sourabh across the room, lost a flip-flop and then stumbled as I bent down to retrieve it. Subhash Ghai looked up from watching the scene they had just shot on the monitor. He took off his glasses.

'What happened?' He waved his hand at my limp.

'Cramp.'

'Eat salt.

'Okay.'

'I have to correct you on one thing,' he said. 'It has been troubling me since we talked. This is distracting me from my work.' He smiled.

I stood nervously looking down at the floor. Subhash Ghai was wearing shoes that looked like slip-on wine gums, the same colour as the burgundy ones I used to pick out of packets when I was about nine.

'You talked of this industry as Bollywood. This is a very wrong thing to call it. We are not trying to copy Hollywood. We are making films for an audience of a billion people. Over 80 per cent of these people don't have enough food in their bellies. Our country does not provide its people with pool halls, basketball courts and video parlours, so we make films for them that will let

'We create total fantasy'

them forget their lives for three hours. We create total fantasy, not the polished reality that Hollywood portrays. Never forget that, never forget that we are making films that allow people to believe for three hours that they are not poor and hungry.' Subhash Ghai put his glasses back on.

'Thank you,' I said. 'But it is hard not to call it Bollywood when that is what a very high percentage of your audience calls it.'

'We are the Hindi film industry and we make films in Hindi to make people feel better about life. This is our job.'

'Okay.'

'Okay, now we are shooting again. I hope you will enjoy watching us work. You must be sure and remember we are making this for people in villages who will see this on a dirty screen or wall. I make films for them, and for the people in the big cities who can stop struggling for a while and watch. I am happy that rich middle-class people go but if I am only making films for them I cannot call myself a Hindi film-maker.' The showman peered at me over the top of his glasses again and went back to work.

I returned to crouch by my pillar, escorted by Sourabh. I checked over my shoulder to ensure that Hrithik had not been close enough to hear my dressing-down, but fortunately he was safely back in make-up and out of earshot. I smiled at him again just in case.

As I squatted down a gaggle of women, young men and children was herded on to the back of the set. I asked Sourabh where they were from.

'People are coming all the time.'

'Could my driver come and watch?' I asked.

'Why not?'

A message was sent and Sanjay appeared almost immediately, his head bobbing at the back of the gaggle. He was waving to me and grinning behind the gawky young men and giggling children. Two young boys at the front of the group were plucking nervously at their shorts. A thin woman in a bright holiday sari smacked both of them on the head.

'Have you been talking to any of the younger directors around?' Sourabh asked me.

I told him about Sunil and *Snip!*, and a couple of other young directors who had also made cross-over films of the same kind, English-Indian, Birmingham *Balti*, the whole *masala* cool, Injun underground scene.

'These guys really don't understand this industry. It is all very clever and such but now you are watching the master at work.' He nodded his head toward Subhash Ghai. 'He understands, he truly has his finger on the pulse of India.'

I thanked Sourabh for his advice. He went back to join Subhash*ji* behind the camera. Two men came to stand on either side of me, one with a pistol tucked into his belt, the other carrying an AK47. The two boys in shorts at the front of the gaggle started squeaking. Hrithik was coming back on to the set.

They rehearsed again. It was not going well. The rehearsals continued. Hrithik was working hard, forcing himself through the scene. His body language was stiff and he strangled his lines. The gaggle behind me began to chat. Subhash Ghai lost patience with them and they were herded away, gazing back over their shoulders for a last look at the nervous boy in the tight T-shirt. The man beside me was jiggling his AK47 against the pillar. He was told to shut up. Lights were moved. Hrithik was checked again for hair and make-up. The girl in the clingy skirt and platforms was fiddling with her eyelashes and rolling over the edges of her boots. Subhash Ghai said something to Hrithik. He laughed. He relaxed. The scene was shot. The great aluminium tea kettle appeared and everyone flopped on to various pieces of Barbie's bedroom furniture.

I looked around, hoping that Sanjay had not been herded away with the gaggle, but he was still there, comfortably ensconced with one of the assistants in a corner. He had a cup of tea in one hand and a smile on his face as wide as the ocean at the end of the garden.

Hrithik was sitting on one of the sofas with the same two girls he had been with when I arrived. They were all back in dark glasses. The girls were laughing, occasionally looking at me and then whispering. Hrithik was concentrating on a tray that had been put in front of him. He was mixing one of his power shakes, stirring the pale green gunge with the end of a pen. He drank it in one go and shook his head. As he put the glass down he called one of the assistants and walked out into the garden.

The assistant came over to where I was still lurking under the arc-lights.

'Hrithik has some time for you now,' he said.

I followed him out into the garden. Two chairs had been put beside the swimming-pool, facing each other. Hrithik was at the end of the garden looking out over the beach. He walked back towards the chairs when he saw me coming out of the house and we sat down facing each other.

'I'm Justine Hardy. I hope your assistant told you that I would be coming to see you?'

Hrithik took off his dark glasses.

'Oh yes, of course, he did.' He leant across to me with his hand held out. I shook Hrithik Roshan's hand. He looked straight at me. I was staring into the face of a beautiful boy behind a mask of film make-up. I was staring into those eyes. Everyone describes them as green. They are not. They are soft hazel melting to dark brown, flecked with light, wide open and vulnerable. He smiled warily and we sat facing each other, he in a tight see-through T-shirt, and me in a not quite-so-tight pink one. Hrithik looked down for a moment and then back up into my eyes. He was waiting for me to say something. He seemed confused but he smiled a tired, polite smile.

'I'm sorry, have I come at a bad time?'

'No, no, I'm sorry. I have to say I didn't realize it was today. Would you like tea?' He moved his chair towards me and winced as he did so.

'Are you okay?'

'Oh *yaar*.' He smiled. 'Actually I am just one big mass of injuries, bad knees, sore back. All this dancing, you see.'

'I was with a dance teacher who said that you dance like Gene Kelly.' Pinky Ali's bit was in straight off.

'That's so nice but really just not true at all.' He stretched out over the back of the chair. The position exaggerated the weight of his built-up shoulders and the narrowness of his hips.

'And the ladies at my beauty salon think that you are getting too thin.'

He started laughing.

'You have a beauty salon? I thought you were a journalist.'

'No, no, I just talk a lot to some ladies at my local beauty salon, and they all love you,' I paused. 'Very much.'

His laugh moved from polite to real.

'Fantastic, perhaps they can give me some advice. I have so much of work and all this dancing, I cannot keep the weight on.'

'Mrs Kanwar makes very good *gajari halwa*.'

Hrithik pulled a face.

'Just too much *ghee*, you know, I really hate all that grease. If your Mrs Kanwar could make *mishti doi*, that would be a very different thing. I love that stuff.' He paused for a moment at the thought of the creamy sweetened Bengali curd. 'God, you know I really love that stuff. And you know this dance thing, I'm really not so good. I am going to get caught soon. I had so much time to prepare for the dancing in *Kaho Naa . . . Pyaar Hai*. Now there is just not that sort of time and everyone is going to see soon that I am just not so hot at all, that maybe I am just a really ordinary dancer.' The tired, polite smile returned. 'You know I am so tired all the time. I can't remember not being tired.'

'It's a pricey game.' I joined the women of India in wanting to protect him.

'Pricey?'

'The cost to you, it takes a lot out of you.' I was watching his hands tapping on his knees.

'You know, I'm not so sure about this star stuff.' He looked away over my shoulder. 'I just wonder what it would be like if it could all just stop and I could get on with learning to act.' His fingers were drumming faster.

'Yoga is good,' I said.

'What?'

'Yoga is very good for dance injuries, tiredness, stress, well, for most things really.'

'Is this so?' His body softened into his chair.

'It is.'

'You must tell me more.' His smile opened up and he looked straight into my eyes again. 'Pink is a good colour for you,' he said, pointing to my T-shirt.

I was back at Bar Indigo again and a year had disappeared. I was looking into those *filmi*-star eyes.

'Because it matches my eyes?' I peered down at my T-shirt, coming over all English in the face of a compliment from a megastar.

Hrithik laughed again, and those eyes flickered with light.

'No, the eyes are blue, the same colour as this fantastic car I have. I love this colour.' He laughed.

'Is that the best thing about the fame, is that the biggest prize?'

'Maybe it is, maybe.'

'Someone else asked me to ask you that.'

'Your beauty salon friends?'

'No, a man with a dog.'

'Okay.' He wrinkled his forehead and went on laughing.

'What about screen kissing?' I was running through my list.

He stopped laughing.

'What?'

'Will you do a real screen kiss at some point?'

Hrithik froze, the tips of his fingers pressed together in front of his mouth.

'I was just chancing my luck,' I said apologetically.

'Hey, no problem, no problem. You know we're not really doing that kind of thing right now, though.' The light had left his eyes. He shifted in his chair. I had departed from the script.

We scuttled back to safer topics: his favourite date is 14 January, the day he met Sussanne at a set of traffic lights and the day that *Kaho Naa . . . Pyaar Hai* was released five years later. I already knew that.

He likes Ferrero Rocher chocolates a lot, but then there is no accounting for taste and I knew that too.

He does not feel he has any control over his life any more. He agrees with Mr Taraporewala that he feels giddy up on the pedestal.

He likes the motto 'The finest steel has to go through the hottest fire'.

He wants to try and take a month off every year, but he did not look convinced that it would happen.

We talked about yoga and Gene Kelly, fast blue cars and the risk of a hit in the shadows of the industry's underworld. Then an assistant came over to tell him that he was needed back on set.

He got up and kissed me goodbye. He smelt of hot clean hair and limes.

'Doesn't it frighten you that your picture is all over the city, that you can't go anywhere without being confronted by huge versions of yourself?' I asked as we walked back to the house.

'I love it. The only thing that frightens me is that it might stop.' He laughed and half raised his hand to me.

The laugh was brittle this time. His mask was back in place.

I sort of forgot to ask him to sign Severin's card and Mira's T-shirt. I am not popular.

Sanjay stopped the car just as we drove away from Beach House. He wanted to show me Hrithik's autograph. In fact he'd got three, one for his son, one for his nephew and one for himself. He had done better than me.

'He liked my pink T-shirt,' I retaliated.

Sanjay shrugged and drove on.

'He is greatest star ever. This I am being told, that he could be big star in Hollywood too.'

'Yes, he probably could if he wanted to.' I had my head pressed against the window.

'You think he could be bigger star than he is now?'

'Yes, I think so.' We were approaching the rag-pickers again on the dumps near Andheri Station. They were now like ghosts in the haze of fading light.

Sanjay started to laugh. 'Not possible to be bigger star than he is now.'

'It's not so great,' I mumbled against the window.

'What is this?' Sanjay turned around.

'Well, you get to be a big star and you get whisked to the front of the queue, you get the best table in the best restaurant in town, you can get just about anything you want, people bow and scrape to you.'

'What is bow and scrape?' Sanjay was watching me in his mirror.

'Everyone being *chamcha*, sycophants. But is that really so great? You can't walk down the street any more without being hassled, you have to watch your back the whole time when you are out in public, you can never have a bad hair or dodgy skin day.' I sighed and Sanjay looked at me in the mirror.

'*Hari Om*,' he said, as though protecting himself from my apparent madness.

'It's okay I suppose if you don't mind giving up everything in your life that you once thought was important, if you realize that the guns and bullets are sometimes real and that they get used.'

'Why so sad?' Sanjay asked, his brow knitted in his reflection. 'He has number one car, you know, Benz number one car.'

'You're right, he does have a Benz.'

We were at the Andheri Station traffic lights. Two boys were next to us in a small, battered Maruti with the windows wide open. The soundtrack to *Fiza* was pouring out with the playback singers cranked up to full volume. Sanjay smiled and bobbed his head in time.

Okay, come on then, bring on the dancing girls. Let them burst out in a sea of sequins. Swell the music over an alpine slope, just one more time, one more wiggle, a final twirl. A last dewy-eyed close-up. A lingering gaze. Lips to neck. A Mercedes Benz. Hazel eyes that turn on and off. Just a boy. Fade out.

Welcome to Bollywood.

The End.

Welcome to Bollywood

handwritten: I⊖H
13583
24/2/06

Acknowledgements

OKAY, HERE I go, in the spotlight, up on the podium in my spangly frock, all you lot looking on and waiting. I will try not to cry. My heartfelt thanks to Roddy Sale, my charming host in Bombay, a beautiful performance; to Rajiv for his encyclopaedic knowledge of *filmi* mags and for his telephone skills; to Lisa for light in Delhi, and to Paddy for being home there; to Nitin Upadhye for his determination in taking photographs; to Sunil Sippy for giving access to all areas on *Snip!*; to Mr Tivarekar for letting the dead speak; to Pinky Ali and Madam Deepa, whose real names have been changed; to Richard for being the best support around; to Gail who has picked me up all along the way; to Natasha for all her advice; but perhaps most of all to Hrithik Roshan, Bollywood Boy, because without him . . . fade to black, credits, swelling orchestral score.